ECOLOGICAL STUDIES
OF FAMILY LIFE

ECOLOGICAL STUDIES OF FAMILY LIFE

Arlene Vetere
University of Southampton

and

Anthony Gale
University of Southampton

with

Sue Lewis

Claire Jolly

and

Shirley Reynolds

JOHN WILEY & SONS
Chichester • New York • Brisbane • Toronto • Singapore

Library of Congress Cataloging-in-Publication Data:

Vetere, Arlene.
    Ecological studies of family life.

    Includes indexes.
    1. Family. 2. Family life surveys. I. Gale,
Anthony. II. Title.
HQ518.V48   1987   306.8′5   86-19056

ISBN 0 471 91253 0

British Library Cataloguing in Publication Data:

Vetere, Arlene
    Ecological studies of family life.
    1. Family — Research
    I. Title II. Gale, Anthony
    306.8′5′072   HQ728

    ISBN 0 471 91253 0

Printed and bound in Great Britain.

Contents

Foreword

> We shall not cease from exploration
> And the end of all our exploring
> Will be to arrive where we started
> And know the place for the first time.*

T. S. Eliot's quotation is used by Gurman and Kniskern (1981) to introduce their exhaustive review of family therapy outcome research which appears in their own *Handbook of Family Therapy*. The quotation is very appropriate since it touches on a crucial facet of such research. Outcome research is essentially 'spiral'—it appears to make little progress and seems to go round in circles. A view from above does indeed reveal only circles but a view from the side reveals a shallow spiral with tangible gains being made as it progresses upwards.

Studying families seems to be essentially similar to this. We all are acute observers of families—we have great personal knowledge of the machinations of our own families derived from firsthand experiences and yet in our professional roles this firsthand knowledge is somehow dismissed or forgotten. Our knowledge is not 'scientific' or respectable enough to warrant further discussion. As an undergraduate I studied psychology for three years and yet the family was not mentioned once. Even the so-called social psychologist who taught us about human groups failed to give a single lecture on the family.

It is truly bizarre that psychologists have so long failed to focus research attention upon the family. This reticence has been strangely shared by anthropologists who have studied families but families from other cultures rather than their own. Sociologists have been much more prepared to study features of families and family life but they have tended to fight shy of studying the interior of the family. Perhaps there are powerful taboos against penetrating too deeply into the life of families but it is clear that these taboos need to be lifted if a true psychology of human behaviour is to be developed.

---

*Reproduced by permission of Faber and Faber Limited and Harcourt, Brace and Jovanovich, Inc. from 'Little Gidding', in *Four Quartets*, © 1943 T. S. Eliot, renewed in 1971 by Esme Valerie Eliot.

Arlene Vetere and Tony Gale's *Ecological Studies of Family Life* is a modest yet pioneering book which seeks to encourage researchers, therapists and all students of human behaviour 'to arrive . . . and to know the place for the first time'. It challenges us to take the family seriously—to develop a fine-grained understanding of the intricacies of family life. This understanding has to be at a new level and on a new basis. Our personal knowledge of families is not to be belittled. Biographers, diarists and novelists are amongst the best psychologists that have ever been published. But there remains the daunting task of using the ever-improving techniques of psychology to enrich our understanding of family processes and family structure.

I was not party to the birth of the project reported in this book but I was very happy to be drawn in as a consultant (and godparent) when the project was beginning to take its first unsure but energy-filled steps. From my privileged position as consultant I was able to benefit from the exciting ideas and discoveries that were being generated by the research group but I was also able to share (albeit at secondhand) some of the heartaches and difficulties that the project members experienced. As a family therapist I am quite used to leaving a session with a family feeling emotionally drained but such an experience pales into insignificance compared with the experience of having to live with a family for several days at a time. At least when the session is over it is possible to relax and to use the support of colleagues to talk oneself down. Participant observation is needless-to-say entirely different—the only escape from the family is at night when everybody has gone to bed. The messiness and lack of control that is inherent in participant observation perhaps explains its unpopularity.

The multidimensional approach adopted by the research team is very attractive to me since it contains many of the elements that I would want to see included in a package which attempts to reflect the richness of family interaction. I can vouch for the value of the extensive participant observer data generated by the project since one of the families that I had in therapy was observed by team members. The value of such data to me was very clear since I was able to correct some major errors in the therapy that I was undertaking with the family. It is clear to me that such an approach is a necessary first step in developing our understanding. Laboratory studies of the behaviour of families are not to be dismissed but their artificiality needs to be understood by examining how families behave in their natural environment. An ethologist would not expect to develop an understanding of the behaviour of mountain gorillas by studying them just in the laboratory or even in a zoo. Observation in the wild (which often comes close to being participant observation) is the most convincing method currently available.

The attempts to develop Gottman's sequential analysis methods will, I am sure, help to stimulate other researchers to adopt his exciting methods. Obviously there are still methodological problems to be ironed out but the approach will directly appeal to family therapists who attempt to delineate the precise punctuation of a given sequence of behavioural events generated by families they are working with. I have also particularly enjoyed the team's extension of personal construct theory based ideas to encompass family construing. A former student of mine, Harry Procter, was a pioneer of this approach with schizophrenic families but it is obvious from the work outlined in this book that it is possible to generate a defensible method for examining any type of family. Family therapists through their addiction to conceptual frameworks derived from General System Theory have tended to treat family members as interchangeable objects lacking consciousness. This book will undoubtedly act as an antidote to this type of mechanistic, dehumanizing error. As Arlene Vetere eloquently argues, GST has its value as a starting point for generating an adequate theory of family interaction but it cannot be considered as anything more than a starting point. This is perhaps an unpopular thing to say but I hope that family therapists can demonstrate their ability to abandon their treasured shibboleths in favour of richer and more demanding theories which can begin to adequately reflect the richness and complexity of the behaviour patterns that are generated within families.

I am glad to be able to welcome this book as an important point of departure in the struggle to achieve such a theoretical development—but I do have two regrets about it. The first is that such a book was not readily available either in 1959, when I began my career as a psychologist, or in 1977 when I began training as a family therapist. My second regret concerns the sad fact that no further research will be produced by the Southampton project. This book will, I am sure, become a much quoted source of information for a wide range of researchers and professionals interested in the family but we will all be left with a sense of frustration. Clearly a research unit is required to take this work forward yet the likelihood of such a unit ever being organized in this country, given the current political climate, is almost zero.

This is a somewhat sombre note on which to end but I am sure that it will not prevent you from reading this book with the enthusiasm it deserves. I am equally sure that Arlene Vetere and Tony Gale have produced a book that has the potential to inspire other researchers to follow in their footsteps. Family research is uniquely exhausting and exacting as this book so clearly demonstrates but its rewards cannot be underestimated. As a family therapist I feel very privileged to work with families who, in the main, are remarkably trusting and hence are prepared to lay themselves open to intense forms of intervention. It is equally true, as again this book demonstrates, that families can be remarkably generous in allowing researchers to have access to them.

Families are willing and able to respond to the needs and demands of researchers but the $64,000 question remains—will researchers be able to respond to the challenge laid down by Arlene Vetere and Tony Gale or will they play safe and keep to more traditional avenues of research which until now have appeared to be academically more respectable?

Reference

Gurman, A.S. and Kniskern, D.P. (1981). *Handbook of Family Therapy*. New York: Brunner Mazel.

Andy Treacher
Principal Clinical Psychologist
Department of Child and Family Psychiatry
Royal United Hospital, Bath

Preface

This is an unusual book. While there are many books about the family and about family therapy, few have been written by psychologists. The family has been a major concern in sociology, social anthropology, social history and psychiatry, but for several reasons, it has been neglected by psychology. Our own research involved living in the family home with volunteer families for extended visits of a week or more. By using the method of participant observation we hoped to learn about family life in the raw. The book explains how we developed this research technique for our family research and how we have attempted to analyse our findings in a systematic fashion.

We have written this research monograph as a collaborative enterprise. Most of the authors were active in participant observation and had direct experience of living in the private world of our volunteer families. One of the authors is a statistician; she assisted in the development of the work by helping us to analyse our data. She has also helped us by offering a very critical view of our methodology, the reliability of our observational methods, and the robustness of our techniques for coding and classifying our family observations. Finally, one of the couples who allowed us to live in their home, have given an account of their own family problems, seen through their own eyes.

We have tried to make our book user-friendly and we hope it will appeal to a number of researchers and family therapists, as well as to psychiatrists, social workers, and educational and clinical psychologists. Several of the chapters offer a novel account of a set of problems for the first time, and we hope they will therefore prove attractive to undergraduates or professionals in training. These include a discussion of the potential of family study for psychological research and theorizing into individual development; a critical evaluation of the General System approach in the context of individual and social behaviour; a discussion of several major theories of family behaviour together with a general prescription for future theories; and, finally, consideration of the special ethical issues which arise in family research.

We also offer several levels of description and analysis. Already mentioned is the short chapter contributed by one of our families. For each of the families studied, we offer an analysis based on three key theories (structural theory, choice-exchange theory, and distance regulation theory), together with detailed illustrated extracts from our original participant observation diaries. The aim of the family vignettes, the formal analysis, and the illustrative examples, is to bring the families to life for the reader. However, we suggest that this approach could be developed further for professional work with families. We have also used film, repertory grids, sociograms, and sequential analysis to try to capture key aspects of family life. Finally, we offer a repertory grid analysis of all the families studied as seen through the construct system of the key researcher in the team.

The psychological study of the family is still in its infancy. Many of the concepts of family communication developed in the 1960s have proved elusive and difficult to operationalize. Several major reviews of family interaction studies have painted a rather gloomy picture of progress achieved so far. While we are not the first researchers to use the participant observation technique in the family home, we believe our methods and general approach to family study offer some promise for the future. Research funds were limited and we did not achieve all that we set out to achieve. However, we believe that we have established a new style of family research which can be taken up and developed by others. We have not been afraid to identify conceptual and methodological faults in our approach. Hopefully, we have been able to point to potential hazards and will therefore have made the journey easier for future explorers.

The work took several years from initial conceptualization to the completion of the main body of empirical research. We wish to thank the Committee for Advanced Studies of the University of Southampton and the Psychology Committee of the former Social Science Research Council (now the Economic and Social Research Council) for providing research funding for what must have seemed at the time to be a risky and audacious stab in the dark. More detailed acknowledgements to the many individuals and groups who gave us practical help and advice throughout the project are given at the end of Chapter 1.

Arlene Vetere   *University of Southampton*
Anthony Gale   *July 1986*

CHAPTER ONE

The Family: A Failure in Psychological Theory and Research

Arlene Vetere and Anthony Gale

Introduction

This book describes our research with families. We lived in the homes of a dozen families as participant observers, for extended weekends and periods of a week or more. To do this, a single researcher moved into the home, observed family behaviour, joined in family activities, and maintained a tape-recorded diary of family events. Our aim was to subject the family's behaviour to systematic psychological analysis.

In psychology, measurement instruments must be reliable and capable of objective description if they are to be used to test theory. By comparing the experience of more than one observer in the same home, we hoped to test the reliability of our participant observation method. In some cases, we supplemented our observer's account by other methods, the use of repertory grids, and films of family activities. Some families were also asked to give their account of the research and one family has contributed part of this book, by describing their life as they saw it. From our recorded observations, transcripts were prepared, which, in their turn, were subjected to a variety of analyses, designed not only to measure the power of the participant observation method but to reveal aspects of family life and the nature of relationships among family members.

Earlier workers have observed in the family home. However, ours is the first attempt to challenge directly the methodological problems which such work entails. Apart from problems of sampling, bias, reactivity, and subjectivity, we are also concerned with the ethical implications of research which intrudes into the private lives of others; such ethical issues, which affect the progress of the work, impose constraints on the ability to report the data and, indeed, can create conflict between the several roles of the observer. Nevertheless, we believe our research creates a number of problems which must be faced by psychology as a whole and are not merely special difficulties created by the naturalistic method.

1

Why Study the Family?

Introductory texts written for students of psychology do not have the word 'family' in the contents page and rarely in the subject index. There is a simple reason for this: psychology has not studied the family. It is difficult to justify family research in psychology without engaging in rhetoric or clinical speculation, largely because there is so little formal evidence available. Yet we believe the family to be important for a number of reasons.

Within our culture the job of socialization, of acquiring the rules, roles, and norms of the culture is largely left to the family. The child becomes a social creature through interaction with the family. In the simplest terms this means that a large proportion of the child's time is spent in interaction with family members. But while psychology has focused on child development it has been within the context largely of dyadic relationships: mother–child interaction, and more recently father–child interaction, and sibling interaction. The family *qua family* has not been treated as a unit of analysis, with special characteristics or rules of organization, which shape not only the behaviour of the child, but feed back to shape the family itself. Family theorists in other disciplines think of family influence as an important determinant of behaviour throughout the life cycle, but psychology has focused primarily not only on the child but on the early years. Yet if we are to emphasize the family as a source of variance in individual behaviour, then our description must cover school experience, peer influence, adolescence, courting, the couple in marriage, the effects of marital breakdown, children leaving home, retirement, death, and bereavement. Given such a long list of sources of influence on personal behaviour, it is evident that pre-occupation with the early years and the caretaker role can only offer a glimpse of the family's role.

Family life lasts a lifetime. A couple who set up home together bring with them the traditions of two families. Over the years, and in producing a family of their own, they negotiate an elaboration or development of what they have learned in the past. Not only do they recapture part of the life of their families of origin, but they replicate in real flesh and relationships the symbols and signs of their culture. Roles about gender, childhood, affection, responsibility, and personal rights, are transmitted through the media, through film and advertising, so that family members are constantly reminded of the family values of the culture. Whether physically present or not, family members, as intimate others, are present in the mind of each individual.

As divorce becomes more common, the pattern is even more complicated, because existing families can become welded together, joining two elaborated subcultures under one roof. And the single parent, while also offering a contrast to the nuclear family, nevertheless carries the responsibilities which society normally imposes on couples, so that family experience takes the form of a single adult with one or more children.

A common-or-garden Martian psychologist will observe how much time is spent within the family, how much effort is devoted to it, and how much of our beliefs, ideals, and goals, seem to stem from family experience. As a behaviourist, he or she would observe regular relationships between events in the family environment, individual behaviour, its contingencies and consequences. Given the amount of time spent in the family he or she would expect it to yield information about the reinforcement histories of its members. One of the few behavioural psychologists to study patterns of family interaction is Patterson (1969) who explored the contingencies which parents and children offered each other, particularly in the context of negative reciprocity. But his work focuses on the present rather than the past, deals with dyads more than whole families, and because of its behavioural orientation, does not consider the phenomenology of family members.

Behaviour is governed not only by immediate rewards and punishments (the proximate causes of behaviour) but by values and beliefs. An account of family life cannot be limited to the mere present. Families carry with them across generations beliefs about gender-related behaviour, the expression of emotion, and the rights and wrongs of authority and decision-making. Such factors determine the intensity of positive and negative emotion in the atmosphere of the individual family. Clinicians have identified extreme beliefs of this nature as a source of pathology; for example, communication theorists have talked of powerful family 'myths' which constrain individual behaviour for the sake of family loyalty (happy families do not have secrets, do not argue, do everything together . . .).

Why Has Psychology Neglected the Family?

Why then has psychology neglected the family? Other disciplines have not been so chary of studying the family, for example, anthropologists, sociologists, and social historians have long traditions of treating the family as a central focus for scholarship and empirical research. While their interest has been in the family as a social institution, or in rites of passage, rather than in detailed accounts of processes of interaction or the investigation of personal experience, psychology has much to learn both from the theoretical constructs and the methodologies employed. One of the intersections between these disciplines and psychology has been in the study of the exotic, the kibbutz, the open family, the commune, and other special arrangements. This has led to a distorted view of the family because it is based on unusual styles of living in the absence of normative data.

Interest in the family as a social institution was focused on certain key traditional questions: what constitutes the family and how is its membership defined; is the family universal and therefore a reflection of certain biological imperatives; does family life over the passage of time demonstrate invariance; have certain family functions been removed from the family and taken over by other social institutions? Such questions are not within the ambit of traditional psychological concerns nor are established psychological methods appropriate to their solution.

Historically, traditional psychoanalysis and its offspring have emphasized the relationship between the infant and other family members. But the family in question is seen through the eyes of the intrapsychic conflicts of the individual; the parts played by family members are written in a predetermined biological script in which the actors have little room for manoeuvre. However, a major contribution of the psychoanalytic tradition has been the concept of defence mechanisms, devices designed to reduce anxiety and ego threat. These have been borrowed from the individual context by family clinicians to explain family dynamics. For example, unresolved conflict between the parents (the analogue of intrapsychic conflict) can be projected on to a child who then bears a symptom. The symptom serves two processes: firstly, to deflect concern away from the parents and, secondly, to express the anxiety in the child's pathology. Such accounts are open to the same criticisms as the original intrapsychic theory: they do not explain why particular defence mechanisms are chosen, why a particular child becomes the victim, or even why a particular symptom (i.e., enuresis, anorexia, school refusal) is chosen.

The psychometric tradition is guilty of the fundamental attribution error of accounting for an individual's behaviour in terms of traits and personal characteristics, rather than contexts or person-situation interactions. The role of the family in influencing behaviour is downstaged in favour of personal characteristics within the person, such as intelligence, personality, and individual differences in motivation. These internal dispositions are seen as primary causal factors in the determination of behaviour.

Even social psychologists, concerned with inter-individual behaviour, have tended to shun natural groups. Rather, much experimental social psychology has been developed with artificially created interactions, set up in the laboratory, often between subjects who have never met each other before, have no history of affiliation, and have no investment in a common future. In contrast, we may assert that families have a deep personal involvement, a long history of association, a ferocious commitment to the future, and a reluctance to accept outsiders without a long period of initiation. Paradoxically, those social psychologists engaged in a revolution within their discipline and who have rejected the laboratory-based, experimental approach, might light upon the family as a true social context within which social acts have personal and shared meanings.

We also need to accept the possibility that study of the family is in some sense rocking the boat. It is more than a coincidence that some of the more passionate advocates of antipsychiatry were at the same time contemptuous of many aspects of the contemporary nuclear family (e.g., Cooper, 1971; Laing and Esterson, 1964). These authors saw the family as the basic underpinning of much which they found unacceptable in society as a whole. The family was seen as the major stumbling block to personal freedom, a straightjacket into which the individual is trussed and tied at birth, and from which he/she never escapes. Society's institutions were seen as replicates of the oppressive processes of family life, the abuse of power, the blackmail of intimacy, and the restriction on personal experience and exploration. Psychologists need to ask themselves on at least one occasion in their professional lives, whether they be researchers or practitioners, to what extent they might be sustaining the status quo in our society. Perhaps the family is too hot to handle!

Professional psychologists, in educational, clinical, and occupational fields are likely to conduct their business with individuals. If family stress is seen as a cause or consequence of individual disorder, little will be done to interact with the family. The training of these applied specialties in Britain includes little appreciation of group behaviour, never mind family behaviour. For example, models of school refusal see the child's difficulties as stemming from maladaptive learning, where the school is a phobic stimulus, or as a reflection of separation anxiety involving loss of the mother. Lip service is paid to the notion of family pressures which serve to keep the child at home, but while this can involve treating school refusal as separation anxiety on the part of the *mother*, the mother's anxiety is rarely seen as a secondary condition to conflicts between the spouses. Nor is the mother-child relationship seen as a substitute for spouse affection and support. Thus the educational psychologist does not venture into family change procedures. Say a clinical psychologist is faced with a female client suffering from depression. In contrast to the psychiatrist who operates with medical models of psychiatric disorder, the psychologist might wish to explore the client's cognitive frameworks and attributions. The notion that the disorder is somehow offering secondary gain to others or to the client, because it serves to deflect attention from more fundamental problems of family relationships, is rarely considered. Thus a housebound housewife, formerly employed and enjoying the status and personal esteem which stems from work, may be reacting to a change in role, in which her husband, children and in-laws consider her responsibilities as mother and wife to be more important. Even she herself may not be aware of the loss which this change of function implies. In such circumstances, the depression has to be seen, not as a personal possession of the wife (i.e., as *her* depression) but as a result of the interaction between family expectations, transmitted role definitions, and the secondary gains which family members derive from her helplessness. The implication is that the therapeutic process would involve the whole family and not the wife alone, or even the marital pair.

Again, occupational psychologists tend to operate within the working context and see employees as leaving their families at home when they come to work. Only dramatic changes in life circumstances, such as divorce or a bereavement, are acknowledged as potential sources of reductions in working efficiency. In contrast, we would claim that events in the home and everyday conflicts concerning decision-making and priorities may impact on individual effectiveness at work. The search for sources of motivation to work and job satisfaction has not included consideration of family process.

We do not wish to underestimate the consequences of a family-based approach to applied psychology, nor the implications for both training and practice. Family work is particularly taxing, and calls for an institutional base from which the individual practitioner can draw succour and support. Many professional psychologists are expected to plough a lonely furrow and to work as effective practitioners without further supervision or specialized training.

Other caring professions have a long-established casework tradition which has not precluded seeing the client in their home base. Social workers rarely consider individual problems out of context and, indeed, are required quite often to assess the quality of family environment in which their clients live. Even so, it is not clear that practice is guided by a formal theory of family process, nor that observations are made of interactions among several family members in a variety of circumstances. There is also the danger that the focus on family process may distract attention from individual variables; for example, it is not easy to explain why a particular parent engages in child abuse, or why a particular child appears as victim, if one focuses on interaction at the complete cost of individual variables.

We have already mentioned Patterson's work and the behavioural approach to family problems. We must point out, however, that behavioural and psychodynamic approaches have different implications and outcomes. As Gurman and Kniskern (1978) argue, behavioural approaches, by focusing on the presenting problem, can miss the point. Say parents are concerned about the uncontrollable tantrums of a child. A behavioural approach will encourage them to identify the antecedent circumstances to an outburst, their own reactions, and the possible rewards which the child achieves. The parents will then be given a behavioural toolkit for reshaping the child's behaviour. The child is therefore accepted as being an essential ingredient of the problem and the criterion of therapeutic success will be the elimination of disruptive behaviour. In contrast, a psychodynamic style family approach may see the child's behaviour as a mere reflection of major problems elsewhere in the family; thus focus on the child merely handles the symptom, not the communicational disorder. The outcome criterion is improved communication, say, between the parents, *as well as* the loss of the child's disruptive behaviour. Thus in reviewing outcome studies, Gurman and Kniskern assert that behavioural treatments are less successful. We appreciate that it is easy to overlook positive side-effects of the behavioural approach; for example, in working together to deal with the identified patient's 'problem' the parents might well have to improve their capacity to communicate, to share responsibility, and work as a team. But the family therapy approach would regard these effects as primary consequences of therapeutic intervention.

Traditions in Family Research

We must not create the impression that psychology has totally ignored the family. Communication theorists have an established tradition of formal research. But such research is more likely to have been conducted in the laboratory than in the home. Even so, family research is plagued with practical difficulties. As Raush, Greif, and Nugent (1979) comment: 'It is far easier to give questionnaires or to conduct laboratory experiments with captive populations of college students than to study families in interaction. In every respect — sampling, time and personnel considerations, instrumentation, data-coding, and analysis problems — the investigator of family interaction is faced with uncertainties and with necessities for compromise' (page 478). We comment below on the ways in which such problems have affected family research.

Bateson (1958) is usually credited with the observation that the child's self-image emerges through interactional patterns with close intimate others. This image is maintained and adapted through communicative behaviour. Such assumptions provided the spur for empirical research into family experience and the transmission of distress and mental illness. It is claimed that families with a schizophrenic member exhibit unusual ways of sharing feelings and a world view. These deviant patterns of communication give rise to schizophrenic behaviour in a particular family member. Three major groups are associated with this work and share a common set of beliefs. Thus Bateson, Jackson, Haley, and Weakland (1956) in their theory of schizophrenia elaborated on the double-bind hypothesis and subsequently claimed to demonstrate in experimental studies of decision-making that family members can communicate contradictory information either within channels (i.e., speech) or between channels (i.e., speech and facial expression).

The concepts of 'schism' and 'skew' were developed by the Lidz group (e.g., Lidz, Cornelison, Fleck, and Terry, 1957). The *skewed* family is organized around one central pathological family member (usually the mother) while *schismatic* relationships are characterized by chronic hostility and mutual withdrawal between all family members. In both types of family, age and generation boundaries are blurred and behaviour is inappropriate both in relation to the parents' mutual roles, and in their interaction with the children. These effects combine to produce distorted identity development in the child. Clinical observation led Lidz and associates to distinguish the two types of family.

Bowen (1960) has a similar formulation; however, he emphasizes the development of rigid and extreme family roles, which in their turn lead to polarization. Thus his emphasis is on schism and marked family conflict which he calls *emotional divorce*. For example, his *omnipotent-helpless* polarity could involve the *over-adequate mother* and *peripheral father*. This view also developed from clinical observation and interview.

Wynne, Ryckoff, Day, and Hirsch (1958) are the third major group. Their emphasis was upon the importance of healthy ego development and adequate identity formation. This, they claim, is inhibited by families in which there is inadequate opportunity for selecting and testing different roles during development, either within or outside the family. Families with a schizophrenic member fail to provide a stable and coherently meaningful environment. The key concept of Wynne *et al.* is *pseudo-mutuality*, which is a lack of true complementary role opportunities; communication and interaction are disjointed, involving roles which are either too rigid or too loose and ambiguous.

Thus we see that these different groups emphasize the way in which the family works to deny individual experience and the formation of a separate identity and sense of self. For comprehensive and evaluative reviews of such approaches see Mishler and Waxler (1965) and Raush *et al.* (1979).

Before turning to criticisms which have been made of such theories, we must draw attention to their lasting contribution. First, by seeing the illness as a developmental process within a distorted familial environment, such approaches distracted attention from the medical model concepts of schizophrenic illness. Within that environment *relationships* rather than personality or individual pathology, became the focus of interest for treatment. Secondly, they drew attention to particular aspects of interpersonal relationships within the family, for example, the *double-bind* and the associated concepts described above (schism, skew, pseudo-mutuality, undifferentiated ego mass, emotional divorce, etc.). Finally, these clinical approaches created an active thrust for research which focused on four major areas: conflict, dominance, affect, and clarity of communication.

Criticisms of the Communication Theorists

The research which followed these seminal ideas involved the description of allegedly abnormal patterns of communication in families with a schizophrenic member, sometimes including controls in the form of other families which contained other disorders and handicaps. In damning reviews of this work by Frank (1965), Fontana (1966), and Jacob (1975) much of the research was seen to be defective. Studies failed both in design and in their ability to identify actual patterns of communication which were unique to families with a schizophrenic member. Nor were the communication researchers able to show, where deviant communication was demonstrated, how it was related causally to pathological behaviour in individuals. For any such study to be convincing it must demonstrate several things: that the behaviours observed necessarily lead to the appearance within the family of a deviant member (i.e., are not observed in 'normal' families); that they are exclusively related to schizophrenic pathology (rather than say delinquency or depression); and that they are not the *result* of the presence of a schizophrenic member, rather than the cause. Even where appropriate relationships are demonstrated, it then has to be explained why a *particular* family member becomes schizophrenic rather than another. One of the most systematic and orderly studies in the field, that of Mishler and Waxler (1968) nevertheless achieved a very small yield in terms of 'significant' results.

More recently, after several years of inactivity in this field, the focus has switched to the role of the family in relapse in schizophrenia, rather than as a primary cause. Families shown to be highly emotionally expressive (HEE) can induce exceptionally high relapse rates in patients who are free of drug treatments, out of hospital, and in contact with their family for more than 35 hours per week. The combined effects (off drugs, out of hospital, high contact with HEE relatives) can lead to 92 per cent relapse (Vaughn and Leff, 1976). However, in such work, the causal modelling and the quality of research is much more subtle than the earlier studies of the 1960s and the measurement of degree of expressed emotion is objective and reliable.

Looked at thirty years later, the communication theorists' approach seems to have achieved little in practical terms. Certainly, it changed our ways of thinking about the family and led to a series of studies, which on the whole proved to be inconclusive. The case for faulty communication as a primary cause of individual pathology has not been proved. It remains open whether better research designs and more adequate measurement techniques would reveal more specific causal relationships.

Straus and Brown (1978) in their inventory of the family measurement literature, comment on the limited availability of techniques for describing and measuring the family as a whole. This problem (of sampling *all* family members, rather than parents and/or dyads) is still with us (see Olson and Markoff, 1983). Even so, very few of the measures which have been devised for infra-familial sampling satisfy basic scientific requirements. Straus and Brown state that more than half of the available instruments provide no evidence of reliability, and something like 70 per cent fail to pay attention to validity. The classic review of Riskin and Faunce (1972) failed to locate more than a handful of family-interaction studies which were methodologically sound.

The several criticisms of the available research included: lack of conceptual clarification (leading to poor operationalization of key concepts such as 'communication'); failure to obtain measures of inter-judge agreement; low inter-judge reliability; absence of blind raters (i.e., the diagnostic status of families was known); lack of demographic comparability of experimental and control groups; and lack of comparability of treatment status (i.e., experimental group hospitalized, control group living at home). To these criticisms we might add the fact that the majority of studies were problem-driven and not theory-driven (see Hodgson and Lewis, 1979). Thus full and adequate consideration of the nature of the variables selected for examination and the measurement techniques employed is rare.

Selecting a Research Strategy

Faced with such difficulties, we had to make major decisions as to research strategy, at the beginning of our own work.

Psychologists with a laboratory orientation will throw up their hands in horror, when reading of our approach to data acquisition. Our aim was to gain access to the private life of the family. This required access to the family's natural ecology, the home. To gain understanding of the meaning of events in the home, we were obliged to become participant observers. To become participant observers we had to constrain our freedom of action and degree of control over events, since it was inevitable that the family would react to our presence. An exceptional or excessive presence would have pushed family behaviour beyond its normal or habitual range. Therefore, we were obliged to have only one observer in the home at any one time (rather than two or three), to eschew all mechanical recording devices which might influence behaviour and/or constrain freedom of movement (cameras, tape-recorders), and to follow the family around as much as possible, participating in family events. As observers we were almost passive, controlling events, not as if within the laboratory, but inadvertently: because of the family members' interpretation of our attitudes and beliefs, because of our own actual or perceived personality attributes, or because the families with whom we stayed were in need of help with personal problems. This brief description of the research problems encapsulates the decisions which were made: to observe rather than manipulate, to observe in the natural context, to minimize reactivity, to engage in extensive sampling within each family, to measure reliability, and where possible to test for validity. In addition, we drew upon an existing taxonomy of group behaviours which could enable formal operationalization (Borgatta, 1962). The full role of the observer as participant is described in Chapters 4 and 6.

What are the consequences of such naturalistic research? The laboratory offers all the formal requirements of a systematic science: reliability of measurement, control over experimental manipulations, control over systematic and random error, and, perhaps most important, control over the rate of gain of psychological information. Because we are almost pioneers, and because our approach was so new and hazardous, we chose a naturalistic research posture. We were not in the business of manipulation but observation. We did not understand and therefore we sought understanding. We had read what others had done, were dissatisfied with their approach, and sought to improve upon it. We wished to see the world through the eyes of family members. But all system was not thrown to the winds. We attempted to insert different observers in the same home, to counterbalance the order of their presence, to check on the reliability of observation, of observers, and of our behavioural taxonomy. What is the value of such an uncontrolled approach to psychological research? (In Chapter 12 Sue Lewis demonstrates the extent to which our approach has been deficient and the results non-generalizable).

There are several arguments in favour of a naturalistic approach in family research. First, observation and systematic description form the basis upon which sound theory can be built. Following the analogy from anthropology and biology such observation needs to be ecologically valid. In family research, this implies observation in the home. Only there can we sample a full set of conditions under which the family has to function, across a wide range of moods and settings. Such conditions, reflecting long-established patterns of interaction within a specific environment, cannot be reproduced within the laboratory. However, since the initial description has a purpose, to help to develop theory, it is therefore guided by longer-term goals and necessarily selective. But apart from formal theoretical orientation, there is what we might call *implicit theory*, namely the assumptions and prior conceptions of family life which each researcher brings with them as a form of bias.

New Methods in Social Science

London and Thorngate (1981) have considered the extent to which the methods of the natural sciences have borne fruit for the social sciences. They draw attention to the special characteristic of '*amplification processes* . . . the myriad of processes that can make incidental and nonincidental events, however small, unsuspected progenitors of larger happenings or surreptitious contributors to the evolution of such happenings' (page 206). Such events can only be appreciated in retrospect. They can be convergent (if their effects lead to the theoretically expected) or divergent. Such amplified fluctuations can occur quickly or more slowly. Unfortunately, much psychological research absorbs such events into the error term, denying their causal significance. This is acceptable in the convergent case but not in the divergent case. For the family, for example, the sudden death of a marriage partner, as a result of a chance motor accident caused through someone else's drunkenness, has gross and far-reaching divergent amplification effects. Such effects, in systems terms, are difficult to anticipate as emergent properties of the existing system: 'It is difficult to imagine a classical investigation of the causal relationships affected by divergent deviation emerging from chance events or fluctuations. Controlled experimentation in the social sciences, as ordinarily understood, aims to keep fluctuations within limits and to inhibit any escalation of accidental effects. Yet it is just this practice that hampers the investigation of phenomena that develop outside the laboratory in ways that are circumscribed or proscribed outright inside the laboratory' (page 210).

London and Thorngate suggest a variety of ways in which such phenomena can be captured. Observation in the preserved situation and context is one approach. In such situations one can observe the freely evolving pattern of events. But of course the rub is that we cannot extrapolate to context-free generalizations. Moreover, viewed in historical terms, a set of observations might oblige the observer to shift from one disciplinary boundary to another, to appreciate what London and Thorngate describe as the *causal collage*. To grasp the meaning of events, vivid personal descriptions by participants will serve to trigger recognition of their salience in others, more than will the dry ritual reporting of science.

To capture such events and to ensure that they are less likely to be overlooked, London and Thorngate recommend extensive sampling of the individual case, particularly over time. They recommend what they describe as *orientative sampling*: this (a) sensitizes the observer to salient variables, and (b) leads the way to eventual isomorphic mapping onto larger populations. However, the role of the researcher which London and Thorngate describe is different from that of the camera or standardized instrument of measurement. It loosens the grip of the experimenter on the subject, just as Jourard's (1969) approach of self-disclosure narrows the status gap between investigator and subject.

We hope that the reader will take the view, having completed this book, that we have sampled family life in the raw, and described it in its natural vividness. Our own view is that given additional resources we could: (a) have used our experience to train observers to a higher level of reliability, and (b) have created a data set with greater generalizability. There are differences in viewpoint among us and we are not ashamed to reveal them, as Chapter 12 by Sue Lewis demonstrates. We must accept that our sample is small, consisted of families in contact with social agencies, and that our stay with families was brief, albeit much longer than others have achieved. London and Thorngate suggest that the benefit of orientative sampling is that one requires no prior assurance that the sample is representative; a phenomenon is explored at the outset with an openness to experience. Our research, therefore, represents the beginnings of a research programme.

Special Problems of Naturalistic Research

Finding volunteer families

The notion of working in natural contexts has several practical consequences for research strategy. Gaining access to organizations in the real world for pure research rather than practical application is notoriously hard. Such organizations may be seen as gate-keepers to the research domain, and many months of careful negotiation can lead to zero outcome and a sense of depressed resignation. In the present study we were obliged to take an indirect route, via child guidance clinics, and to live with families who were under some form of treatment. The early families in the study had problems of school refusal, later families had a variety of communicational difficulties. None of the families was a context for severe psychopathology or psychosis.

We remain puzzled as to how authorities like Kantor and Lehr (1975) managed to secure access to 'normal families'; unfortunately, they provide no methodological detail. One has to ask why some families will volunteer and others will refuse, and speculate on the extent to which such characteristics will influence what is observed. Westley and Epstein (1969) demonstrated that it was the families with least disturbed members who agreed to participate and/or persisted with their study.

In the present case, some of our refusals appeared to arise because the presence of the observer might itself have set off a divergently amplifying set of events, including major changes in spouse relationships. On several occasions, we sensed a strong positive attitude towards us by one spouse, and a strongly conflicting view on the part of the other. It seemed that one member might have an emotional invest-ment in the status quo and that our intrusion would disrupt homeostatic mechanisms which sustained current interactional patterns. The keen invitation of the other spouse, in contrast, may have reflected a desire for change and an improvement in their personal status. Refusal was therefore a defence. In general, the one characteristic common to the families we studied was that they trusted us as social scientists (not clinical experts) and that they saw our involvement as one possible way out of their current difficulties. In Chapters 8 and 10 one family gives their view of their own life and our impact upon it.

Finding participant observers

Not only are volunteer families hard to find, but so are participant observers. The work entailed separation from one's own domestic circumstances, a possible six-teen hours per day of intensive observation, a denial of much of personal identity for prolonged periods, and a willingness not to disagree or to assert one's opinions. Moreover, the experience of observing others has the effect of changing one's percep-tion of one's own domestic ecology; relationships and attitudes come under a new and penetrating searchlight. Somehow, the observer has to have a friendly authen-ticity, a confidence which is expressed in manner and not in words or action, a sense of unconditional positive regard (in Rogerian terms) which provides authority, yet without threat or judgement. The lack of evaluative judgement implies not only an acceptance of the family's beliefs and lifestyle, but a willingness to learn from the family and to respect their particular world view, however discrepant from one's own. None of us would claim to satisfy all of these requirements all of the time!

Establishing a relationship between observer and observed

In addition to these consequences of participant observation, there is a formal requirement to establish a working relationship with all family members and their acquaintances. These are people of different gender, age, and status, with different expectations of the observer. They include members of different ethnic groups, different religious beliefs, and different social classes from that of the observer.

The relationship between experimenter and subject is not the same as the relationship between observer and observed. In particular, the intrusion into the lives of others raises great problems of confidentiality and consent. It has not been easy for us, for example, to select many observer transcript passages for inclusion in this book, since we would be embarrassed (or even ashamed) to reveal them. These were intimate secrets, conveyed in the heady reality of family interaction processes. Luckily, our relationship with several families has been such that they have granted us permission and/or have agreed to contribute to the book. The full set of ethical issues we encountered is discussed in Chapter 5.

Difficulties of systematic observation

Problems of sampling and analysis are also considerable. Our shortest stay was for four days, including a weekend. Each hour (or as near to the hour as possible) we recorded privately, on a handheld tape-recorder, what had occurred in our field of view. The temporal order of events, as well as their emotional colouring, was recorded from memory and not from real-time actuality. One strange effect of the neutral role is that one feels oneself having less personal investment in events. Indeed, it is not easy to detect the personality of the observer in many of our transcripts. However, to suggest that sampling and recording were person-free, or free of the cultural preconceptions of our observers, would not only be flying in the face of reality, but a denial of elementary principles of perceptual experience. The ordinary observer is not accurate; hopefully, as trained observers we were superior. Unfortunately, there was no external validation available, other than the interpretations of other observers. We kept observers apart until all reporting and analysis was complete (a difficult task when two people work in the same room!). Samples of diary extracts, showing the family as viewed by different observers, are given in Chapter 9.

The Need for Good Theory

In 1971, Hill offered a list of five strategies for the development of family theory and research. His efforts led to a multidisciplinary venture, which in turn was translated into two major volumes (Burr, Hill, Nye, and Reiss, 1979). The five strategies were as follows:

1. seek out *general* theories which, although developed for other purposes, have been applied in the family domain and whose constructs are embodied in family theories whether in an explicit or implicit form (for example, general system theory);
2. locate, codify, and systematize *partial* theories of the *family* (for example, Jackson's double-bind);
3. find theories developed in other contexts which could be pressed into explanations of family behaviour (for example, dissonance theory, or equity theory);

4. locate, codify, and systematize research propositions and findings, ranging from simple exercises in data-gathering to metatheoretical analysis of theory construction;
5. integrate, cross-relate, and systematize all the information gathered from 1 through 4.

This vast enterprise, on the admission of Hill and his associates, was never fully realized in the volumes which they published (Burr *et al.*, 1979). Nevertheless, it remains a sound strategy for the development of psychological theory and research into the family. But there are several impediments to progress particularly within the discipline of psychology. First, few psychologists are familiar with the language and concepts of sociological theory and research. Yet many sociological concepts have surface similarity with psychological concepts; certainly, the object of many sociological enquiries could be translated into objects of psychological enquiry. Secondly, Hill's programme for the development of family research involves an extremely broad range of competence *within* psychology, stretching from inter-personal interaction, developmental theory, organizational psychology, and group behaviour, as well as involving concepts of the self, and theories of a phenomenological nature. While such theoretical traditions may be brought to bear upon the family itself, they nevertheless neglect the appraisal of the impact of the *external* culture and social norms upon family life. For example, there is ample evidence that social class factors have their influence on academic attainment, but we know little about how these macro variables are tied together by family process.

In Chapter 3 we ask the question: What are the requirements for good theories of family behaviour? We examine several key theories in the light of these requirements and make recommendations for future practice. In Chapter 2 we consider in detail a key theoretical approach in family theory, the General System Theory approach (e.g., von Bertalanffy, 1968). While the systems approach has clear benefits, they may only be at a surface level; the approach does not always live up to its promise when pressed into use for the description of complex behaviours in complex environments.

How This Work Began

Anthony Gale first came into contact with family work while teaching in Cardiff. Sue Walrond-Skinner and Emilia Dowling of the Cardiff Family Institute invited him to participate in their research. This developed into a teaching interest. Subsequently, Arlene Vetere joined his course on The Family and became fascinated and enchanted by the work of Jules Henry, described in his *Pathways to Madness* (1973). She then decided to devote the following years to participant observation of family life, starting with four families who had a school-refusing child. This work formed the core of her doctoral thesis. On the basis of this pioneering work, we received further research funds.

We have included a description of the way the work developed because the story is instructive. Anthony Gale is by training an experimental and laboratory scientist and Arlene Vetere, as a student of psychology, had not been introduced to non-quantitative methods. The proposal to carry out this research met with derision and disbelief by many of our colleagues, who regarded our approach as risky, irresponsible, and lacking in the rigour of real psychology. We are grateful to our colleagues for their opposition, which sharpened the pleasures of the work. Our diaries of family life, some of which are extended descriptions of family life over more than a week's observation, strike us as being the stuff of real psychology. Moreover, our work raised a great number of theoretical, methodological, and ethical issues which would never have confronted us with such force within the laboratory.

The experience of family work has enriched in several ways our lives as psychologists. One of the reasons for writing this particular introduction to the book is to convey our astonishment that psychologists continue to ignore the family not only as a source of human experience but as a context for the development of psychological research and theory itself.

The Structure of This Book

In Chapter 1 we have tried to identify the key themes which run through the book: the importance of family life to the individual, the neglect of the family in both academic and applied psychology, the need for good theory in family research, and problems in research method, and in naturalistic research in particular. We devote Chapter 2 to a critical consideration of General System Theory, from its early beginnings, through to its application in the family context. Such a critique is important because so many family researchers and therapists refer to systems concepts without considering their limitations. We feel there is a danger that smart-looking terminology can be used to create a false sense of systematic thinking and theorizing.

Chapter 3 reviews, again within a critical framework, a sample of important theories of family behaviour and ends with a prescription for theory construction in the field. Family research calls for special methods of investigation. Chapter 4 reviews the history of the participant observation method, its advantages and disadvantages, and its appropriateness for family study. Work with families involves intrusion into their private lives; it also raises difficulties for the researchers themselves and for their relationships not only with the family but with other professionals in contact with the family. These ethical issues are considered in Chapter 5. The remainder of the book is devoted to our own study: the development of the family scenario (Chapter 6); the analysis of participant observer data (Chapter 7); the use of interviews, films, and repertory grids (Chapter 8); descriptions of nine families from different theoretical viewpoints together with a view of them through the eyes of two participant observers (Chapter 9); a couple's view of themselves and their family problems (Chapter 10); and, an attempt to characterize the families studied in general terms, via the construct system of one observer (Chapter 11). In spite of our intentions, our research did not achieve all its objectives; in Chapter 12 we offer a critical evaluation of the project made by a statistician, which sets out a list of requirements for future work. We end with an appraisal of the research together with suggestions for its potential in applied fields (Chapter 13). Because of limitations of space the account of our data is in the form of illustrative examples. The original data are lodged in the Department of Psychology at the University of Southampton and are available, with appropriate safeguards in relation to confidentiality, to serious researchers. The data consist both of the original diaries and the computer analyses.

Finally we wish to acknowledge the financial support provided by the Psychology Committee of the former Social Science Research Council (now the ESRC) and the University of Southampton Committee for Advanced Studies, who funded the work. Several professional colleagues introduced us to individual families. We are indebted to the Hythe Child Guidance Clinic, the Wessex Unit for Children and Parents, and the Chippenham Child and Family Guidance Centre. Throughout the work we received constant encouragement from Andrew Treacher who has read and commented on parts of the manuscript. But our biggest thanks must go to all the families who allowed us to enter their homes, treated us as family members, and who taught us so much about family life.

References

Bateson, G. (1958). *Naven, 2nd edn with Epilogue*. Stanford: Stanford University Press.
Bateson, G., Jackson, D. D., Haley, J. and Weakland, J. H. (1956). Toward a theory of schizophrenia. *Behavioural Science*, **1**, 251–264.
von Bertalanffy, L. (1968). *General System Theory*. Harmondsworth: Penguin.
Borgatta, E. F. (1962). A systematic study of interaction process scores, peer and self-assessments, personality and other variables. *Genetic Psychology Monographs*, **65**, 219–291.
Bowen, M. (1960). A family concept of schizophrenia. In: D. D. Jackson (Ed.), *Schizophrenia: An Integrated Approach*. New York: Basic Books.
Burr, W. R., Hill, R., Nye, F. I. and Reiss, I. L. (Eds) (1979). *Contemporary Theories About the Family*, vol. 1, *Research Based Theories*. New York: Free Press.
Burr, W. R., Hill, R., Nye, F. I. and Reiss, I. L. (Eds) (1979). *Contemporary Theories About the Family*, vol. 2, *General Theories/Theoretical Orientations*. New York: Free Press.
Cooper, D. (1971). *The Death of the Family*. New York: Pantheon.
Fontana, A. F. (1966). Familial aetiology of schizophrenia: Is a scientific methodology possible? *Psychological Bulletin*, **66**, 214–227.
Frank, G. H. (1965). The role of the family in the development of psychopathology. *Psychological Bulletin*, **64**, 191–205.
Gurman, A. S. and Kniskern, D. P. (1978). Research on marital and family therapy: Progress, perspective, and prospect. In: S. L. Garfield and A. S. Bergin (Eds), *Handbook of Psychotherapy and Behaviour Change: An Empirical Analysis*, 2nd edn. New York: Wiley.
Henry, J. (1973). *Pathways to Madness*. New York: Vintage Books.
Hill, R. (1971). *Payoffs and limitations of contemporary strategies for family theory systematization*. Paper presented at NCFR Meetings in Estes Park, Colorado, August.
Hodgson, J. W. and Lewis, R. A. (1979). Pilgrim's progress III: A trend analysis of family theory and methodology. *Family Process*, **18**, 163–173.
Jacob, T. (1975). Family interaction in disturbed and normal families: A methodological and substantive review. *Psychological Bulletin*, **82**, 133–165.
Jourard, S. M. (1969). The effects of experimenter's self-disclosure on subject's behaviour. In: C. D. Spielberger (Ed.), *Current Topics in Clinical and Community Psychology*. New York: Academic Press.

Kantor, D. and Lehr, W. (1975). *Inside the Family: Towards a Theory of Family Process.* San Francisco, California: Jossey-Bass.

Laing, R. D. and Esterson, A. (1964). *Sanity, Madness and the Family.* London: Tavistock.

Lidz, T., Cornelison, A., Fleck, S. and Terry, D. (1957). The intra-familial environment of schizophrenic patients: II. Marital schism and marital skew. *American Journal of Psychiatry,* **114**, 241–248.

London, I. D. and Thorngate, W. (1981). Divergent amplification and social behaviour: Some methodological considerations. *Psychological Reports,* **48**, 203–228.

Mishler, E. G. and Waxler, N. E. (1965). Family interaction processes and schizophrenia: A review of current theories. *Merrill-Palmer Quarterly of Behaviour and Development,* **11**, 269–315.

Mishler, E. G. and Waxler, N. E. (1968). *Interaction in Families.* New York: Wiley.

Olson, D. H. and Markoff, R. (1983). *Inventory of Marriage and Family Literature,* vol. 9. London: Sage.

Patterson, G. R., Ray, R. S., Shaw, D. A. and Cobb, J. A. (1969). *Manual for Coding Family Interactions.* New York: Asis National Auxiliary Publication Service.

Raush, H. L., Greif, A. C. and Nugent, J. (1979). Communication in couples and families. In: W. R. Burr, R. Hill, F. I. Nye and I. L. Reiss (Eds), *Contemporary Theories About the Family,* vol. 1, *Research Based Theories.* New York: Free Press.

Riskin, J. and Faunce, E. E. (1972). An evaluative review of family interaction research. *Family Process,* **11**, 365–455.

Straus, M. and Brown, B. W. (1978). *Family Measurement Techniques.* Minnesota: University of Minnesota Press.

Vaughn, C. E. and Leff, J. P. (1976). The influence of family and social factors on the course of psychotic illness. *British Journal of Psychiatry,* **129**, 125–137.

Westley, W. A. and Epstein, N. B. (1969). *The Silent Majority.* San Francisco, California: Jossey-Bass.

Wynne, L. C., Ryckoff, I. M., Day, J. and Hirsch, S. I. (1958). Pseudomutuality in the family relations of schizophrenics. *Psychiatry,* **21**, 205–220.

CHAPTER 2

General System Theory and the Family: A Critical Evaluation

Arlene Vetere

Introduction

It is now fashionable for social scientists to describe family structure and behaviour in 'systems' terms. Concepts derived from General System Theory (von Bertalanffy, 1956) are bandied between the social science disciplines, with little concern for the rigorous definition of terms. For example, families are variously described as open systems, homeostatic systems, error-activated negative feedback systems, and so on. Sadly, such jargon often provides a smokescreen for sloppy, ill-disciplined thinking which has a superficial attraction. For example, does a structural description of a family's *boundaries* have explanatory power? Can we predict from structural descriptions which family members will exhibit symptoms?

The concepts of General System Theory are applied to the understanding of human social phenomena for which they were not originally developed. There is a danger that the area of family study will fragment and become empirically contentless, rather than realizing the promise of a coherent theoretical view of the family afforded by General System Theory, unless a concerted effort is made by social scientists to clarify concepts and define terms before translating them into operational definitions and specific observations. We shall return to the origins of General System Theory in the fields of biology and control engineering to clarify some of the muddles surrounding 'systems' concepts. Then we examine their potential for application to family study.

Systems and System Levels

A whole which functions as a whole through the interdependence of its parts is known as a *system*. General System Theory attempts to understand and explain how this obtains in the widest variety of systems. Thus the theory (a) seeks to classify systems

18

according to the way the parts are organized or interrelated, and (b) to describe typical patterns of behaviour for the different classes of systems as defined. The term 'system' spans the physical, biological, and social world, so that we can speak of a solar system, geophysical systems, economic systems, molecular systems, and so on. For example, in biology, the organism is seen as a system of interdependent parts, each of which consists of many *sub*systems. The human body nicely illustrates the complexity of a biological system, with its skeletal system, nervous system, endocrine system, behavioural system, perceptual-subjective system, and so on. Describing and explaining the complex relationships between these human systems presents a real challenge to theory and methodology.

Systems research is concerned with the concept of organized complexity. Within the model of organized complexity, there exists a *hierarchy* of levels of organization. A biological example of a hierarchy is organism – organ – tissue – cell – organelle. Each level of organization within the hierarchy is more complex than the one below and each level is characterized by *emergent properties* that do not exist at lower levels and as such are not reducible to previous events. Our example of a biological system has emergent properties, such as reproduction, self-organization, and self-reflective behaviour. Of course the question arises as to the origin and construction of the emergent properties. Our ignorance of the basic properties of some systems components leads us to speculate that the novel properties of the system are present in potential form, emerging when the components interact in a particular way.

A hierarchy of systems is possible because of the concept of 'open' systems. If a system is 'open' for at least one property, it can exchange materials, energies, and information with its environment, constantly building up and breaking down its components. Thus open systems can be considered subsystems of some higher order systems, for example, the individual as a member of a family, the family as a part of society, and so on; and since each subsystem can be subdivided into sub-subsystems, a hierarchy of systems is produced.

What is General System Theory's Starting Point?

During the 1930s von Bertalanffy formulated a General System Theory as a working hypothesis. As a biologist, he wanted to account for the organization of the parts of the organism and how this organization maintained and regulated the organism's functioning. According to von Bertalanffy (1962), General System Theory developed in parallel with a number of attempts at model building and abstract generalization, all concerned with the means by which 'information' is transmitted within and between systems. For example, information theorists developed the principles of information transmission, suggesting that it is a measurable quantity, while cyberneticists studied communication and control based on the idea of circular feedback. Von Bertalanffy describes a change in the intellectual climate, post-war, conducive to the development of his ideas. Sadovsky (1972) points out that system technology arose during World War II with the new military technology when technical devices were seen to be an entire complex of conditions, necessary for the adequate *functioning* of the device, and not merely the process of design and construction itself. Mechanical engineers and later, electrical engineers, wanted to build and run mechanisms which worked. The formal structure of a system was often known but its range of behaviours was often not documented, either by way of empirical studies or experience. Thus von Bertalanffy found that other scientists shared his thoughts, particularly those connected with modern automation in applied fields.

The Problem of Complexity

The analytic method of physical science attempts to reduce the *complexity* of observable phenomena by examining the relationship between pairs of variables while holding other variables constant. It is possible to analyse and interpret the particular reduction by a method of hypothesis testing within a theoretical framework. This is a powerful method for advancing our understanding of certain phenomena. However, it rests on the assumption that the parts of the whole (the variables) remain the same while analysed independently as when they are playing their part in the whole. It further assumes that the rules governing the assembly of the parts are clear-cut.

But the crucial question is whether and to what extent the methods of reduction can explain complexity (Checkland, 1981; Rapoport, 1968). Biologists and particularly social scientists are aware of the increased complexity of their subject matter, which has dense connections between the many different interacting parts, thus making it hard to examine a particular reduction in a controlled experiment; for example, decision-making processes in social institutions.

Within biology there is the problem, referred to earlier, of the emergence of new phenomena at higher levels of complexity, for example, reproduction and self-organization. Within the social sciences, the self-reflective behaviour of humans which entails 'freedom' of choice provides many possible outcomes for behaviour rather than only one possible one. This suggests that human social behaviour will not be reducible to general laws but rather to situational analyses which take account of the actors' attribution of meaning and predict certain behaviours in certain contexts. So far, reductionist thinking has been unable to solve the problems posed by the emergence of a set of phenomena which are higher order with respect to those of the natural sciences. (See Boulding, 1956, for an excellent discussion of the nature of systems in our universe and a classification of these systems into a hierarchy.)

Do We Need a General Theory of Systems?

Attempts to construct general theories of system behaviour, particularly of living systems, have been criticized for being more 'general' than 'theory' (Buck, 1956; Lilienfeld, 1978). It is argued that the science of living phenomena, particularly social behaviour, is inexact and vague and does not provide any means for resolving differences among researchers. It is not our intention here to debate the philosophies of science, but it is worth noting that: (1) methods of sampling behaviour and data analysis continue to improve (see our discussion of London and Thorngate, 1981, Chapter 1), and (2) it is increasingly demonstrated that some living processes are regular and amenable to systematic observation and measurement (Miller, 1980). It remains to be demonstrated that behavioural phenomena are too complex and numerous for meaningful classification and exact measurement.

Perhaps it is more fruitful to ask whether we need a *general* theory of systems. What would we require of such a theory? For example:

1. would it integrate and explain the available research data and generate a common research language;
2. would it operationally define purposive behaviour and the dynamics of change;
3. would it specify the conditions under which the elements will be observed and determine how novel observations are collected in order to increase our understanding of underlying principles;
4. would it provide common units of measurement that allow cross comparisons of research at different system levels?

Such requirements have serious implications for General System Theory as a general theory of systems! Our next task is to evaluate General System Theory within the logical positivist framework for describing theories and their functions as developed by Hall and Lindzey (1957) in their critique of personality theories. We shall set out the key constructs and relevant assumptions of General System Theory and examine the relationships between the constructs. The theoretical constructs will be examined for the clarity of their operational definitions and whether these definitions translate the constructs into observations and predictions. Finally, the coherence of General System Theory with both the existing data and new data generated by the theory will be examined.

Characterization of the Theory: The Key Constructs

General System Theory is designed to describe and integrate the general characteristics of systems and to analyse and understand system function. Hall and Fagen's (1956) definition of a system is widely used: 'a system is a set of objects together with the relationships between the objects and their attributes. The objects are the component parts of the system, the attributes are the properties of the objects' and the relationships tie the system together' (page 18). Hall and Fagen's definition is general and it is impossible to think of anything or any combination of things which could not be conceptualized as a system. A concept which applies to *everything* is logically empty. However the 'definition' is not intended to be a definition in a mathematical or philosophical sense and as such is not amenable to precise and clear description. The problem resides in the nature of the concept to be defined, that of organized complexity.

The literature of General System Theory is diverse and difficult to track down. There exists a heterogeneity of approaches to the definition of system (Ackoff, 1960;

von Bertalanffy, 1962; Open Systems Group, 1981), many of which emphasize the interaction of components and all of which are incomplete, often relating only to the abstract analysis of the selected empirical domain. There is a gap between the general qualitative definition and the techniques of analysis available. In other words, we still lack well-developed research techniques directed at mutually interacting components.

The terms 'objects', 'attributes', and 'relationships' (Hall and Fagen, 1956) will be elaborated to clarify the definition of system. The 'objects' are the parts or components of the system and those parts are unlimited in variety; for example, in the physical sciences, the parts of the system are physical in nature, such as atoms, stars, springs, bones, and gases.

These objects have, among others, the following 'attributes': atomic weight, number of electrons; temperature, distance from other stars; spring tension, displacement, and so on.

The 'relationships' in Hall and Fagen's definition are those that 'tie the system (or the constructs) together'. It is these relationships that make the notion of 'system' useful. We understand events directly by perceiving whole sequences of acts rather than their parts, for example, the actor and their social circumstances. But if we restrict our attention to the observable gross patterns of those wholes, we may not make much progress toward understanding the particular behaviours. We can, for example, more clearly understand the action of an organism if we understand how the components of the act are integrated by its nervous system, perceptual-subjective system, and behavioural system.

When studying physical systems, researchers often substitute abstract systems with analogous relationships and the problem becomes a mathematical one. Physicists, chemists, and engineers adopt this practice: this is the creation of the mathematical model. A system must possess certain properties before it is amenable to this form of analysis. For example, the attributes must be quantifiable and finite, and the relationships between the objects and their translation into observable behaviours must be known. Very few systems possess all these qualities and it is more likely to occur in simpler, mechanical systems than the biological systems of living organisms.

System Boundaries and System Environment

Our discussion of open systems so far implies the existence of an environment in which the system behaves, and interacts with other systems and the environment. Hall and Fagen define the 'environment' of a system as follows: 'for a given system, the environment is the set of objects a change in whose attributes affects the system and also those objects whose attributes are changed by the behaviour of the system' (page 20). In order to define an environment then, all the factors affecting or affected by the system must be known, but the subdivision of the universe into system and environment is often arbitrary. Again this task is somewhat easier in the physical sciences than in the biological and social sciences, where differentiation is complex.

We have already discussed the ability of systems to subdivide hierarchically into subsystems, which in turn can be subdivided into sub-subsystems, components, and so on. Thus a system at one level may be considered a subsystem at another. A system is said to exist within an environment, which is defined as a function of the hierarchical level chosen and modifies the behaviour of the system and may be modified by it. Thus the 'boundary' between the system and the environment should be clearly drawn. Boundaries delineate the components belonging to the system and those belonging to its environment. They demarcate appropriate system behaviour and the admission of members and other imports into the system.

Boundaries of social systems are often determined by the function and behaviour of the system, for example, the personnel, export, and maintenance departments of a factory, so that boundary definition is often a pragmatic issue. As a rule of thumb, researchers tend to select boundaries such that the components within the system have a higher level of interaction among themselves than with components outside the system, while recognizing that a component can belong to two or more different systems at the same time. So in our factory example, a member of the personnel department could belong to the staff social club and attend shareholders' meetings, and so on. This discussion of boundaries now leads us into consideration of open and closed systems and how they differ.

Open and Closed Systems

In 1933 von Bertalanffy put forward the idea of the organism as an 'open' system. Most organic systems are open; hence they exchange materials, energies, and information with their environments, continuously building up and breaking down their components. A system is 'closed' if there is no import or export of energy in any form, such as information, heat, physical materials, and no change of components. An example of a closed system is a chemical reaction taking place within a sealed, insulated container. Closed systems are isolated from their environment and subject to the Second Law of Thermodynamics. This states that the entropy (measure of disorder) of a closed system will always increase toward a maximum, achieved in equilibrium (Prigogine, 1947).

Open systems, unlike closed systems, can achieve a *steady state* which depends upon continuous exchanges with their environment (von Bertalanffy, 1950). The organism is able to adapt to changes in its environment *and* to maintain a continual steady state or homeostasis, to use Cannon's (1938) term; for example, the human body maintains a steady state of body temperature, despite fluctuations in environmental temperatures. Adaptive mechanisms facilitate system response to changing internal and external (environmental) requirements and maintenance mechanisms ensure the various subsystems are in balance and the whole system is in harmony with the environment. These counteracting forces sometimes generate stresses within the system, which are not always dysfunctional.

The steady state of an open system, which has continuous exchange with its environment, is said to exhibit *equifinality* or, metaphorically, to have a goal of its own. Equilibrium states in closed systems are determined by the initial conditions. This means that closed systems have direct cause/effect relationships between the initial conditions and the final state. In contrast, open systems can attain a time-independent state, independent of initial conditions and determined only by the system parameters. Thus final results can be achieved with different initial conditions and in different ways. Open systems are not constrained by the simple cause/effect relationships of closed systems, so that social groups, for example, can attain their goals with varying inputs and varying internal behaviour. It would seem, therefore, that there is more than one way to achieve organizational objectives!

Feedback and Control

The maintenance of the hierarchy within open systems involves a set of processes in which information is communicated for the purposes of regulation and control. Cybernetics, or the science of communication and control (Weiner, 1948), studies the link between control mechanisms found in natural systems and those developed in man-made systems. Technological devices exhibit 'equifinality' or 'purposefulness' in a way that resembles living system behaviour.

Cybernetics studies patterns of signals by means of which information is transmitted both within and between systems. Information transmission is essential for *control*. Thus the capacity of a system to execute control depends on the amount of information it can process and store. All control processes depend upon *communication*, or in other words, upon a manual or automatic flow of information in the form of instructions or constraints.

The idea of information is prior to that of feedback in cybernetics. Weiner noted the importance of what control engineers call *feedback*. He defined it as 'the transmission of information about the actual performance of any machine (in the general sense) to an earlier stage in order to modify its working'. For example, servo-mechanisms, such as central heating thermostats, are man-made systems which operate on the feedback principle. They correct their performance by comparing their current state with some pre-set goal and modify their performance on the basis of the 'observed' difference. Such feedback systems also occur in living systems, for example, posture control in the human body. The nature, degree, and polarity of feedback in a system powerfully affects the stability or instability of a system. This can best be demonstrated by discussing the polarity of feedback.

Feedback can be both *positive* and *negative*. In negative feedback the modification is such that the difference between actual and desired performance is reduced, thereby ensuring *stability*; whereas positive feedback processes induce *instability* by reinforcing any modification in performance (Maruyama, 1963). Thus we see that feedback is a crucial concept in understanding how a system maintains a dynamic equilibrium between the maintenance and adaptive capacities.

Ashby (1956) demonstrated that continuing effective control in a changing environment needs a 'controller' with a variety of responses which can match the variety of the environmental information. This is the Law of Requisite Variety, which together with the Principle of Equifinality, are two *descriptive* laws about the behaviour of systems. There are few laws about system behaviour in *general*, although physicists and control engineers can predict the behaviour of individual physical systems.

The concept of information has been shown to be a powerful one in cybernetics. Although it is an abstraction, it has considerable explanatory power and is capable of generating testable predictions. However, the precise definition of information does raise some problems. Engineers are not concerned with how information is obtained by attributing *meaning* to data. The quantitative measure of 'information' in information theory is concerned with the efficiency of the process whereby a message becomes a signal and is transmitted and received. Engineers are not concerned with content. When considering the application of General System Theory to family study, information within feedback cycles cannot be assumed to be devoid of meaning. This raises problems for family researchers.

The Link Between Man-Made and Natural Systems

Systems that are 'living' in the biological sense share many common attributes with systems that are not. These common attributes are a product of the system's organization. Some researchers generalize the concept of organism to organized system, where organized systems include organisms. The behaviour of all organized living or non-living systems can be studied with certain methods. These are concerned with:

1. the *structure* of the system, i.e., the way in which the system receives, stores, processes and recalls information;
2. the *function* of the system, i.e., the behavioural response of the system to environmental stimulation, using the processed and stored information;
3. the *evolution* of the system.

If it is accepted that structure, function, and evolution are fundamental to all organized systems, then the concept of organism can be broadened still further to include whole complexes of living organisms, for example, human societies (Haire, 1959). We consider a specific example, the family group, in the latter part of this chapter. We also question the appropriateness of the biological model of social organization.

The Present Standing of General System Theory

In the light of the discussion so far, what can we say about the present status of General System Theory?

There is a need for a body of systematic theoretical constructs which can bridge the various scientific disciplines and their separate bodies of theory. Such a meta-theory would facilitate discussion of the general relationships within and between the empirical domains of the various disciplines. The use of the general system view can be seen as a direct response to the fragmentation of the scientific community into separate subdisciplines with their increasingly narrow fields of vision.

General System Theory is conceived as a set of related definitions, assumptions, and propositions which deal with reality as an integrated hierarchy of organization of matter and energy (Miller, 1980). In contrast to technical methods of describing systems which rigidly describe a set of objects and prescribe research methods, General System Theory is usually formulated on a higher level of abstraction, without regard to specific content (von Bertalanffy, 1968). It is concerned with the formal aspects of systems and constitutes an interdisciplinary area (Mesarovic, 1964). However, we must be cautious as this approach is in danger of becoming empirically contentless as it becomes increasingly general. The formulation of rigorous definitions becomes problematic as the gap between the content of formal, abstract disciplines and empirical reality widens. Scientists risk failing to understand each other and of losing sight of the real content for investigation in a given discipline, unable to integrate or be integrated!

In the realms of chemistry, physics, anatomy, and descriptive social science, adequate descriptive models of static structures have been developed. But even at the simplest level, the problem of the adequate description of complex structures remains to be solved. Advances have been made in the field of cybernetics and in the theory of self-maintaining or open systems. However, there is still much to learn about the control mechanisms which operate in the social world and, in the meantime, processes of self-maintenance remain somewhat mysterious. The fit between the conceptual system and the empirical findings is poorest in the study of groups, organizations, and societies, where sophisticated quantification is rare. This is, of course, the concern of the social sciences.

According to Warr (1980), it is not appropriate to set ideal standards for theory development and formulation, but rather to examine the characteristics of theories as they are put into practice by scientists. General System Theory might be more appropriately described as a *conceptual framework* which spans a wide range of disciplines and links up with more limited theories or models. As a conceptual framework, General System Theory may, according to Warr, stand without implied methodology. However, for those researchers working within General System Theory's frame of reference, a theory which is open to refutation or confirmation through observation is more useful than a conceptual framework.

The picture that emerges from the literature is far from that of a unified theory. It remains an open question whether much progress can be made with attempts to construct a unified theory of systems on a rigorous axiomatic basis. Medawar and Medawar (1977) suggest progress has been slow because reductive analysis is the most successful explanatory technique ever used in science. The counter-position to reductionism, based on holism and emergence, does not provide as clear a philosophy. The writings of von Bertalanffy show little development from the 1940s until his death in 1972 and have been subject to recent sharp attacks (Berlinski, 1976; Lilienfeld, 1978).

The definition of system given by von Bertalanffy is more a description of a class of events than a logical definition. Lektorsky and Sadovsky (1960) take this criticism a stage further by declaring that the 'description' lacks logical elegance. The main flaw in the theory lies in the lack of both adequate methods of analysis and synthesis of systems. The rules to establish and apply system principles are not well formulated. Probably no one would disagree that General System Theory has opened up new avenues of investigation and discourse, but the relationships between its abstract theoretical constructs and empirical facts remain tenuous, particularly in the study of human social phenomena. And it is to the study of family life that we now turn.

The Application of General System Theory to the Study of Family Life

The major barrier to the rigorous study of family interaction has been inadequate operationalization of the collection of data. It is clear that most family researchers are calling for a unified model for describing and explaining what happens in families. They require a theory of family behaviour which is comprehensive and able to generate testable predictions. Such a theory must be internally consistent and contain a set of relevant interrelated assumptions capable of operational definition. Thus can our family researcher move from abstract theoretical predictions to empirical observations. The model or theory would provide a common vocabulary, thereby facilitating communication among family process researchers (Group for Advancement of Psychiatry, 1970).

A family theory must satisfy the following requirements:

1. describe and explain family structure, dynamics, process, and change;
2. describe invariant interpersonal structures and emotional dynamics within the family and the transmission of distress onto individuals;
3. account for the family as the interface between the individual and culture, i.e., how does the family mediate between external environmental events and individual development, thus acting as a filter through which the child interprets the world;
4. describe the processes of individuation and differentiation of the family members;
5. predict health and pathology within the family, i.e., provide a source of hypotheses about family function and what causes dysfunction;
6. prescribe therapeutic strategies for dealing with family dysfunction;
7. account for the seemingly antithetical functions of stability and change, particularly when viewed within the family's developmental cycle.

These themes are developed further in Chapter 3 in relation to specific theories of family interactions.

General System Theory has been hailed by many family researchers as the guiding conceptual framework for describing the family. The family system is conceptualized thus: as a series of relationships between the interrelated systems of the individual, the family subsystems, the family system, and the family's environment. The individual family member is conceptualized as an organized system, living within multiple systems, large and small, with psychological, biological, and social characteristics. The family systems approach assumes family organization consists of the patterned activities of a number of individuals, which are thought to be complementary or interdependent with respect to some common goal or outcome. The governance of the individual and the family's effective functioning is discussed in greater detail in the context of specific theories of family interaction in Chapter 3 (for example, Minuchin, 1974; Kantor and Lehr, 1975).

Family researchers were searching for a model that would allow them to study complex organization and interaction in family systems. They appropriated General System Theory and the biological model of social organization, arguing that family groups could be conceptualized as 'organisms' or 'open systems'. Families were said to exhibit all the features of organized systems, although it was acknowledged that their degree of organization varied as did the robustness and viability of the family systems. Families were thought to be amenable to the same analysis as biological organisms and to be subject to similar principles of organization, such as feedback and control, equifinality, emergence, purposeful behaviour, and so on. We shall discuss the dangers of the fallacious analogy later in the chapter.

Family Systems Constructs

The basic unit of analysis for the family systems researcher is the *family system*. Applying Hall and Fagen's (1956) definition of system to the family, the 'objects' are the family members, the 'attributes' are the psychological characteristics of the members, and the 'relationships' are the interrelations between the members. This is clearly a physicalist simile. People are not just physical 'objects'. The non-physical attributes of people, such as the capacity for self-reflection, have more than a modulating effect on behaviour. Harré (1979) argues that it is the group as a whole and not only the individual which creates, maintains, and discards such attributed qualities as 'unassertive', 'competitive', and so on, by means of group interaction.

Implicit in this definition of the family is the existence of a boundary which separates those elements belonging to the system and those belonging to its environment. The boundary is drawn round the system such that the elements within the system interact more frequently amongst themselves than with elements outside the system. However, families are living systems with changing membership, and boundaries are not passively observed physical limits. Minuchin (1974) (see Chapter 3) argues that family boundaries are defined by rules that prescribe who participates and how they participate. Most family researchers use the household kin group system for the purposes of observation. Once the boundary has been 'drawn', families are then classified on a continuum from open to closed, based on the flexibility or 'permeability' of the boundaries. Thus a family would be described as *open* if the family members have a high level of exchange with the outside community and *closed* if low (see Kantor and Lehr, 1975).

When identifying the 'objects' within the system, some researchers designate each family member as an object. However, family membership is not constant over time. This problem of fluid membership is sometimes overcome by positing a set of standardized roles which can theoretically exist in all families, for example, the four-role family system of Parsons (1955) or the multiple-role system of Kantor and Lehr

(1975). Parsons' system consists of instrumental leader, expressive leader, instrumental follower, and expressive follower. Kantor and Lehr postulate the following roles: mover, opposer, follower, and bystander. The role itself is central to the analysis. Thus the family members can share a role, adopt more than one role or leave a role without disturbing the system. This can be useful, but misleading. It does not take account of expansion or contraction in the family system from the point of view of the individual.

Family researchers often specify the nature of the 'relationships' among the 'objects' in terms of family rules. These are said to prescribe the family's response to a wide range of environmental inputs. Although 'rules' are used by family researchers in a *prescriptive* sense, they are unable to explain, for example, the determinants of obedience or the imposition of sanctions, other than in *descriptive* terms.

Adaptability and Change

The major contribution of General System Theory to the study of the family has been to demonstrate the value of system adaptability. We have already discussed how this requires the balancing of both the homeostatic tendency and the capacity for transformation. The interchange of these apparently contradictory functions maintains the system in a provisional equilibrium, with the opportunity for growth and change guaranteed by this instability (Selvini-Palazzoli, Boscolo, Cecchin, and Prata, 1978).

The primary function of the system is to mediate between internal and external change, or pressures to change and the behaviour of the system. The system is defined as its structure and its structure is defined as the network of relationships among the component members. The relationships are defined in terms of interactions that are mediated by communication, information exchange, and the transmission of meaning. Thus the system functions to develop networks of operations suitable for coping with the varied and changeable environmental inputs and internal stresses to which it is subject.

Feedback Processes

Family systems theorists are concerned with family *rules* at several levels, identifying hierarchies of feedback and control. Engineers do not speak of 'rule-governed' systems, but are concerned with formulating laws that describe system behaviour. The two modes of discourse interconnect in the attempt to identify feedback processes.

Feedback processes are believed to be centrally characteristic of social systems (Buckley, 1967). A system is described as having feedback if it has the ability to 'recognize' its own output as input at some later stage.

Whether the system can monitor its progress towards a goal, correct and elaborate its response, and even alter its goals, depends on the complexity of its feedback structures. The term 'recognize' raises problems of interpretation as it is: (1) an 'individual' word, and (2) ill-defined within psychology. Its use by family researchers will be discussed within the framework set out by Broderick and Smith (1979) for understanding feedback levels.

A simple feedback loop obtains when a family output is subsequently processed as input. The result of this feedback will depend on the family rules. It might amplify into a positive feedback spiral. For example, according to the family rules, an external stress might result in internal conflict, which then feeds back into the system as increased stress, and so on. This escalating spiral would continue to operate until the system broke down, unless other feedback mechanisms were present.

Cybernetic control is the next level of complexity in the feedback structure. This is essential for system stability. Output from the system is fed back and compared to some family criterion or standard via a monitoring unit. Any deviation from expected behaviour is corrected. This is the negative feedback process. The system is able to switch from one set of available family rules to another set, but the system cannot 'learn' or 'create' at this level. For example, a family with rules teaching that child disobedience is punished and child obedience is rewarded, might become immobilized when faced with child drug addiction or attempted suicide. There may be no rule in the family's repertory to deal with the unprecedented behaviour. Thus the family must generate a novel rule in order to cope and this takes us on to level three or morphogenesis.

The morphogenic processes (literally form or structure changing processes) are the positive feedback or deviation amplifying processes by which social systems grow and innovate, as necessary for their survival. Morphogenesis is said to occur when the family realizes its usual mode of responding is not adequate for the exigencies of the situation. Family members might react in different ways, such as talking to confidantes or mental health professionals. Much of the writing on therapeutic change concerns change at this level. Thus at levels two and three, the system can reflect upon its goal-directed behaviour: selecting among existing sets of family rules at level two and generating new rules for responding at level three, thereby changing the system's structure.

Families are said to be capable of a higher order of change, level four, when the basic goals of the system are challenged. The conversion of a Catholic family to the faith of the Jehovah's Witnesses provides an example of this order of change. There is virtually no writing dealing with this level of change, other than anecdotal descriptions and speculations as to the processes involved.

The Transfer of Models: Criticisms

When considering the way in which family process researchers utilize the General System Theory framework, it must be asked whether they use methods of genuine quantitative analysis or merely arguments in favour of 'treating the system as a whole', exploiting sophisticated language to throw a smokescreen over sloppy, ill-disciplined concepts.

Family researchers often lack clear *conceptual* definitions, necessary for *operational* definition. It is rare that theoretical concepts are operationally defined within the framework of testing specific predictions, as Hodgson and Lewis (1979) point out. Our criticisms can be directed at both: (1) the transfer of systems technology and (2) the use of the biological analogy in the attempt to understand family behaviour. We shall discuss these two points separately.

The semantic basis on which the systems technological approach has been developed as the means of explaining *social* behaviour is based on loose definitions of the term 'system'. This can lead to fallacious analogy whereby superficial similarities lead to empty conclusions about any collection of variables that is included under the heading 'system'. Within the engineering sciences, the transfer of technology requires that certain conditions be met and certain assumptions about systems must be made explicit. Within the realm of family research, the parameters describing family behaviour are neither undisputed nor incontrovertible.

Social organizations are born, develop according to internal constraints, and die. The organismic analogy of social organization, favoured by some historians and many sociologists, is eschewed by von Bertalanffy (1962). Social organizations are not 'organisms'. A biological organism is something quite different from a social group consisting of distinct individuals. Rapoport and Horvath (1959) see some sense in demonstrating quasi-biological functions in organizations, for example, they maintain themselves, they sometimes reproduce, they respond to stress, and they die. Haire (1959) has argued that a biological model of social organizations requires us to search for lawful processes in organizational growth and development, modelled on such processes in living organisms. This need not imply biologism or the reduction of social to biological concepts, but rather that system principles apply in both fields.

Straus (1973) and Hodgson and Lewis (1979) pointed out that the family systems approach had not generated enough empirical research suitable for an evaluation of its methodological sophistication. At present, there are still not enough examples of links made between the abstract formulations of General System Theory and the reality of everyday family interaction. The main problem posed by General System Theory for family researchers is the relationship between order and disorder. How can we account for the energies of creativity, leadership, and imagination which lead the group into pastures new?

There is much overlap between the description of system behaviour and the explanation of system behaviour. Criticism of General System Theory tends to polarize the two domains so that researchers find difficulty in exploring and using the area of overlap. Is it fair, for example, to expect the theory to explain biologically determined changes in system and individual behaviour? In terms of the family's developmental cycle, one such change might be adolescent sexual development. Minuchin's attempt to take account of biologically determined developmental changes within his Structural Theory of the family is discussed in Chapter 3.

In conclusion, General System Theory provides a framework for describing complex, time-related interactional behaviour for which traditional sociological and psychological theories are not conceptually or methodologically suited. General System Theory focuses our attention on the role of each family member in the genesis and maintenance of behavioural dysfunction within the family and takes account of the nature of the cultural variables impinging on the family.

The systems movement is a discipline that spans the boundaries of the social and natural sciences, fostering communication and linking and integrating much fragmented contemporary theorizing and research. The task now for family researchers is to construct a theoretical language adequate to the task of describing and explaining interaction in families.

References

Ackoff, R. L. (1960). Systems, organizations and interdisciplinary research. *General Systems,* **5**, 1–8.

Ashby, W. R. (1956). *An Introduction to Cybernetics*. London: Chapman and Hall.

Berlinski, D. (1976). *On Systems Analysis*. Cambridge, Massachusetts: M.I.T. Press.

von Bertalanffy, L. (1950). The theory of open systems in physics and biology. *Science,* **3**, 23–29.

von Bertalanffy, L. (1956). General System Theory. *General Systems,* **1**, 1–10.

von Bertalanffy, L. (1962). General system theory: A critical review. *General Systems,* **7**, 1–20.

von Bertalanffy, L. (1968). *General System Theory*. Harmondsworth: Penguin.

Boulding, K. (1956). General systems theory: The skeleton of science. *Management Science,* **2**, 197–208.

Broderick, C. B. and Smith, J. (1979). The general systems approach to the family. In: W. R. Burr, R. Hill, F. I. Nye and I. L. Reiss (Eds), *Contemporary Theories about the Family*, vol. 2, *General Theories/Theoretical Orientations*. New York: Free Press.

Buck, R. C. (1956). On the logic of general behaviour systems theory. In: H. Fiegel and M. Scriven (Eds), *Minnesota Studies in the Philosophy of Science*, vol. 1. Minneapolis: University of Minnesota Press.

Buckley, W. (1967). *Sociology and Modern Systems Theory*. New Jersey: Prentice-Hall.

Cannon, W. B. (1938). *Wisdom of the Body*. New York: Norton.

Checkland, P. (1981). *Systems Thinking, Systems Practice*, Chichester: Wiley.

Group for the Advancement of Psychiatry (1970). *Field of Family Therapy: Report No. 78*. New York: Mental Health Materials Centre.

Haire, M. (1959). Biological models and empirical histories of the growth of organisations. In: M. Haire (Ed.), *Modern Organizations Theory*. New York: Wiley.

Hall, A. D. and Fagen, R. E. (1956). Definition of system. *General Systems Yearbook,* **1**, 18–28.

Hall, C. S. and Lindzey, G. (1957). *Theories of Personality*. New York: Wiley.

Harré, R. (1979). *Social Being: A Theory of Social Psychology*. Oxford: Blackwell.

Hodgson, J. W. and Lewis, R. A. (1979). Pilgrim's progress III. A trend analysis of family theory and methodology. *Family Process,* **18**, 163–173.

Kantor, D. and Lehr, W. (1975). *Inside the Family: Towards a Theory of Family Process*. San Francisco, California: Jossey-Bass.

Lektorsky, V. A. and Sadovsky, V. N. (1960). On principles of system research. *General Systems,* **V**, 171–179.

Lilienfeld, R. (1978). *The Rise of Systems Theory*. New York: Wiley.

London, I. D. and Thorngate, W. (1981). Divergent amplification and social behaviour: Some methodological considerations. *Psychological Reports,* **48**, 203–228.

Maruyama, M. (1963). The second cybernetics: Deviation-amplifying mutual causal processes. *American Scientist,* **51**, 164–179.

Medawar, P. B. and Medawar, J. S. (1977). *The Life Science*. London: Wildwood House.

Mesarovic, M. D. (1964). Foundations for a general systems theory. In: M. D. Mesarovic (Ed.), *Views on General Systems Theory*. New York: Wiley.

Miller, J. G. (1980). *Living Systems*. New York: McGraw-Hill.

Minuchin, S. (1974). *Families and Family Therapy.* London: Tavistock.

Open Systems Group (1981). *Systems Behaviour.* London: Harper and Row.

Parsons, T. (1955). Family structure and the socialisation of the child. In: T. Parsons and R. F. Bales (Eds), *Family, Socialisation and Interaction Process.* Glencoe, Illinois: Free Press.

Prigogine, I. (1947). *Etude Thermodynamique des Phenomenes Irreversibles.* Paris: Dunod.

Rapoport, A. (1968). Foreword. In: W. Buckley (Ed.), *Modern Systems Research for the Behavioural Scientist.* Chicago, Illinois: Aldine.

Rapoport, A. and Horvath, W. J. (1959). Thoughts on organization theory and a review of two conferences. *General Systems,* **4**, 87–93.

Sadovsky, V. N. (1972). General systems theory: Its task and methods of construction. *General Systems,* **17**, 171–179.

Selvini-Palazzoli, M., Boscolo, L., Cecchin, G. and Prata, G. (1978). *Paradox and Counter Paradox.* New York: Jason Aronson.

Straus, M. (1973). A G.S.T. approach to a theory of violence between family members. *Social Science Information,* **12**, 105–125.

Warr, P. B. (1980). An introduction to models in psychological research. In: A. J. Chapman and D. M. Jones (Eds), *Models of Man.* Leicester: The British Psychological Society.

Weiner, N. (1948). *Cybernetics.* Cambridge, Massachusetts: M.I.T. Press.

CHAPTER THREE
Some Theories of Family Behaviour

Anthony Gale and Arlene Vetere

Introduction

We have devoted a chapter to consideration of General System approaches and their weaknesses because the concept of systems is used so frequently within theories of the family and in psychotherapeutic family treatments. We now examine a number of theories of family behaviour, including that of Minuchin (e.g., 1974) which provided the key theoretical guidelines for our own research.

Why are theories necessary in family research? Some of our earlier work was consciously atheoretical, to ensure that in acting as participant observers we would not anticipate which variables were most salient and thereby rob ourselves of potentially rich data. However, once we had overcome the initial shock of living in other people's homes and learned to appreciate the drawbacks of the technique we were developing, it became apparent that theory was needed to guide our observations. Theory was essential to help us identify those aspects of family life upon which observers should focus, thereby reducing the burden of processing a constant stream of social events.

If family theories are necessary, it is also sensible to ask whether they are actually possible. One of the most comprehensive undertakings in this respect is the pair of volumes edited by Burr, Hill, Nye, and Reiss (1979a,b). They attempted to locate theories in anthropology, sociology, and psychology which could be used to understand family life. They also explored theories specifically devised with family life as their focus. Much of what follows is based upon the authoritative presentations made in those two volumes. However, it must be said that Burr *et al.* failed completely in their ambition to provide a general workable brief for family theory, or to devise a set of constructs whose common and shared meanings would make interaction between theories feasible (Hill, 1979). It is also apparent that different theories operate at different levels of description (from specification of macro variables such as levels of divorce or general incidence of family abuse, down to patterns of interaction within the family, and the phenomenal experience of different

34

family members). Somehow, social science has as yet been unable to link these levels of description within one conceptual framework. Thus after much effort, several conferences and working meetings, Burr *et al.* offer a depressing evaluation of their own achievements. Nevertheless, their two volumes are the most sophisticated collection available, although for a variety of reasons the theories of Kantor and Lehr (1975) and Olson, McCubbin, Barnes, Larsen, Muxen and Wilson (1983) are not considered.

What is a Good Theory of Family Behaviour?

The positive and negative features of existing theories can be used to construct an ideal model for a theory of family behaviour. Our view is that such a theory must be formal and systematic and that such formality operates at several levels. Thus a *theory* is not just a loose set of ideas, and is unlikely to get very far if it depends on one or two key constructs (such as 'double-bind', 'scapegoating', 'schism', 'skew', and so on). One reason for the need of several key concepts is that the family is associated with an enormous range of human behaviours; thus there is a great deal to explain.

Such concepts need to be defined with precision, not only to indicate the set of events to which they refer, but also to ensure that their relationship with *other* key concepts may be determined. Thus one needs not only the concepts and their definitions, but a set of rules for relating them in terms of their hierarchical structure, their degree of mutual influence or indeed, their functional independence. For example, several theories of family behaviour recognize the expression of affect, positive emotion, and affiliation as important determinants of family behaviour. Now suppose they also consider power to be of importance. There is then a necessity to show how affect and power are *related*; for example, is power used to gain affection and vice versa, is the achievement of power a stronger reward than that of positive affection, and if so, are there gender differences in their relative potency, and so on . . . ? This aspect of theory construction, the development of clear definitions of constructs and the rules which relate them, involves a great deal of effort. Even so, such work needs to be done if the theory is to be taken to the next stage, that of empirical operationalization.

In simple terms, a good theory should be able to help us identify what variables are worth examining and how such variables should be measured and evaluated. It should tell us which variables are important and which are trivial. In the case of family life, a good theory would help to explain family events, and would indicate which aspects of family life are relevant to the particular issues and questions which concern us. Say we were interested in child abuse. A theory of family interaction should be capable of telling us how much effort to expend on the investigation of particular variables, such as social class, parental personality, or childhood experience of parents. A practical consequence of such theoretical power would be both to provide an explanation of why a particular family is in difficulty and to offer appropriate means of promoting change. The theory would also provide us with relevant criteria for assessing change and the consequences of particular interventions.

To recap on our specification, a good working theory needs: *precise definition of key terms, rules for relating the key terms, means of translating the theory into observables, including the types of variables to be measured, and sufficient clarity and lack of internal contradiction to enable us to interpret research findings or practical applications with confidence.*

What Particular Family Facts Does a Family Theory Need to Explain?

Hill (1979) listed those areas of interest which emerge in most discussions of family life and family theory: *social class; religion and ethnic identity; age, gender, and generation; life cycle stage and family size; power support; and role allocation.* Hill was unable to integrate this broad set of themes within one conceptual framework, largely because each theme has evolved within a different disciplinary tradition and the key terms do not have semantic equivalence for different theorists or research domains. Apart from the theoretical disadvantages, this leads to a practical difficulty: because the same term has different meanings, researchers cannot converse with each other. Since we are psychologists, with a particular interest in the observation of patterns of publicly observable behaviour, our own requirements for theory are less ambitious in terms of the full range of variables which Hill listed. Nevertheless, we can identify a number of problems which need to be resolved before psychological work on family process can really get off the ground.

Gale (1984) listed a number of features which a good family theory should contain. First, many theories specify a number of needs or motives which drive family behaviour. In the absence of an agreed notion of individual human motivation within general psychology, it seems strange to talk of family 'needs' as if the family is some sort of augmented individual. Moreover, the difficulty is even greater when it is evident that much family stress is said to arise as a result of a *conflict* of individual needs. Family members seem to pull and push in different directions. Thus a workable theory must sort out the ways in which the family as a group differs from the family as a collection of individuals, and must provide a specification for determining individual and family needs, the ways these are negotiated, and the conditions under which they come into conflict and/or are changed. This issue is often sidestepped by theories which focus on structure rather than dynamic processes. The challenge is a difficult one because, as we know from individual motivational theory, needs can be biologically or socially determined. There are even psychologists who deny the utility of the concept of needs and regard their specification as a circular process. It is also an explicit feature of family life cycle theory (see below) that needs of family and individual members change over time. Personal needs alter with personal development, the demands of sex-typical roles vary over time and at different rates, and the outside world penetrates with varying impact onto the lives of individual family members. While we do not expect a theory of family behaviour to necessarily provide a detailed specification in such a difficult area, it is a negative characteristic of a theory if it sidesteps the problem or allocates little attention to it. We think the use of 'person-talk', borrowing the vernacular or even theoretical terminology applied to individuals, to be misleading in the context of *family* behaviour. A preferable analogy would be to use the model of organizational behaviour. Even so, most organizational theories are not primarily concerned with individual needs, insofar as they seem unrelated to the key goals of the organization.

A second and related problem is the notion of the psychological reality of family life. A good theory needs to ask: Who's reality? Within family research the key advocate of the phenomenal approach is Laing (e.g., Laing and Esterson, 1964). We assume that the phenomenology of each individual member is different, and while the family may have a set of common meanings for family events, meanings which are in some sense private from the outside world or the world of the researcher, there are still discrepancies among family members in their personal interpretation of events. Such discrepancies will in their turn influence the behaviour of individuals and their interactions with each other. A number of researchers and theorists talk of 'the family' as if any respondent member in some sense represents an organismic view. Thus for example, in much research, one of the parents speaks for the family. Olson *et al.* (1983) claim that their own research, in which both parents were asked to complete questionnaires and in which adolescents also gave their views, is particularly novel. Even so, we should note that the correlations between family members' responses were particularly low. Thus even the very well-developed questionnaires used by the Olson group, with high reliability and alleged validity, fare rather poorly when more than one family member is asked his/her views about key aspects of family life.

Our own approach implies that *all family members* need to provide data about family life, if one seeks to describe the family's experience in any comprehensive fashion. We have to confess that in our own research, with its dependence on *observation*, the reality observed is in several respects that of the observer. Moreover, because our observers are passive, they do not seek actively to gain information, for example, about the perceived *past history* of the family. We accept that our argument, pressed to extremes, will imply that there is no common reality and that each of us lives in soliptical isolation. However, our appeal is for theory which recognizes the problem and which, in specifying operational means of measuring family beliefs, requires the sampling of the views of several respondents, including their perceptions of past history and the family myths attached to it.

Several authors have called for effective family taxonomies; certainly, several theories of family behaviour provide them. While redolent of a medical model approach to psychiatric disorders, there can be no doubt that taxonomies can assist in the difficult problem of classifying family behaviours. Unfortunately, the issues already raised in relation to motivation and psychological reality need to be resolved *before* a workable taxonomy can be developed. There is a danger in having an impressive yet misleading taxonomy. A worse problem is that taxonomies refer to objects and organisms which are relatively fixed in character or whose future is reasonably invariant. In contrast, the complexity of family life and experience can make prediction extremely difficult and it is hazardous even to describe a family as the *same* family once there has been alteration in its membership or a dramatic change in life circumstances. The use of taxonomies, therefore, can be a false science.

Finally, explicit or implicit *value systems* seem to control many of our choices in life and the ways in which we allocate personal and other resources. Quite often, within one person, there are conflicting values; certainly, within families, values concerning gender role, authority, autonomy, and the expression of feeling, differ in a variety of ways. For the theorist or researcher, there is a great danger of applying one's own value system (often derived from personal family experience or reactions to it) either consciously or unconsciously, to the specification or evaluation of family behaviour. A good theory of family behaviour presupposes a theory of personal values, the manner in which such value systems arise and change, and the ways in which they relate to actual behaviour. Such a theory will also need to explain the relationship between family values and sociocultural values and norms and the ways in which they support each other or come into conflict.

Thus a good theory of family behaviour needs to contain concepts relating to *motivations, psychological reality*, and *values*; these need to be *related* in a formal fashion, both to each other and to actual observable behaviour; there must also be a specification for the *measurement* of individual and family actions which reflects these important variables and their relationships; such specification of key concepts and modes of measurement might well generate a *taxonomy* of family behaviour, allowing for convenient subclassifications of styles of family life. Since the family is not constant over time and passes through various evolutionary stages, the theory must also describe and account for *development trends*. This is a difficult brief to satisfy. Many of the problems it raises are central issues in psychology itself and involve the building of bridges between branches of psychology which rarely come into contact with each other: *biological* factors determine many individual needs and growth patterns; *social interaction* determines patterns of *behaviour* in individual family members and family subsystems; *individuals* perceive, think, and feel differently about family events; and *values* govern desires and choices about styles of family interaction. We should not forget however that non-psychological events, such as illness, war, contraception, unemployment or death, can have a major impact upon the psychological reality of family life, and indeed change the very structure under consideration. Family-cycle theories (see below) emphasize the very predictability and inevitable impact of such events on both structure and process. Many clinical theories, embedded in the current problems of the family under treatment, seem to neglect how common and yet powerful such life events are.

In the brief review of some major family theories which follows, we shall give a description of the key features of the theory, together with an appraisal of the extent to which it satisfies the requirements we have set out above. Given the limited resources available to us in our own research, we have been obliged to constrain our approach in several ways. We have chosen a relatively limited theoretical framework and have sampled only certain aspects of family behaviour. This opens us to a set of criticisms which justifiably we share with other family researchers.

Minuchin's Structural Theory (1974)

Minuchin's structural theory is based upon his clinical experience of families in distress. Major accounts are given in *Families of the Slums* (1967) which focused on executive behaviour and leadership in single-parent families; *Families and Family Therapy* (1974) which provides an analysis of the key constructs, with particular emphasis on *enmeshment* and *disengagement*; and *Psychosomatic Families* (1978) where conflict, its avoidance and resolution, are a particular focus and styles of parent-child interaction are specified in some detail. *Structure* refers to the family's organizational characteristics, the subsystems it contains, and the rules which govern interactional patterns among family members. Thus an aim of therapy is to alter organizational patterns, particularly where modes of communication among members are seen to be dysfunctional.

The theory has five principal features:

1. the family is a system which operates through transactional patterns;
2. functions of the family system are carried out by bounded subsystems;
3. such subsystems are made up of individuals on a temporary or permanent basis, and members can be part of one or more systems, within which their roles will differ;
4. subsystems are hierarchically organized in a way which regulates power structure within and between subsystems;
5. cohesiveness and adaptability are key characteristics of the family.

At the apex of the family hierarchy is the *spouse subsystem*, which historically is antecedent to the development of the other subsystems. Its functions include affectional exchange, decision-making, gender role specification, and role allocation in relation to executive and economic supports. It serves as the primary link between the family and the outside world and acts as a model to the offspring in the execution of its functions. Thus, within the Western nuclear family it is expected to support biological and economic needs, as well as mutual emotional support and friendship. Socialization requirements are expressed through the *parental subsystem* which is vested with authority and power and which has to satisfy the conflicting demands of nurturance and protection on the one hand and the encouragement of autonomy and responsibility on the other. Adaptability within this subsystem is necessary both because of developmental changes within the offspring and the varying pressures which age-related expectations bring to bear from society as a whole. The *parent–child* subsystem seems to be particularly concerned with affectional bonding and gender identification. In hierarchical terms it presupposes the effective functioning of both spouse and parental subsystems. Finally, the *sibling subsystem* (a particularly novel feature of the theory, which nevertheless receives only modest attention) is the social context within which the child learns to cooperate, to cope with jealousy and competition, and to prepare for peer-related activities in later life. Experience within the sibling subsystem provides models for friendship and equality of relationship in contrast to the relative submissiveness required within the parental and parent–child subsystems.

The extent to which Minuchin's definitions are mutually exclusive is not clear. For example, it is not possible to list a set of behaviours which delineate spouse, parental or parent–child subsystems in absolute terms; some overlap of function is of course likely in a structural framework. As we pointed out in our discussion of the pitfalls of systems approaches, such difficulties are common, and the distinction between attributes of units and relationships among units is often difficult to draw. In the case of physical systems, say a motor car engine, attributes and relationships of components are easy to specify and measure independently. But with people in groups, particularly intimate groups with a long history, such clarity is hardly possible. A submissive person is only understood in the context of a dominant other; a dominant person can hardly be dominant in the absence of a partner. Thus, it is difficult to describe the characteristics of the parental subsystem, in isolation from the context and relationships within which it functions.

For Minuchin, the functional demands of each subsystem require different skills and different patterns of behaviour. *Boundaries* around systems protect their functional integrity, limiting interference from other systems. Such boundaries are defined by *rules* which specify who belongs to the subsystem, the roles that operate within it, and the categories of behaviour that are acceptable. *Clear boundaries* are optimal and offer clearly recognizable and accepted rules. Thus a clearly bounded spouse subsystem will exclude interference from offspring or other relatives. Clarity of boundaries is therefore seen as a measure of the family's functional efficiency. However, *rigid* boundaries imply a lack of flexibility and *diffuse* boundaries imply the undermining of the subsystem's integrity by constant interference from external agents, leading to ambiguity and chaos in the construction of stable rules. Thus a diffuse boundary around the siblings and the intrusion of parents or grandparents into its transactions will rob its members of their capacity to negotiate and make joint decisions.

A particularly useful aspect of Minuchin's approach is his translation of the concept of boundaries and relationships into simple diagrammatic forms. The *maps* of the family which can be drawn using these conventions may then be used to represent subsystems at various stages of their evolution, the presence of strong affectional or conflictual relations, the strength or permeability of boundaries, and the existence of triangular modes of conflict resolution. Clinicians may use such maps not only to describe the family as it is, but the desired alternative organization which is the objective of therapy. Such diagrammatic representations, altered on an iterative basis as the therapist comes to understand the family's organization, give the theory a capacity for objective and practical implementation (see Chapter 9).

The concept of *cohesion* is central to the theory and reflects both emotional bonding of members and their individual autonomy. Cohesion is greatest in the *enmeshed* family, where relationships are intense and there is extreme concern for the experience of individual members, and boundaries between individuals and between subsystems are diffuse. It is likely to act against the autonomy of individual members. In contrast, cohesion is lowest in *disengaged* families where boundaries are rigid, members lead separate lives, and communication is poor. Thus cohesion is an important indicator of the transactional patterns of family members. At some stages in the family life-cycle, a degree of enmeshment is necessary for the discharge of age-related functions. We should also note that excessive enmeshment in one subsystem (for example, between a mother and young child) may be associated with disengagement elsewhere (in the spouse subsystem).

One effect of diffuse boundaries can be the blurring or even reversal of roles across generations and the disruption of norms of authority and power. A grandparent might seek to take over the power of an adult daughter, thereby depriving her of her competence in her roles as spouse and mother. Such cross-generational influence might even extend to a third generation, so that grandmother, mother, and grandchild all become locked in a close affiliation at the expense of their participation in other appropriate subsystems. Another example is that of the *parental child* who by virtue of inadequacy in, or the absence of, a same sex parent may acquire parental, executive or affectional functions and a degree of delegated authority which might be quite incompatible with his/her role as a child or sibling. That is not to say that a child should not learn lessons of nurturance and care in the family context, or the bearing of responsibility for younger siblings. However, if there is a blurring of boundaries between roles, the child is more likely to become symptomatic.

Adaptable families are able to alter roles and relationships in response to pressures for change. The precise way in which this happens for functional families is not specified in great detail by Minuchin. In contrast to the adaptable family, the family which cannot change may develop pathology in one of its members as a means of diverting attention from more fundamental sources of stress. Thus an inability to resolve conflict within the spouse subsystem may lead to the creation of diffuse boundaries around the parents and the drawing into the spouse subsystem of a child who then becomes the focus of attention. This child may then become the *identified patient* and its pathology will serve to maintain the family in its present state, i.e., as an *homeostatic* mechanism for resisting change. The notion that the identified patient is not the true patient is thus the key rationale for the use of family therapy, which seeks to alter family organization as a primary goal in treating individually expressed pathology.

Cohesion and power are revealed by the examination of family relationships. Minuchin pays more attention to cohesion than to power; however, we believe the following account to be a fair interpretation of his views. An *alliance* is a working bond between members without creating conflicts with others. In contrast *coalitions* operate at someone else's expense; for example, a *detouring coalition* shifts unresolved conflict onto others, sometimes in the form of pathology, leaving the original pair intact. In *triangulation* a third party is drawn in by either member, to form a coalition against the other. The triangulated child, for example, might find itself torn between the loyalty and affiliative demands of both parents, or drawn into a strong relationship with one at the expense of the other and of the spouse subsystem. Power is expressed through hierarchical arrangements; for Minuchin the parents' role includes power over children. A child (as in the case of the parental child) might have power thrust upon it, because of the inadequacy of a parent.

Behind the accounts of the development of pathology is an implicit belief in the notion of psychic conflict and the need for it to be discharged if it exceeds some limit. This psychoanalytic view of conflict and its translation into defences is imposed on the family as an organism and operates as it would in the mind and behaviour of one of Freud's patients. Thus a family *scapegoat*, as in the original biblical use of the term, is identified by group collusion, as the bearer of the family's ills. Similarly, some of the mechanisms we have described above are parallel to defences such as projection, displacement, repression, and rationalization.

Because Minuchin's theory was devised for dealing with families with problems, it does not say enough about normal family process. The tasks and modes of interaction of different subsystems are to a certain extent assumed; when they are expressed it is very much in terms of a Western and middle-class ideal, although of course much of Minuchin's experience was with socially deprived Puerto Rican families. While the behaviour of a parental child is not necessarily seen to be dys-functional, Minuchin appears, in his therapeutic strategies, to wish to reinstate the power and authority of parents. This may well be appropriate in the circumstances but it does mean that Minuchin operates with a limited set of *values* about how families *should* behave. Many of the criticisms of Parsons' view of family life, the functions the family discharges and the gender roles of parents, may be directed at Minuchin's approach. Moreover, the emphasis on structure means that *dynamic* processes are neglected. For example, the concept of *enmeshment* is more a *descriptive* device than a causal or explanatory construct. Minuchin can describe the way the family is, but not how it arrived at that point. Thus it is not clear why particular children should become scapegoated, or identified patients, or parental children. A more com-plete theory should be able to predict in advance which member is likely to succumb.

Even so, as we have already indicated, the structure itself is not easy to specify and the concept of 'boundaries' suffers from being a physical entity (as drawn in a map), an expression of relationships (involving positive and negative feelings), and as a shorthand for the specification of a set of behaviours and the rules which govern them. While *power* is an important variable for Minuchin, it is not easy to express within the conventions of his mapping procedures.

Minuchin's view of the family is that of the outsider describing the family as seen in the eye of the camera. While his therapeutic approach does involve becoming a temporary member of the family and even identifying temporarily with some member at the emotional expense of others, he pays little formal attention to the problem of differential phenomenology. For example, given our own view of the problem of the psychological reality of family experience, we would expect different family members to draw different maps of the family's subsystems.

This emphasis on the family as observed was, however, particularly helpful to us in seeking a theoretical basis within which we could govern our own observations of families. The concept of subsystems and their differentiated functions enabled us to construct appropriate frames within which to scan and classify family behaviours. Thus while the theory has faults when set aside the requirements for a *general* theory of family behaviour, its focus on the here-and-now was particularly useful.

Life-Cycle Theories

It is impossible to ignore the notion that families pass through a series of phases, whose characteristics are determined by changes within members, the impact of external events, and the influence of sociocultural norms and requirements. There are several theories within psychology which have the concept of *stages* of development as a central principle of growth. Perhaps the most influential, so far as family theorists are concerned, is that of Erik Erikson (1965) who developed the *eight stages of man* in which the individual is faced by clusters of challenges, potential hazards, and ultimate achievements. Thus the adolescent confronts the basic challenge of *identity versus identity confusion*; the hazard of this stage of development is a failure of society to provide clearly defined roles and standards of conduct which, in turn, may be compounded by membership peer groups which share the child's confusion or provide well-defined alternative roles; the ultimate characteristic to be achieved is a sense of *identity*, a clear notion of what one is and what one's roles in life might be. Thus, appropriate conditions need to be made available if the adolescent is to move smoothly to the next stage of growth.

The notion of *critical phases in development* is common to Freudian, Piagetian, and ethological theories. It contains a number of important elements, as follows:

1. as the organism develops it passes through stages at which it is sensitive to particular types of stimulation or experience;
2. the organism is thus open to certain experiences for a specifiable period of time;
3. by interacting with the appropriate stimulation, the organism acquires species specific skills and is enabled to move smoothly to the ensuing stage;
4. inappropriate stimulation (too much or too little, or the wrong type) leads to developmental stunting or to the development of inappropriate and maladaptive behaviours.

Erikson's theory is a particularly good example of a lifespan view of stages of development. The extent to which such principles of development are generalizable has been challenged both within ethology and developmental psychology. In the human case, the critical phase approach seems unduly fatalistic and inflexible, implying that failure to complete an earlier stage condemns the individual to subsequent incompetence and inability to grow. In this sense it is similar to theories of innate intelligence and the notion that biologically determined factors act as limits to functional effectiveness. Nevertheless, the notion of stages, linked together in a life cycle, has proved attractive to family theorists. Thus the family is seen to pass through a series of phases in growth, at each of which there are special challenges to be overcome. A family which is flexible and adaptive passes through such life transitions without too many hitches. We should note the paradox that while the definition of stages itself involves different aggregates of family membership and different interpersonal relationships some theorists nevertheless still wish to talk of the *coping skills of the family*, or *family strengths*, as if the family is in many senses invariant. Thus as in trait theories of personality, the family is seen to have traits or dispositions which it carries with it over time. It is worth noting here that not all families are of the Parsonian nuclear variety; many modern families have single parents, are reconstituted combinations and so on.

A typical set of stages would be as follows: courting couples, couples without children, childbearing families with children in the preschool years, families with school-age children, families with adolescents at home, launching families (adolescents beginning to evolve separate lives), empty nest families, families in retirement (e.g., Olson *et al.*, 1983). Each of these eight stages, in offering different challenges, makes different demands on family members and determines to some extent the nature of their relationships. Moreover, skills which are effective at one stage of development may not only be inappropriate to the next or later stages, but might prove to be malfunctional and harmful. The emotional closeness which characterizes parents and very young children may inhibit adjustment at the launching stage.

Let us take the example of the couple without children and the challenges that face them. First there is some withdrawal from the family of origin and the acceptance of the intimacy of the other partner's family. This emotional detachment is paralleled by a change in relationships with existing friends and the incorporation of residual relationships of the partner. At the same time, as a sense of common identity is developing, which in our culture is paralleled by individual autonomy, the couple need to see themselves as a couple as well as individual selves. Negotiation over roles and power is required, as new decisions need to be made and the number of experiences shared becomes greater. We should note that our educational system provides no explicit warnings (to the couple, their friends or their families) of the changes in role, attitudes, and behaviour which the formation of emotional relationships in adulthood requires.

Thus, in common with Erikson's general theory of individual growth, it should be possible, within a particular cultural context, to provide a checklist of developmental challenges and hazards, and the types and varieties of skills which each stage demands, for each of the different participants in the family scene. Even more important is the theoretical significance of the concept of stages, as an antidote or reminder for those theories which seek to conceptualize the family in terms of a small set of constructs. We have already questioned the value of the expression *the family*, namely the notion that it is an entity, which while changing remains essentially the same in many respects. Personality theorists, concerned with the simpler case of individual growth, have had considerable difficulty with such a view of constancy of traits; and the current prevailing view is to emphasize *interactions* between individual characteristics and the complex set of differing environments in which the person is to be found. Given that a family is made up of different individuals, at different stages of growth, the concept of *the family* is difficult to grasp. The second caution is that any theory which purports to be a theory of family behaviour *must* show how the key variables or factors within the theory *are altered by the passage of time*. While this is a theoretical problem it also raises practical difficulties for empirical research, for it calls for *longitudinal* rather than *cross-sectional* designs. As with ageing research, it is possible, within a cross-sectional design, to confound a particular group with a particular stage of development. To follow the ageing analogy, persons of 20 and 80 years will have had different educational opportunity, different childhood diets, different welfare provision, different early political and economic experiences, and so on. Thus, to examine the influence of different stages of the family life cycle, we need to follow a cohort of families over time; it is not sufficient merely to sample sets of families simultaneously, at different stages of development.

It follows that for a variety of practical reasons, family life cycle theories, while they have considerable construct validity, are not easy to put to test. On the other hand, their implications for *other* family theories are considerable.

The Choice-Exchange Theory of Nye

Nye's (1979, 1982) theory of family behaviour is a development and application of exchange theory as formalized by Thibaut and Kelley (1959). The general assumption of exchange theory is that we avoid costly behaviour and seek rewarding roles and experiences. In the process of selecting appropriate outcomes, rewards and costs are estimated so that some rewards will imply some costs and vice versa. The theory is therefore a rational theory in which the person's perception of rewards, costs, and the level of satisfaction which they are able to derive from situations, determine ultimate choices.

The theory has five key features:

1. the concept of rational choice;
2. a set of rewards which family members seek;
3. the costs or efforts which they seek to avoid;
4. the comparison level which an individual uses to determine the appropriate level of reward which they believe they deserve;
5. the notion of reciprocity in interpersonal relations.

This is a general theory of human behaviour, applied in the particular context of family life. Because it is a rational theory, much of the research carried out by Nye involves the use of questionnaires and interviews, designed to elicit reports by family members of the costs and rewards which marriage and parenthood entail.

The concept of rewards and costs and the notion of exchange are powerful in explaining why individuals might sustain a set of behaviours or remain within a relationship, which from the outside might seem to be disadvantageous or even hazardous. Thus the theory enables us to explain why parents devote so much effort to the rearing of children, why individuals tolerate an apparently unsatisfactory marriage or physical abuse, and why divorce, which in the past was less acceptable, is now associated with more favourable attitudes.

Rewards may take any form, namely, status, cash, power, affection, social and physical support, environments, climates, and psychological satisfaction. *Costs* are any status, relationship or activity which is disliked. Uncertainty, which creates an unpleasant psychological state in the form of anxiety, is also seen as a cost. We seek to achieve a state of *profit*, i.e., a condition in which we gain the best relationship between rewards and costs. Reward can take the form of accepting a cost which is less effortful or distasteful than another cost; thus a woman may choose to live with an abusing husband because the cost of being on her own and the need to secure economic support for herself and her children is seen to be greater than the cost of being abused. Similarly, one reward may be rejected for a more satisfactory alternative. Moreover, in determining rewards, we consider the opportunity cost of particular actions, since they delimit our choice or freedom to act in other ways. Thus marriage and the commitment to a sexual partner may be seen to have several associated rewards in exchange for which one nevertheless reduces the opportunity for sexual relationships with others.

An individual will persist in a behaviour if it does not imply a cost below the *comparison level*, i.e., if the alternatives available are seen to be less rewarding and if the behaviour itself and its rewards are seen to be appropriate to the person's needs and rights.

Nye lists a number of rewards which have particular power: social approval, autonomy, security and certainty, shared values, money, and reciprocal equality. Each of these will be compared in relation to each other as well as to costs, in particular situations. Moreover, some may offer immediate reward while others require delay before gratification becomes available.

Nye considers the problem of values and beliefs and the power which they hold over our behaviour, restricting certain choices. He is inclined to reduce such beliefs to the principle of social approval/disapproval. He appreciates that some critics are unable to accept such an hedonistic view of altruistic or religious behaviours.

A powerful aspect of the theory is that it recognizes individual and group differences in the values assigned to particular rewards and costs. It is therefore able to cope with variability in individual behaviour, without sacrificing certain general principles. For example, he asserts that women's need for sexual gratification is lower than that of men. Sexual activity will therefore be seen to have a lower reward value than alternatives. However, it may constitute an acceptable cost on occasion in order to secure other rewards. Within a family, different members will have different notions of cost and reward in relation to family life. Moreover, as the family passes through its developmental stages, the effort required by different members varies. Thus the newborn child receives constant reward with very little effort or cost; later the child is expected to reward others in exchange for rewards and to acquire the notion that reciprocity is desirable.

One particular area of research which has been explored by Nye and his associates is that of marital communication. Communication which involves anger, negative emotional experiences, or lowering of personal status, might be seen to be effortful and costly. Switching off discussion in such circumstances, even if it is treated in a negative way by a spouse, may be less costly than engaging in full debate.

In terms of our set of requirements for good theory, the choice-exchange approach can be seen to be satisfactory in several ways. The actions of all the family members can be seen in terms of personal rewards and costs, so that the theory is sensitive both to *family* beliefs and behaviour and to those of the *individual*. The general underlying principle of need seems to rest on the basic biological principles of reward and punishment, approach and avoidance, and the associated balance between positive and negative affect or pleasure versus pain and/or anxiety.

What is not clear, however, is the extent to which individuals can report accurately on their choices (rational or otherwise), or whether reasons given by individuals might be *post hoc* rationalizations or reconstructions. Indeed, rationality may play little part in our decisions, particularly when they relate to emotionally significant others. It is also not clear whether the theory can predict an individual's behaviour *ante hoc* or suggest how an individual might behave in the future under certain circumstances. To a certain extent, therefore, the specification of rewards in particular contexts may be *post hoc* and even circular (i.e., this action was taken because it was rewarding). While many theories of family behaviour seem more able to explain stability and homeostasis, rather than change and adaptation, it would be a great bonus for exchange theory if it could predict change *in advance* rather than after the event. The theory suggests that the way to change an individual's behaviour is by rational discussion, by reference to principles of reciprocity, and by conscious deliberation. It is not clear how such an approach can be applied to young children, to the emotionally disturbed, or to the ill-educated. Moreover, while Nye recognizes that emotional states are difficult to reduce to rational choice, it is hard to see how individuals appear to be overtaken by emotion in their family relationships in a manner which is both involuntary and costly. The theory seems very much one for the educated middle-class adult possibly trained in economics or accountancy!

Some critics may see exchange theory as reductionist and a negation of certain aspects of human experience. But in contrast to many systems approaches, it acknowledges the importance of self-reflection, the evaluation of alternatives, and the notion of conscious choice. For many psychologists, these attributes of persons, while difficult to demonstrate or measure, are the basis for distinguishing human beings from other systems.

While the exchange theory is capable of generating a rich set of research issues and questions within the context of family life, it was not an appropriate theoretical approach for our own work. Given our commitment to observation and our use of families with young children, the notion of securing rational accounts for personal behaviour seemed impractical to us. Nevertheless, the principle of being sensitive to the presence of positive and negative affect in the social-psychological space of family life, was one which guided some of our measurement and classification of behaviour.

Symbolic Interactionism and its Relevance to Family Life

This brief exposition is based upon a paper by Burr, Leigh, Day, and Constantine (1979) in which they demonstrate the relevance of some of the key concepts within symbolic interactionism approaches to the understanding of family life. We say 'approaches' because the symbolic interactionist tradition is set within a complicated fabric of individual theorists and differing disciplines. We limit ourselves to concepts which have some generality, namely:

1. the importance of symbols and their meaning;
2. the notion of a public and personal self;
3. role, role enactment, role transition, and role strain;
4. human beings as actors as well as reactors.

The basic tenet of symbolic interactionism is that our world is symbolic as well as physical; by interaction within our social world we not only acquire symbols and their meanings but alter our own being and nature. The infant at birth is asocial and then learns its culture. This is not a passive but an active process because the individual is in constant interaction with the symbols which surround them. The child only becomes a differentiated being and acquires a sense of personal identity as a result of interaction with other people and things. Thus recognizing others as selves is a precondition to the awareness of oneself as self.

Because we are in constant interaction with our world, its meanings are not only incorporated into our own sense of being, but are altered by us. In the development of our sense of self, at least two parts of the person can be recognized, a social self (or Mead's *me*) and a spontaneous and unpredictable self (Mead's *I*). The *me* is that which is easily recognized by others, it is well organized, it interacts with family, intimates, workmates. Within that social self, the variety of roles which the individual has to sustain is incorporated. Thus the role of mother, student, widow, doctor, friend are all acquired by the social self. The meaning of such roles and their requirements is part of the culture in which we live and it is part of human experience to acquire and react to role specifications.

The person is not passive in this relationship with the world, as we have seen, since *transaction* is a constant feature of human experience. Because the individual reflects upon experience, individual behaviours, contexts, and groups, have personal meaning for that individual. Thus there is a distinction between *acts*, i.e., observed behaviours as recorded by a camera, and *actions* which incorporate in the mind of the participant, the *meanings* of those acts.

For much of the time we are in harmony with our social world and the roles we enact are fulfilled smoothly, convincingly, and in accordance with our own expectations and those of others. However, role fulfilment can be affected in various ways. For example, as the family moves through stages of its life cycle, new demands and new role requirements are imposed on its members. The role of the elderly widow is not that of the busy mother and housewife. The role of the primiparous parent is not that of the young lover. Transition from one role to another can cause strain, excessive effort, and anxiety. Clarity of role definition aids transition. For example, the adolescent hovers between the roles of child and adult; the theory would predict that clearer specification of the new roles which the adolescent must fulfil will ease the transition to adulthood. Such specifications are to be found within the culture, the symbols which are available to us as clues to role requirements. Currently, the specification for adolescence may be less clear than it was when children were able to enter employment upon leaving school, and to take on a range of associated responsibilities.

One source of evidence of role strain may be when the spontaneous self intrudes upon the smooth performance of role requirements and the individual, in an emotional way, seems to be unable to accept the social behaviours expected of him/her.

Within the context of family life the concept of role is clearly salient. Each family member has a number of roles which he/she must fulfil. The specification for such roles is constantly present. In childhood, models are displayed before us, not only within the home but within the media, in literature, and within the culture at large. These tell us what it is to be a mother, father, sibling, and so on. Moreover, within the course of family interaction, role requirements are often specified and prescribed, to the extent that family members will be reminded of what is expected of them and spontaneous deviations from role will be punished. The particular and special meanings attached to certain roles and functions, the idiosyncratic ways in which a particular family operates, will be in constant negotiation between family members.

Family stress will occur when roles can no longer be fulfilled in a smooth and integrated fashion. The causes of such stress might be non-psychological events which create major life changes. These may intrude from the outside world or may arise from spontaneous changes within family members.

Independent of the present research, we have developed a study of family photographic albums as symbolic representations of family life, within the symbolic interactionist tradition. Family photographs may be seen to represent symbols of family meanings at different levels. The arrangement of family members within Victorian family photographs may be compared with the contemporary arrangement; there are clear implications for the notions of gender roles and child–adult relations. Parents are no longer necessarily in the centre of the photograph, male adults do not need to stand behind and above their spouse, children may be held by male adults and so on. Within the individual family photograph, proximity and display of individual family members may give clues to particular relationships within that family. The display within the home of photographs of different members, their number, prominence, and proximity to other symbols will again inform us of their value. The very process of selection of family photographs by the individual will help to convey the meaning and affectional significance of the individuals they portray. Thus just as public symbols (such as television advertisements) tell us about gender roles and expectations, so family albums give symbolic representation of the interior of family life.

In the absence of a notable quantity of research in which the symbolic interactionist approach is applied to the context of family experience, it is not easy for us to offer an appraisal in terms of the criteria for good family theory, set out at the beginning of this chapter. Because the approach is interactionist and because people are not only changed by, but themselves change, the symbols which surround them and their meanings, our positivist prescription for clear definitions and precise relational rules between constructs may be seen to run in direct contradiction with symbolic inter-actionism. Similarly, the notion of operationalization of constructs implies the potential for objective measurement. This again will be difficult when an observed event represents mere acts rather than action. However, the theory is strong in relation to our requirements for a specification of values, and the need to tap the psychological reality of family life for its individual members. In this sense, participant obser-vation, if it allows the observer to translate acts into actions by learning to appreciate the meaning of events for the natural participant, will be approved of by symbolic interactionist theorists. However, it does not of itself as a technique guarantee the *validity* of the observer's interpretations, unless positive steps are taken to secure from family participants their own *accounts* of events.

Olson's Circumplex Model

The circumplex model of Olson and associates (e.g., 1979, 1980, 1983) is one of the most modern and systematically developed models of family behaviour. Published as a series of papers, a reasonably full statement may be found in a single volume entitled *Families: What Makes them Work* (1983). The development of the model has been associated with the use of cluster analysis techniques, the production of family and marital interaction scales, and several empirical studies, some of them of considerable magnitude. The theory is said to contrast with those derived from clinical experience because it focuses on normal patterns of family interaction and emphasizes *family strengths* rather than weaknesses. Nevertheless, clinical studies and theories were one of the starting points for the circumplex model and the key constructs were derived from an extensive study of the literature which yielded elements or factors with high communality in content across theories: *cohesion, adaptability*, and *communication*.

The key constructs of the circumplex model are:

1. three key dimensions (cohesion, adaptability, communication);
2. a taxonomy of three family types (balanced, mid-range, extreme);
3. three key aspects of family adjustment (stressors, family coping, family resources).

Cohesion, adaptability, and *communication* are dimensions derived from more than fifty concepts within the family and marital interaction literature; they represent connectedness-separation, flexibility and ability to change, and communication. *Cohesion* includes emotional bonding, boundaries, coalitions, time, space, friends, decision-making, and interests and recreation; families may operate at four levels of cohesion: from enmeshed, through connected, separated, and disengaged. The central levels are seen as adaptive and the extremes problematic. *Adaptability* involves power structure, role relationships, and relationship rules. It also ranges through four levels, the central levels being seen as more effective for family functioning: from rigid, through structured, flexible, and chaotic. In principle, therefore, the Olson scheme allows for 16 family types. Cohesion and adaptability are arranged in a two-dimensional matrix in which each level of the two variables is shown as a circle, so that families fall within the bounds of three concentric circles. The sixteen types, in turn, enable them to make predictions about the family's capacity to cope with normal and extraordinary life transitions. *Communication*, their third key construct, is seen as a *facilitating* dimension. At its positive pole it includes empathy, reflective listening, and supportive comment, and at the negative pole, double messages, double binds, and criticism. These negative attributes prevent the expression of feelings and restrict movement and change.

The Olson (1983) presentation (Olson, McCubbin, Barnes, Larsen, Muxen, and Wilson) is somewhat misleading. In principle, they could have followed standard factor analytic techniques to derive their key dimensions. Characteristic features of family life could have been entered as items. The factor loadings for the different factors and/or their extent of independence would then have emerged. Within the circumplex model, which resembles a diagram representing a two-factor space, cohesion and adaptability are presented as orthogonal. It thus appears that in factor analytic terms the items underlying each factor are independent. However, the construction of the dimensions and the scales derived from them does not appear to have benefited from such a formal analysis. Secondly, very little attention is paid to the problem of relating the *communication* construct to the other key constructs of cohesion and adaptability. Communication is omitted from the diagrammatic presentation, and appears to be in some sense correlated with both the other variables. It is in one sense in the model, and yet otherwise absent. Thus the conceptualization of the relationships between key variables is less clear than it might be. Olson *et al.* (1983) set out a series of hypotheses about how particular types of family will react to transitions and life stresses, but we were unable to determine how the hypotheses were derived, in a formal way, from the theory. Hypotheses concerning communication, for example, suddenly appear within the text, when communication has had only the most casual definition. It is possible that communication is at right angles to the other two dimensions. All three dimensions may lie in three-dimensional space, but we need to know whether they are orthogonal or oblique in their relationships. Unfortunately, the specification of individual items and their content is not given in any detail.

Thirdly, Olson *et al.* (1983) offer a table showing that their concepts are to be found in other theories. Their claim is that they have tapped into a host of existing and related constructs. This may well be the case, but it is only part of the story; for example, Kantor and Lehr specify three key family *targets* or motives (affect, power, and meaning) *as well as* three *access* dimensions (space, time, and energy). For Olson *et al.* cohesion appears to include features which come under affect, space, time, and power for Kantor and Lehr, while it includes also decision-making, which is a power dimension for Kantor and Lehr. At the same time the Olson concept of *adaptability* is equated with the power dimension!

While we accept Olson's claim that cohesion has many parallels in other theories, it is in our view misleading to suggest that its semantic content is identical across theories. Hill (1979) warned against the dangers of assuming that things with the same name are indeed the same things. We believe that Olson *could* have achieved what he claims to have achieved, but it would have required a more sophisticated set of techniques. As it stands the key dimensions of the theory have more apparent validity than substance. Thus, in our view, the theory fails (1) to provide clear definitions, (2) to show how the key concepts are related, or (3) to provide formal means of operationalizing the key constructs. The circumplex model may be a useful aid to thinking about family process; but it is not a formal theory. Moreover, we question whether the measurement devices are related to the analysis of key constructs in a formal fashion.

It is not clear what parallels *meaning* and *values* within the Olson approach. While there is considerable emphasis on family strengths and adaptive processes, we have to ask, 'adaptive for what?'. Frequently, there is talk of 'healthy' or 'functional' families without recognition that our definition of healthy and functional may differ. The absence of conflict in a family could have a variety of outcomes; one needs a set of value judgements to determine their quality. We have a suspicion that Olson and associates have an image of a middle-class, purposeful, and achieving American family as their ideal. For example, in their major empirical study of 1200 families, they mention only in passing that all their respondents were members of the Lutheran church; we would wish to challenge their claim that they have secured a representative sample. We can also ask, 'healthy for whom?'. The emphasis seems to be on 'the family' without reference to the conflicting needs of members. Thus Olson and his associates express concern and surprise at the low level of correlation between family members' responses. Such surprise can only be possible if one treats the family as an homogenous group, with common needs, common perceptions, and agreed procedures for the achievement of common goals.

The Distance Regulation Theory of Kantor and Lehr (1975)

The distance regulation theory of Kantor and Lehr, described in detail in *Inside the Family: Toward a Theory of Family Process* (1975), is the most comprehensive theory devised specifically for the description of family life. It is also a theory about normal everyday life in everyday families. Kantor and Lehr are critical of theories based on psychopathogenic families. Such theories, they claim, have focused on the unusual, exotic, and bizarre and have therefore created a distorted perspective on family life. The theory has six major components:

1. three family subsystems;
2. three family goals (or targets);
3. three key dimensions (or access dimensions) for achieving the goals;
4. several dozen different mechanisms used for implementing 2 and 3, i.e., the six target and access dimensions;
5. a taxonomy of three family types;
6. a set of four parts or roles which family members may play.

The theory is a *systems* theory, in which the family is seen as being complex, open, adaptive, and constantly processing information. The information which is processed is information about *distance regulation*. In other words much of family communication is used to attain subsystem goals, by conveying information about what distances between members are proper or optimal. 'Distance' is used in both a literal and metaphorical sense. It can therefore refer to quite explicit distancing mechanisms (like locks on doors) or to much more subtle means of holding people together or apart. 'Feedback' is a particularly important concept for the theory since it involves the processing of incoming information by comparing it against some comparator or set of standards, and then effecting an output which, in its turn, links the system to the input. Many of the mechanisms of family action described by Kantor and Lehr can be seen as devices for sustaining existing behaviour or promoting change. Unlike several other theories, stabilizing and change mechanisms are given equal attention. Kantor and Lehr refrain from offering precise definitions of positive and negative feedback in the context of family life.

Their concept of family subsystems, unlike that of Minuchin, is particularly vague, because it is concerned with different domains of description rather than with functions. Their intention is to distinguish the family as a whole unit, from interpersonal acts, and personal acts and phenomenology. They therefore talk of three subsystems, and the interface between them. For example, an adolescent's goals (personal subsystem) may be in conflict with everyone else in the household (parents plus other family members or the family subsystem). The conflict will take the form of discussion and argument within an interpersonal subsystem (adolescent plus mother). Thus it is a truism that in all activities, two and possibly three subsystems come into action. While it is appropriate to recognize the distinction between individuals, groups, and the whole family, Kantor and Lehr do not provide clear means of doing so. For example, each individual is seen as having a social self or family membership and a private self, but we are not told how the two aspects interact, come into conflict or are reconciled. This is an important criticism, because Kantor and Lehr approach family behaviour as if it is a script written consensually by the actors. They never really get to grips therefore with the problem of who sets the goals, how conflict is resolved, whether the script is constructed in a conscious fashion or involves a mixture of voluntary, involuntary, and even enforced action. Thus much of their theory and descriptive data are about the *family unit subsystem*. Such a focus of attention results in part from their emphasis on the description of family actions and upon immediate, rather than distant, causation. Kantor and Lehr pay little more than lip service to causation external to the family, originating within the culture, within peer groups, or other social contexts. The primary focus of the theory is the *social space* within which family members interact. Nevertheless, they are unusual in offering a set of roles or parts for family members to play, and the interplay of these roles in the context of bargaining and negotiating for subsystem power, is called *psychopolitics* (see pages 55–56 below).

The most novel feature of the theory is the introduction of six dimensions of family behaviour. All family behaviour takes place in a *social space*, within which the six dimensions are in constant operation. The principal aims or motives of the family are called *target* dimensions, and these are *affect, power,* and *meaning.* In everyday terms these can be seen as: needs for positive support and nurturance (affect); the expression of status, responsibility, rights, property, dominance, and submission (power); and, values, personal identity, and sense of purpose (meaning). In order to achieve these aims or targets, three other dimensions (the access dimensions) operate within the family's social space: *space, time,* and *energy.* The concept of *space* refers to boundaries and distance between persons and groupings (thus positive affect may be expressed by proximity). *Time* may refer to a general orientation of the family in terms of the perceived importance of past, present or future (e.g., delaying immediate gratification for future goals), or at a micro-level in terms of the degree of synchrony or desynchrony in the actions of family members (e.g., eating together or separately, group or individual leisure activities and so on). *Energy* is described in terms of patterns of uptake, storage, and discharge, and refers at one level to the overall intensity of family experience, and at the micro-level to patterns of eating or exercise-taking. The formalization of the concept of energy is important, since it brings to the theory both a biological orientation and a source of possible dynamic mechanisms to sustain overall activity or promote change.

An important notion is the assumption that *all* family behaviour occurs at the intersection or interface of all six dimensions, even though, for a particular action, one or more dimensions might be predominant. For example: when a family comes to the meal table the provision of food may be seen to be nurturant and supportive (affect); patterns of seating may reflect the use of distance to express affiliation (space); patterns of conversation and who is allowed to speak may reflect status (power); the saying of grace before meals will reflect religious belief (meaning); if meals are always served at certain fixed times then that indicates temporal regulation of the family unit (time); and, the rate at which people eat, the quantity and variety of food provided, or the overall intensity of social interaction at the table, reflect the pace of energy uptake or discharge (energy).

It will be immediately apparent that any of the above examples could be reclassified under alternative dimensions. For example: the preparing of food, seating patterns, saying of grace, temporal regulation, and so on, could all be seen to be a primary reflection of the achievement or maintenance of *power*. That is not an embarrass-ment for the theory. What is important is that for any particular family, all six dimensions need to be referred to if an adequate description of that family's life is to be attained. What is not clear, however, is how one handles discrepancies of perception among family members. Thus what a mother sees as predominantly reflecting meaning and affect dimensions ('good mothers prepare meals at regular hours') may be seen by a child as a reflection of negative affect and the abuse of power ('my mother forces me to eat when I don't feel hungry'). Kantor and Lehr, partially because their own sampling of family life was relatively short-lived, are unable to describe or explain how such a state of affairs comes about or how a con-sensual or majority view is reached.

Thus the 'data' provided by Kantor and Lehr are not very helpful in providing us with a means of classifying family behaviours. They provide several illustrative examples and long descriptions of family interactions (some of which are interlaced with interpretative commentaries). However, they never say where the descriptions come from or how they have arrived at their interpretation (see Chapter 4 for our discussion of their methodology). They admit quite frankly to having a clinical rather than an experimental or systematic approach. This is unfortunate, since a good theory must lend itself to systematic operationalization.

In trying to characterize the lives of individual families Kantor and Lehr employ a set of terms which are related but whose relationships are ill-defined. Thus families develop particular *strategies* for achieving the key target-dimensional *goals*. Below the key goals are *subtargets* or *themes*. Such themes are embedded in social action and give family events their meaning; they can of course be in conflict, as in the case of themes of family cohesion and individual freedom. How one distinguishes these levels of motivation is not clear, nor is the methodology used by Kantor and Lehr to yield interpretations of the lives of particular families. On some occasions they appear to be taking acts at face value, at others they see the themes in question to be more deeply embedded, on others they see congruity between statements made and actions, and on other occasions they claim that there is overt contradiction (e.g., where a parent gives verbal support for the concept of individual responsibility and choice yet at the same time refuses to grant a child a front door key).

A family's set of strategies will be of a particular character which enables a more general description of families as *closed, open,* or *random* in style. This general character implies different types of distance-regulation. Thus the closed family will have a distance-regulation style which serves to interpret, protect, and maintain the family's traditions in the face of potential sources of destabilization. Kantor and Lehr list in detail the distance-regulation styles for each family type, in terms of the six key dimensions (affect, power, meaning, space, time, energy). We should note that they are totally free of value judgement in describing extreme family types and their variants, although they seem to see open families as more adaptive to imposed change and stress and to have a fond liking for the chaos and creativity of the random style family. But unlike some authors there is no implicit preference for particular styles of family regulation; rather, Kantor and Lehr favour variety in family forms.

We do not have space to devote to a detailed discussion of the mechanisms which Kantor and Lehr suggest are used to achieve the family's targets. For each of the access dimensions, a host of mechanisms are proposed. Such mechanisms are grouped in *plans*, which are directed route maps '. . . traffic plans for moving people, things and events through the family's social space'. Plans may be prosynchronous, anti-synchronous or asynchronous, reflecting, respectively, family goals which are enmeshed or closely knit, enforce independence, or allow for parallel, loosely knit activities. Thus in the case of the access dimension of *energy*, the mechanisms deployed within such plans include those required for: locating energy sources, tapping into them, charging up, storing, testing against comparator principles, investing for future uses, allocating to particular activities, withdrawing from particular activities, keeping track of requirements, prioritizing, and transforming from one form (physical, mental) or charge (positive, negative, neutral). Each of these mechanisms has a special name within the theory. But how they interrelate or are organized within plans is not specified, nor is it clear how they were derived, since they could be based on either armchair speculation or actual observations and analysis. Nevertheless, these novel descriptions of family activities and the systematic taxonomy or classification which is set up around the key theoretical dimensions (access and target variables) seem to us to have face validity and to be capable of transformation into formal theory and operationalization. This in itself would be a major research enterprise. Our own research called for a much more simplified scheme. We should note that the mechanisms cater for all the key aspects of a feedback system, in that incoming stimuli are located, directed through the system, compared against prior evaluative criteria, and stored for future use and/or are used as a trigger to action upon the environment. At the same time, the state of the system is constantly monitored.

The final element in the Kantor and Lehr theory is also related to their systems/feedback approach and also offers a taxonomy for the classification of family behaviours within social space. This is the concept of *four player parts. Psychopolitics* is the description of the processes whereby individuals negotiate their roles within the social group. 'It is our belief that each individual seeks and negotiates for a place in the family system, in order that his personality may be affirmed by the family in ways that are compatible with his own needs and optimally, with the goals of the family establishment strategies . . . These strategies are intended to provide him a place within the family in which he can use the space, time and energy available to him in order to gain access to the targets of intimacy, nurturance, efficacy and identity he is seeking' (Kantor and Lehr, 1975 page 180).

The process of constant negotiation is revealed by analysing every family member's behaviour in terms of a four-fold and exhaustive description. Whenever the family members interact, all four categories of behaviour are available for use and may be deployed by any member in order to express the operation of the six key dimensions. These four player parts or roles are: *mover, follower, opposer*, and *bystander*. Within the conceptual framework of player parts, Kantor and Lehr are able to incorporate more specific family role concepts of other theorists and clinicians (this is one of the few places in their book where they refer to other authorities). *Movers* propose actions, but they are counterbalanced by the psychopolitics of *opposition*. To achieve their strategy both movers and opposers need the support of followers. Either a mover or an opposer can of course propose or resist maintenance or change, the extension of personal power or the limitation of the power of others. The follower uses the facilitation of power in others to support his/her own needs; this might involve taking an easy course, in contrast to the effort needed to become a mover. The *bystander* is seen to have a feedback-type role since he/she reflects upon the action of others without being a mover or opposer; by being independent of alliances and maintaining a personal brief, the bystander is free to express a view without being seen as a follower or opposer. The bystander might also make overt comparisons of the behaviour of family members against some set of family standards of conduct. Of course, this device can be used for various purposes, including that of moving or opposing. Thus within an interaction, an individual may change role within the flux of events.

Psychopolitics, like politics in the general domain, is about power and influence. In any observed interaction, any of the four roles might prove to be the more powerful. It is not until an interactive sequence is complete that one can conclude which player-part has proved most successful in negotiation. The term *manifest power* is used to describe the individual who appears to come out the winner after a particular interactional sequence. We are using the term *winner* here not merely in terms of the use of power as a goal in its own right but also in terms of the achievement of personal goals, such as positive affect and affiliation.

Using illustrative examples, Kantor and Lehr show how each of the key components of their theory (subsystems, target dimensions, access dimensions, access mechanisms, family types, player parts) all come together to constitute a general distance regulation theory. Their focus is upon sequences of observable behaviour and inferred inner states and events. Thus a brief sequence like a child knocking on its parents' bedroom door early in the morning can take several pages to describe.

We have devoted several pages ourselves to the description of the theory, because in our view it is a masterpiece of imaginative and potentially practical theory building.

Its strengths reveal its weaknesses; for example, its focus on the observable reveals the difficulty of gaining access to the unobserved, phenomenal, or subconscious world of family members. While Kantor and Lehr see such individual processes as crucial to our understanding of family life, they can offer little more than lip service to them. Thus their description of mechanisms and family styles of action, together with the conceptualization of four player parts, is much more powerful than their concept of individual intentions, personal subsystems, and so on. They claim that they used interview protocols and projective tests with some family members, but it is not clear how these were then used. What is not clear is whether the processes which occur are governed by voluntary or involuntary control processes, or include an element of conscious reflection. There is a constant slipping between the language of explicit organization, automatic obedience to rules, and unconscious determination. This is perhaps inevitable in a scheme which seeks to integrate group, dyadic, and individual processes.

The notion of a general system with feedback systems and informational transmission is translated into several levels of description, exemplified by styles of action, plans for the support of strategies, and mechanisms for implementing plans. However, like other systems theorists, they have not escaped from the concept of the machine, constructed on the basis of a general blueprint, and operating according to the principles followed by the designer, or a script devised by the author. While they acknowledge that individuals have their own motives, that individuals negotiate personal roles and power, that families can remain stable (stick to a general plan) or be subject to change (be flexible), they are nevertheless unable to slip easily between their several levels of description. Even at the level of observable action, we have to ask whether several observers observing the same sequence would be able (as the theory stands) to agree on the classification of the behaviour observed, to describe the mechanisms in use or the player parts enacted, to infer the plan and its parent strategy, or relate these to family-system goals and values.

In conclusion, the Kantor and Lehr theory is one of the most ambitious. It is puzzling that it is only referred to in passing in much of the literature. It contains many of the key variables (at least by name) which appear in other theories. Unfortunately, the very complexity of the theory, in spite of its organization, lays it open to criticism. It is unfortunate that Kantor and Lehr do not give a detailed account of their methodology. If we knew how they sampled family behaviour, or how different types of data (observation, interview, tape recordings) were integrated, it would be easier to see how this complex theory can be operationalized. As it stands, and in spite of its theoretical comprehensiveness, the key terms in the theory have little more status than their vernacular usage. From the point of view of our own research, the theory was too complex to handle in any practical fashion.

Theoretical Critiques of Family Life: Laing and Cooper

The writings of the radical antipsychiatry and antifamily movement are important, because they have implicit theories about family functioning and the role of family experience, both in the development of the individual and in the organization of society in general. As we saw in Chapter 1, it was Laing's enquiries with schizophrenic patients within the family context which drew the attention of psychologists to the potential importance of family processes. It would be improper for us, in reviewing theories of family behaviour, not to give an account of the views of Laing and Cooper, which were so influential within the 1960s and 1970s and which had so much appeal on university campuses at that time. One reason for devoting attention to these accounts is to show that while they have an important message about family behaviour, they are in many respects based more on exhortation than reality.

Cooper's *Death of the Family* (1971) is a remarkable book, written with tremendous feeling and power, poetic in style, and conveying anger, empathy, and contempt at one and the same time. The family is the target of Cooper's attack for the following reasons:

1. the family is the training ground which prepares the individual for emotional slavery and denial of self-autonomy;
2. the autonomous self is seen as an end in itself, as is personal experience, which requires to be untrammelled and validated in its own right;
3. the moral value of an action is in terms of the degree to which it offers personal experience;
4. the family seeks to repress individual expression and to invalidate the self;
5. the family is seen as a model for other organizational and institutional structures in society, which mimic its key features;
6. social institutions such as work, education, and government reflect this process, enforcing conformity and obedience and stifling creative experience and action;
7. these processes are sustained across generations and reflect the selfishness and greed of bourgeois and capitalist society, enabling a handful of grey men, at the top of an elaborated structure, to dominate.

Laing's existential approach was first set out in *The Divided Self* (1960), in which he sought to make the experience of schizophrenics comprehensible and valid. Psychotic behaviour, he claimed, can be understood if viewed within its social context, the power structure of the family. Like Cooper, the self is viewed primarily in phenomenological terms. Laing does not deny that it may be useful to describe people in terms of their physiology, nor, as some have claimed does he deny the possibility of genetic determination of schizoid characteristics. But when talking of persons and *being*, such descriptions fall short. Our relationships with others cannot be captured in physical terms or by analogy with organisms. 'The science of persons is the study of human beings that begins from a relationship with the other as a person and proceeds to an account of the other still as a person' (page 21). When I look at you I may note physical attributes but my language for describing you is in terms of responsibility, ability to make choices, as a self-acting agent, and as someone who has experience, intentions, desires, fears, and hopes. Laing says it is wrong for either type of description (physical or phenomenological) to forget the other, since a description which omits other ways of description will lose its way. Because our understanding of others involves appreciating their phenomenal experience, the exploration of the person takes considerable time and effort.

Laing claims that the schizoid person is turned schizophrenic as a result of constant invalidation of personal experience, imposed by personal and emotional manipulation by the family. In *Sanity, Madness and the Family* (Laing and Esterson, 1964) interviews with 11 psychotic individuals and their families, over a period of five years, are reported. While there is controversy as to whether Laing claims that family interaction *causes* schizophrenia, it is clear that he seeks to demonstrate it has a major role. In particular, he claims that the parents' belief system, and the behaviour which they impose upon and expect of the child, lead to the invalidation of the child's experience and his/her capacity to fully express personal feelings and desires. One adult patient is described by her mother as having been a 'good child'. The mother's description included the appraisal of the child as not being demanding as a baby, easily weaned, clean after potty training, obedient, and never a 'trouble'. Laing claims that many of us would not equate this description of 'good' with 'healthy'; we would expect a child to have illnesses, tantrums, to challenge authority, to be cheeky, grubby, obstinate, and, on occasion, very difficult to handle. His approach is also particularly dependent upon the notion of double-messages, where the child is unable to disentangle the meaning of the statements of others or to establish a stable view of his/her emotional standing within the family; thus statements implying that one is valued may contain disconfirmatory overtones and emotional ambiguity.

The views of Cooper and Laing are important in drawing our attention to key aspects of family life which need to be born in mind in the construction of theory: systems approaches, with their mechanical analogy, fall short of describing the phenomenal experience of family members; personal experience and self-worth are shaped by family influence; family interactions are strongly affected by the value judgements of the most powerful individuals. Of course, if phenomenal experience is a crucial aspect of the description of *persons*, it is not clear how it makes sense to even talk of *the family* either from an external observer's point of view, or as an aggregation of individuals. The family thereby becomes reduced to a system or organization, while the experience of family life can only be gained from inside the selves of the family's members. There is even so a considerable challenge in seeking to tap such personal experience or, indeed, to integrate the different phenomenal views expressed.

Laing and his associates have been subjected to severe criticism. For example, Rachman (1973) takes Laing to task on several grounds. We do not know how Laing selects 'data' from his discussions with patients and their families, thus it is possible that extreme bias has made that selection unrepresentative (Laing acknowledges that bias is inevitable in any evaluation of others). More important perhaps is the criticism that whatever the behaviour of families with a psychotic member, we have no evidence that it deviates from the range of behaviours observed in 'normal' families, nor in families with a member with a different sort of mental illness. Indeed, Laing's account does not explain why his patients become schizophrenic rather than depressed, manic, or perpetually anxious. The necessary control families (i.e., 'normal', or those containing members with non-psychotic pathology) are not included in his investigation.

Even if it were the case that families with a psychotic member do have behaviours which facilitate the development of schizophrenia, Laing does not tell us how the disorder comes to alight on a *particular* individual and not a sibling. Again, the behaviour of families with a psychotic member may deviate from the norm; but it may be that the patient's behaviour *causes* unusual parental behaviour as a reaction to the patient. Thus Laing could have the direction of causation the wrong way around. Even so, will such behaviour deviate from that experienced in a family with a depressed member or indeed with a child with a severe physical handicap? Rachman also points to the strong evidence for a genetic influence on the development of schizophrenia in an individual, the likelihood that close relatives may give abnormal responses on a variety of psychological measures, and the fact that genetic theory *can* explain variations within families. Laing, therefore, can be seen to select one of several alternatives, that family behaviour induces schizophrenia. But is is also possible that any correlation has an inverse pattern of causation or, more likely, that a common genetic factor is responsible both for strange family behaviours (if indeed they are demonstrated to exist) *and* the pathology of the sick member.

In a sense, the views of Laing and Cooper are hardly fully-fledged or systematic theories. Nevertheless, their view of family life has lessons for other theorists to learn. We should not end this brief account without commenting on the radical and revolutionary views expressed by Cooper in particular. To us there seems a contradiction in denying the need for society to shape the behaviour of its members. Cooper's ideal person loves himself (this is a precondition, in Cooper's terms, for our capacity to love others), engages in experience, and denies himself nothing. But one person's freedom can be another's tyranny and oppression. Cooper thinks it right for oppressed groups to bomb property and light incendiaries; the fact that this might curtail the potential experience (and lives) of others is not considered. The denial of the *contrat social* seems perverse. Others, for example Kohut (1977), have considered the importance of self-love, but have not extended the notion to a license for the abuse of others. On the more positive side, Cooper describes communes as places of mutual respect and freedom of expression; he also describes therapeutic communities in which patients are treated as persons, are not labelled or stigmatized and are allowed privacy and dignity. Such states of affairs, which he suggests therefore contradict the more distasteful aspects of family life, are indeed admirable. Whether they follow necessarily from his general premises or whether society as a whole could function on the same principles of interpersonal behaviour, are matters which remain to be demonstrated.

Implications of Theories of the Family for Future Family Research

In this concluding section we consider those general issues which arise from our presentation and evaluation of a number of key theories of family behaviour.

We challenge, first of all, the apparent reification of 'the family'. We have shown that for several reasons, talk of 'the family' may not make psychological sense. In particular, we believe it to be misleading to use *person* words (like need, wish, choose, decide) to describe a group of persons. Many of these terms are used within the literature either in a vernacular and imprecise sense, or in a way which pretends to be formal and derived from theories developed for the description of individuals. Even in that context, our current knowledge is not powerful. Is it not perverse, if we do not have a clear view of how *individuals* are motivated to speculate about the motivation of 'the family'? It is perhaps better to think of the family as a social context for individual development and fulfilment; then we would be less tempted to think of a social context having needs, wishes, and so on.

If there is an adequate psychology of the individual, can we use it to build up a picture of the family as a set of aggregated individuals? There are two drawbacks with this approach. Firstly, the combination of individuals creates a context for emergent properties, the notion that two persons and their relationship come to much more than the mere sum of two persons. Secondly, whenever psychologists study more than one person, there is a shift in perspective such that the persons studied are viewed from the *outside*. If this is a consequence, then there is a danger in selecting a view which is only one view, and which may prove to be non-veridical for the individuals themselves. The challenge is to combine a set of very different universes of discourse within one conceptual framework: individual phenomenology, individual behaviour, and group/family behaviour.

If such a methodology were developed, what variables could it sample? The concepts of *affect, power,* and *meaning* of Kantor and Lehr (1975) seem to us to be an excellent starting point. They encompass notions of positive and negative emotions, decision processes and negotiation, and the exploration of attitudes and beliefs. None of the theorists we have examined, however, has offered a precise account of these domains or shown how, in any description of a sequence of actions and reactions, the three variables may be observed to interrelate. There is no means of generating a checklist for the classification of behaviour and experience. We are inclined to suggest that the claim of Kantor and Lehr, that *all* family events occur at the interstices of several variables, is worth developing in more formal terms. We assume that any analysis which emerged would assign *weightings* of differential value to each of the variables, in any particular case. We are confident in asserting that any family theory or piece of family research which neglects one or two of these key variables (for example, a study of power, which neglects affect and meaning) is likely to be quite inadequate to the task of describing family life. It is worth pointing out that in psychology itself there is a perceptible trend towards the integration of theoretical approaches to cognitive and emotional aspects of behaviour. Such work is not easy, and we could be accused of setting an impossible brief for family research. Our answer would be that theories of the family, such as that of Kantor and Lehr, could point the way for future theorizing in psychology as a whole.

We now offer a brief checklist for guiding the development of family theory. Each of the points made has appeared elsewhere in this chapter, but it is worth enumerating them separately.

A Checklist for Theory Development

1. The theory should be stated with a clarity which ensures that the key variables can be measured and their relationships can be specified.

2. The range of variables likely to influence the particular family facts or events under investigation should be specified; where they are excluded from the theory, then reasons for doing so should be given.

3. The concepts of needs and motives need to be clarified. It is possible to manage without such concepts (see, for example, Skinner, 1971). If needs or motives are claimed to be an essential feature, then the theory should state whether motives are unconscious and inaccessible, or available for self-report. Where the family is said to have motives, the method of measuring them should be specified.

4. There should be a model of sources of family conflict, their identification, and the various ways in which conflict is resolved and/or displaced.

5. Family roles and functions should be described in relation to their impact on emotional, decision-making, socialization, and other salient factors.

6. The different phenomenal views or perspectives of all family members should be recognized.

7. There should be systematic exploration of values and beliefs, both explicit and implicit, together with their interaction with extra-familial belief structures and/or institutions.

8. The family should not be regarded as stationary. A good theory will contain a developmental model (not necessarily a stage theory) which specifies how key family variables alter over time. The model should cater for predictable changes and for the differential effects of, and adaptations to, the external stressors which make their impact at different developmental periods.

9. An explicit goal of the theory should be the precise description of repetitive family behaviours.

10. In devising taxonomies for describing behaviours, a distinction needs to be drawn between *acts* and *actions*. There is a danger of losing contact with validity in the search for simple and reliable measurements.

11. Descriptions are needed which sample individual, dyadic, and larger group interactions. Preferably, the theory should be able to treat such interactions as of equal salience in the description of family behaviour.

12. The various elements which we have already described may be used to devise a taxonomy for (a) the description of different family atmospheres and lifestyles, and (b) the classification of family behaviours, family events, and interactional sequences.

References

Burr, W. R., Hill, R., Nye, F. I. and Reiss, I. L. (Eds) (1979a). *Contemporary Theories About the Family*, vol. 1, *Research Based Theories*. New York: Free Press.
Burr, W. R., Hill, R., Nye, F. I. and Reiss, I. L. (Eds) (1979b). *Contemporary Theories About the Family*, vol. 2, *General Theories/Theoretical Orientations*. New York: Free Press.

Burr, W. R., Leigh, G. F., Day, R. D. and Constantine, J. (1979). Symbolic interaction in the family. In: W. R. Burr, R. Hill, F. I. Nye and I. L. Reiss (Eds), *Contemporary Theories About the Family*, vol. 2, *General Theories/Theoretical Orientations*. New York: Free Press.

Cooper, D. (1971). *The Death of the Family*. Harmondsworth: Penguin.

Erikson, E. H. (1965). *Childhood and Society*. Harmondsworth: Penguin.

Gale, A. (1984). Review of *Stress and the Family* (H. I. McCubbin and C. R. Figley, Eds). In: *British Journal of Psychology*, **76**, 136–137.

Hill, R. (1979). As reported by the editors in Introduction to Burr, W. R., Hill, R., Nye, F. I. and Reiss, I. L. (Eds) (1979). *Contemporary Theories About the Family*, vol. 1, *Research Based Theories*. New York: Free Press.

Kantor, D. and Lehr, W. (1975). *Inside the Family: Towards a Theory of Family Process*. San Francisco, California: Jossey Bass.

Kohut, H. (1977). *The Restoration of the Self*. New York: International Universities Press.

Laing, R. D. (1960). *The Divided Self*. London: Tavistock.

Laing, R. D. and Esterson, A. (1964). *Sanity, Madness and the Family*. London: Tavistock.

Minuchin, S. (1974). *Families and Family Therapy*. London: Tavistock.

Minuchin, S., Montalvo, B., Guerney, Jr., B. G., Rosman, B. L. and Schumer, F. (1967). *Families of the Slums: An Exploration of their Structure and Treatment*. New York: Basic Books.

Minuchin, S., Rosman, B. and Baker, L. (1978). *Psychosomatic Families: Anorexia Nervosa in Context*. Cambridge, Massachusetts: Harvard University Press.

Nye, F. I. (1979). Choice, exchange and the family. In: W. R. Burr, R. Hill, F. I. Nye and I. L. Reiss (Eds), *Contemporary Theories About the Family*, vol. 2, *General Theories/Theoretical Orientations*. New York: Free Press.

Nye, F. I. (Ed.) (1982). *Family Relationships: Rewards and Costs*. Beverly Hills, California: Sage.

Olson, D. H., Sprenkle, D. H. and Russell, C. S. (1979). Circumplex model of marital and family systems: I. Cohesion and adaptability dimensions, family types, and clinical applications. *Family Process*, **18**, 3–28.

Olson, D. H. and Craddock, A. E. (1980). Circumplex model of marital and family systems: Applications to Australian families. *Australian Journal of Sex, Marriage and the Family*, **1**, 53–69.

Olson, D. H., McCubbin, H. I., Barnes, H. Larsen, A., Muxen, M. and Wilson, M. (1983). *Families: What Makes them Work*. Beverly Hills, California: Sage.

Rachman, S. (1973). Schizophrenia: a look at Laing's views. *New Society*, April, 184–186.

Skinner, B. F. (1971). *Beyond Freedom and Dignity*. Harmondsworth: Penguin.

Thibaut, J. W. and Kelley, H. H. (1959). *The Social Psychology of Groups*. New York: Wiley.

CHAPTER FOUR

Benefits and Problems of the Participant Observation Technique

Arlene Vetere

Introduction

What is participant observation? How has it evolved as a research methodology and an assessment procedure? When is it appropriate and when not? We describe the theoretical social roles of participant observation as formalized by Junker (1972). He devised a continuum of relative *involvement* with the research population to relative *detachment*. We illustrate Junker's model with examples from the psychological and sociological literature. Participant observation has a number of advantages as a data gathering technique, particularly in the context of studying the family in the home environment. Special problems arise, however, both for the observer and for the family under observation. The process of participant observation can be understood by analysing it in terms of existing social psychological theories. Such an analysis leads to an improved understanding of the nature of participant observation and its methodological problems.

Historical Development of Participant Observation as a Technique

> While the three of us were in the kitchen Harriet was crying in her room. She cried and cried but neither Dr nor Mrs Jones made a move nor said a word to her. At last Mrs Jones said to her husband, 'If you happen to be passing by the bedroom, would you glide in there and do something about your daughter?'. He asked, laughing, 'Why didn't you simply say, 'Go in and take care of Harriet'?'. She said, 'You know what you would have said if I had done that', and he replied, 'What would I have said?', and she answered, 'You would have said, ''Go to hell!''.' He laughed and replied that he would have said, 'Okay,' but she repeated, 'You would have said, ''Go to hell!'' '.

This quotation is from *Pathways to Madness*, written by the anthropologist Jules Henry in 1973. He was interested in the ways in which some Western nuclear families promote psychoses in their children. Henry's work and writings provided the initial inspiration for our own work. But in contrast with us, he was concerned with

64

psychoanalytic and depth explanations of the behaviour of family members. Henry's research relied on naturalistic observation, a common methodology in the disciplines of ethology, anthropology, and the biological sciences. But in spite of its frequent use, we have found few systematic, formal descriptions of participant observation or handbooks to aid the novice. Such formal models are necessary, however, to guide the participant observer in a number of important decisions and choices: the social role to be adopted; the group to be studied; the number of observations to be made; the sampling frame (where, when, how often); the method of recording; and the retreat from the group under study. We had to tackle all these issues. It is useful to set them in an historical context.

The involvement with a hitherto unknown human group has implications both for the observer and the observed. An analysis of this particular problem has evolved over time. Early field workers in anthropology, like Mead (1930) and Malinowski (1926), emphasized the importance of observing yet not disturbing the social behaviour under study. When one is a member of a social group one is not normally also detached from it. But the social role of the participant observer requires that he or she maintains a neutral stance. Neutrality implies a refusal to become involved with internal factions and alliances within the group. But such willingness to take sides is expected in most social groups. Thus, antagonism can be created by the very ambiguity of the observer's role as a social being within the group. But is the prescription of 'neutrality' possible in practice? Silence and lack of intervention are socially meaningful. Watzlawick, Beavin, and Jackson (1967) comment that neutrality to the point of silence is a form of communication. For example, in a family quarrel, the silence of a third member may be interpreted as an indication of their superior refusal to become involved. Similarly, failure to communicate by the observer can be interpreted as a sign that the observer considers him/herself outside the group, above the group, or more important, lacks interest in the group. Our view is that the observer is a social being who must respond to the actions of the group and to conversational overtures initiated by its members. The rejection of extreme neutrality as a role for the observer is expressed in the views of Vidich (1955) and others who realized that observers make themselves meaningful to people by their very presence. Such presence is impossible to conceal. However, Junker (1972) was the first to construct a formal model of the nature and extent of the social meaning of the observer's presence (see below).

Following the work of Mead and Malinowski, the development of participant observation as a technique has had some notable contributors. Kluckhohn (1940) attempted to explode the myth of what she considered to be 'total objectivity' in experimental social psychological research. She argued that *all* observation is subject to measurement error and showed from her own work how participant observation highlights the problems of reliability and validity. For example, when observing a Spanish-speaking village in New Mexico, she found that indirect interviewing, while helping a woman with her washing was very different from direct interviewing in the woman's parlour or in the office. She did not wait for persons to recall past events voluntarily; rather, she asked 'leading questions'. This technique alters the situation in varying degrees but does not involve the creation of a special situation, which might be met by evasion or misrepresentation. Her range of data was increased in one instance by the use of simulation of behaviour, made possible by participation; for example, through gradual simulation of the Spanish-American woman's fear of witchcraft, she obtained information about jealously guarded beliefs.

In her view, traditional social psychological methods, such as laboratory studies of group interaction, were open to similar criticism. Kluckhohn attempted to overcome problems of inaccuracy in measurement by enabling observers to identify and examine their own biases and analyse their social roles within the group under study. She participated in village dances, seeing them as an opportunity for relaxation, as did the villagers. Her experiences in avoiding drunken or over-attentive men reflected her participation in the community, but were dealt with according to her own rules and standards. Understanding of her social role and social biases was increased as a result of the examination of such experiences.

In our own work with families it is clear that bias operates at several levels during data collection: the *observer's* perception of individual family members, the *family members'* perception of the observer, and the *interaction* between the observer and the family.

Schwartz and Schwartz (1955) drew attention in a very explicit way to the fact that the observer him or herself is a part of the context under observation. This implies that the *interaction* between observer and observed influences the observer, when registering, interpreting, and recording the observations. The very nature of this interaction varies over time and must be seen as a *process* (Vidich, 1955). When observing in natural settings, the researcher's role gradually evolves, through changing perceptions of both observer and observed; each contributes in a dynamic fashion to the other's perceptions, as mutual familiarity increases. Thus, the observer's relationship with the observed is very much like other relationships between people, and progressively less like the relationship between scientist and experimental materials. We may illustrate this process by reference to one of the families we studied. This was a large family in which the father saw himself as an outsider (to his wife and five sons) and constantly sought confirmation of his own worth by seeking out the observer, drawing out advice and opinion, and placing her in the role of social worker. The observer reported that she found this constant demand for attention and support difficult to resist and became wheedled into a role which was not of her own choice. We do not need to mention that, prior to entry into the family, quite explicit descriptions had been given about the desired observer's role.

It is therefore unrealistic to believe that there could ever be a fixed and prescribed role for our observers. Different families and different family members will have different expectations of the observer, and of their own appropriate reactions. We suspect that one source of unreliable observation is the past history of the observer, particularly in the context of their own family life, however much he or she has been trained to be objective. All these perceptions and their interactions are likely to change over time, and the observer is a different person, rather than a standard instrument, when entering the next family to be studied.

As Vidich pointed out, the nature and the extent of the information collected by the observer, and the response to the observer, varies with the group's changing expectations of the observer. A difficulty is that total immersion of the observer within the group is likely to lower sensitivity to bias. Identification of error sources in our own research does not guarantee an adequate means of estimating them or eliminating them. An ideal design would seek to separate out: family perceptions (including interactions between members), observer perceptions, the complex interaction between family and observer, and the dynamic temporal element. Even assuming that the data were available for analysis, we would need a time series model for characterizing the data both as dependent and independent variables (see Gottman, 1979).

Schutz (1970) identified the 'stranger' problem. This is encountered by observers when entering an alien or novel culture. In one's own culture one has the advantage of communicating in one's own language and symbolic systems, which is very much like day-to-day interaction, such as moving to a new neighbourhood or starting a new job. This can prevent attributing to the group under observation, meanings which are alien to their own experience; however, it does not prevent the use of stereotypes and scapegoating mechanisms prevalent in the culture.

One of the most famous and influential participant observation studies is that of Barker (1963) who studied a large group of children and their families in the American Midwest. He drew a distinction between two researcher roles: the *transducer* and the *operator*. The transducer role is illustrated by Barker's own technique. Each researcher, working as an individual, would follow a single child throughout the school day, observing and recording the child's spontaneous behaviour within the various contexts and interactions experienced by the child. Such contexts receive particular emphasis. The presence of the observer was minimized as much as possible. In contrast, an operator would select behaviour for study (Barker chose 'typical' schooldays on the basis of large samples), and then impose *prearranged* units of measurement and constraints upon behaviour (for example, in a laboratory and not in natural contexts). In Barker's view only 'transducer-data' allow for the reliable identification of the 'fundamental units' of the 'behaviour stream'. Moreover, the task of the observer is to identify and measure the situational factors of relevance to the observed person's behaviour. A nice example he gives is of the baseball player, where the rules which operate are so firmly established that individuals are in a sense, interchangeable. The ideal transducer measures events without contamination and with high fidelity.

Thus we may treat each family home as a different situation, with its own 'rules', and these in turn affect the data collected, the role of the observer, and the interpretation of the observer by those under observation. Barker claims that individual environments must be described independently of the behaviour which occurs within them.

Moos and Moos (1976) constructed a taxonomy of the social environments of families, along several psychological dimensions. These dimensions included: *achievement* oriented, *conflict* oriented, and *expression* oriented. They claim that such information about an individual family provides important clues as to the socialization procedures employed within the home and the types of therapeutic intervention which are appropriate for a particular child and its family.

The issues considered above indicate that the term *participant observer* cannot be used in a simple and straightforward sense. Unfortunately, in many textbooks and scientific reports, the term is used loosely, without recourse to conceptual or operational definition. The lessons learned by these key figures in the development of the technique are frequently forgotten.

Junker's Taxonomy

Junker (1972) described the social roles of the participant observer in terms of a continuum ranging from complete participation, through participant as observer, and observer as participant, to the complete observer.

The *complete participant* conceals their observational activity from those under observation, becoming totally involved in the group's lifestyle, behaviour, and concerns. The advantage of this mode of observation is that as a member of the in-group, the observer becomes acquainted with a particular role and has access to 'private' information. This creates the opportunity to obtain rich and veridical data. But complete observation has severe disadvantages. If the observer is found out he or she is open to accusations of spying, there is a danger of forming alliances within the group, and fear of disclosure may inhibit observation outside the in-group. The observer in this mode is therefore under great personal strain apart from the burden of the ethical consequences of deceit. A controversial example of this style of approach is the Festinger, Reicken, and Schacter (1956) study, *When Prophecy Fails*. Researchers pretended to have become converted in order to gain access to a religious group. The group predicted the imminent end of the world based on information relayed to them by beings in outer space. The observers wanted to know what would happen when this prophecy failed. Ethical objections apart, given that the group was not large, the sudden swelling of its ranks by the researchers at a time when public opposition was high, could be seen to have had a biasing impact on group behaviour. Some wags have extended such criticism by suggesting that this famous study was in fact based on one group of Harvard researchers observing another group!

In contrast, the *participant as observer* does not conceal observational activity while engaging in relative involvement with the group. Participation occurs, as in the first mode, thus allowing acquaintance with a group role, but there is freedom to make observations outside the in-group. Disadvantages include a lower degree of access to private information, a need to spend more time participating than observing, group evaluation as an outsider playing a participating role, and, inevitably, some group discussion of the role. Whyte's (1955) *Street Corner Society*, the study of the social structure of an Italian slum, is a good example of this approach. He boarded with an Italian family, learned their language, and gained access to male groups by revealing that he was writing a book. Goffman's interpretation of the experience of patients in asylums (1961) is another classic example. Only by participating could Goffman have brought to light the loss of self-esteem experienced in institutions and the existence of a flourishing parallel underlife in hospitals, allowing patients to maintain a sense of identity and self-respect.

Our own approach with families is that of Junker's *observer as participant*. Here the observer declares the intention to observe from the outset, and this public disclosure ensures relative detachment. There is therefore less restriction imposed by the demands of the role of participation, and private information can be made available if confidentiality is guaranteed. However, as we see in Chapter 5, undertakings about confidentiality can restrict freedom to report on material. A major drawback is that the observer remains peripheral to the group, *in* the world of the group, but not *of* it. Henry, in *Pathways to Madness* (1973), adopted the observer as participant role when living with families who had a psychotic member. Henry was keen to observe how family behaviours served to promote psychotic behaviour in one individual and we offered a sample of his observations at the beginning of this chapter. Barker's work, also referred to earlier, offers another classic example.

Junker's final category, the *complete observer*, is one of complete detachment, without any contact with group members, and allows complete freedom from contamination by group reactivity. The one-way screen in a social psychology laboratory is a good example. The major disadvantage, apart from the ethical issue of observing without gaining prior permission, is that the observer sees *acts* rather than experiencing *actions*; by failing to share the experiential world of the group under observation, the full meaning of group actions is lost. Thus, this mode of observation hardly qualifies as participative.

One intervening category which Junker did not include is the quasi-experiment, where manipulation of an experimental variable is combined with observation. For example, Darley and Latané (1968) asked confederates to feign collapse on the subway, so that they could observe whether bystanders became involved or displayed apathy. The quasi-experiment therefore combines some of the control of the classic experiment with the observation of the behaviour stream in naturalistic contexts.

According to Junker, therefore, participant observation has several identifiable features: participation in the daily lives of those under study as the principal source of data; watching group members in typical situations and observing their reactions; talking with group members; working with them; sharing ritual and social events; entering the private world of their home. The aim is to sample as many settings and moods as possible. For Junker, three main variables distinguish the different levels of participant observation: concealment, confidentiality, and degree of involvement.

Participant Observation in the Home

There are many advantages in participant observation as a research method in the context of family interaction studies, particularly in the early and descriptive, exploratory stages. Data are generated with a range of contexts and detail that capture the 'behaviour stream' of Barker. A particular advantage during the early stages of research is that the researcher becomes sensitized to the nature of family interaction process and the range of variables which need to be taken into account. Working hypotheses can be constructed from this raw experience. In contrast, laboratory studies start out by being overselective and thereby exclude some of the conditions and family situations which are particularly revealing to the researcher. For example, traumatic events, behaviour of individual children with or without siblings, demonstrations of affection, conflict and its resolution, contextually dependent rule following, and so on, are most likely to occur in a natural environment and be suppressed on the researcher's territory. Over and above the selectivity of events and the limited sample range, the laboratory might impose unnatural constraints; in developmental studies, for example, the child may be required to attend for periods which exceed its natural attention span. Participant observation also avoids the difficulties of self-report data, where subjects may be unable to report on their own behaviour either because they are not natural observers of themselves or because they do not have the language skills to classify and express events.

Participant observation data have the unique property of describing the flow and interchange of social behaviour in dynamic movement over time. No attempt is made to freeze behaviour in a brief and encapsulated moment of time. This does not imply that events are not repeated. For example, the participant observer in the home may observe repeated patterns of child misbehaviour and parental disciplining, noting the context, what happens, and who becomes involved. Moreover, the historical and social meaning of events are accessible as is the group's own subculture, its framework of shared meanings, neologisms, myths and symbols. In our example, the response of a second parent to a call for help in disciplining a child may reflect their own prior experience of parenting in their family of origin, or the prevailing cultural norms and evaluations of alternative methods of parental discipline.

The work of Henry (1973), Kantor and Lehr (1975), and Steinglass (1979) illustrates how well suited participant observation can be to the ecological aim of exploring and interrelating spontaneous, interpersonal behaviour and the psychological living conditions of children and families. Henry argues that the home is the optimal setting for the study of 'disturbed' behaviour. A General System view qua Minuchin (see Chapter 3) would see the home context as a crucial element in family behaviour. The work of Henry and others, by exploring behaviour in context, served to shift attention from a medical model which sees aetiology within the individual. The ecological context provides the evidence of interactional processes (see Framo, 1965).

Hansen (1981) followed Henry's example. She used home visits for families who did not respond to therapy in the consulting room. She generated a descriptive and normative data base by living for a week with each of three families whom she considered 'functional' and then attempted cross-family comparisons, tentatively exploring the causes of the differences and supported by verbal reports from family members. Unfortunately, her untimely death made her essentially descriptive data, which were published posthumously, incomplete. Nevertheless, her descriptions are an important contribution to the family research literature.

Special Problems of Participant Observation in the Home

Home observation raises some rather special problems: observational reactivity, researcher bias, and reliability and validity. (We consider ethical issues and their consequences in Chapter 5.)

Observational reactivity

Does the family change its customary behaviours merely because the observer is present? The problem of reactivity, that the object of study is affected by the act of study, is not just a problem in psychology or in family research. As Stapp, a quantum physicist put it: '. . . the observed system is required to be isolated in order to be defined, yet interacting in order to be observed' (1971, page 1303). Thus both isolation of subject matter *or* the addition of a measurement instrument change its habitual modes of behaviour. Observation is therefore an interactive process; what is observed is in part at least an emergent property of the process. The presence of the observer in the home is very likely to have an effect on what would have been the natural course of events. But there is a problem in estimating the *degree* of this effect. Logically, one needs to have access to *true* effects in order to estimate the effects of *measurement error*, but one cannot measure true effects without measurement. Nevertheless, there are ways in which one can get closer to what might have been had there been no observer. For example, if one assumes that reactivity effects diminish with time, repeated sampling will show whether behaviour is stable. Again, one can measure behaviour when different observers are present; if the observers are reliable, then change in family behaviour is more likely to be due to events within the family itself, rather than the interaction of family plus observation. One can also ask family members whether the presence of the observer made an impact upon them. But none of these procedures can provide conclusive proof, for reasons we consider below. Moreover, it is likely that different family members because of age, self-consciousness, a felt need to behave in a socially desirable fashion, a need to sustain pathology in a member, and so on, will react differently from each other to the presence of the observer. This means that the magnitude of the interactive effect is a function of family members present, the context of observation, and the observer. It is not surprising, therefore, that the nature and magnitude of interactive effects are in dispute.

Few studies have dealt specifically with the effects of the observer's presence on parent–child relationships or parent–parent relationships, particularly in the natural setting of the family home. Some authors take the extreme view that reactivity effects are negligible (Behrens and Sherman, 1959; Wright, 1967), while others are more willing to recognize reactivity (Hoover and Rinehart, 1968; White, 1973). Reviews of the available studies indicate that the effect is most pronounced as observation begins (Johnson and Bolstad, 1973; Kent and Foster, 1977). Our post-observation interview with one of the families studied in our project, supports this impression (see Chapter 8).

Reactive effects are themselves a very important source of working hypotheses and should not be seen to be mere artefacts. One needs to ask why particular modes of reactivity have occurred. For example, strong attention-seeking behaviour towards the observer by particular family members, in contrast with others, may say something about underlying family dynamics. Indeed, some reactivity effects may sensitize the observer to the possibility that the *wrong* variables have been selected for study (London and Thorngate, 1981).

Unfortunately, many family therapists and many family researchers do make the assumption that what they observe is the habitual pattern of behaviour of the family. Some therapeutic intervention strategies are explicitly designed to elicit interaction patterns. Our view is that some of the research strategies we have adopted help to clarify the issue but will never resolve it. The truth is that reactivity is one of the crosses that psychology as a whole has to bear (Silverman, 1977; Tajfel, 1981); however, naturalistic observation of groups in their normal ecological contexts, brings us closer to normal modes of behaviour and group interaction than does the special and artificial context of the laboratory (Gale and Baker, 1981).

Unfortunately, in participant observation, reactivity occurs not only within the family, but in the observer. The observer is not a microscope nor a video camera, but a person attempting to observe. In fact, a video camera would not convey much advantage, for the content of the film it captures has to be sampled and analysed by someone.

The bias of the observer

Our observers were themselves members of families and heads of families, with personal experience of being reared and of child-rearing. Since child-rearing practice and indeed interpersonal relationships within families vary considerably, and since there are no rules about what is correct and what is not correct, the observer is likely to be responding on the basis of personal experience and beliefs. Thus it is unlikely that the observer will view the family without some preconceived assumptions about what is or what should be. Perception is seen by many psychologists as an active and interpretative process, and in social psychology, perceptual bias has been shown to affect our perception of others. Indeed, the very presence of attitudes and beliefs and expectations of role is seen to support processes of interaction among individuals. But response to role and role structure is not consciously determined, and persons trained to interact with others, for example, as psychotherapists, need to be trained in order to become aware of their preconceptions.

One of the problems with our own research is that there was no one to train us and that our preconceptions, if actually identified, emerged only as part of the research. In other words, we became sensitive to *some* of our biases only after time, and only *after* the experience of interaction with families. The use of two independent observers, on two separate occasions, was designed to counteract some of our ignorance, as was the procedure of cross-scoring of transcripts (see Chapter 7). The difficulty is that a study of accuracy and freedom from bias presupposes some objective criteria against which an individual observer's judgements may be validated. However, the use of independent observers or raters of observation transcripts can guarantee only reliability and not validity. Without replication from independent sources there can be no validity, yet replication as such merely assures that the observers or scorers are using the same assumptions or conceptual framework. That framework could be invalid. One technique we employed was to ask observers to maintain a personal diary, over and above the observational record, in which any experience during which the observer became aware of personal bias and reactivity could be recorded. This diary also served for the cathartic discharge of emotions generated during the lonely business of observation!

Given our awareness that our observer is subject to the bias of cognitive set and motivated perception, that, at worst, she sees what she expects to see, we can nevertheless formalize some of the potential error sources. These can occur at various stages in the observational process: the observer needs to interpret the family's use of language; she must use language herself to describe the family's behaviour; the language she has available may be more suited to some modes of interaction than others and may be inadequate to the task of describing complex and rapid interaction; and she may differ from other observers, both in the degree of self-discipline in language use and in the stock of descriptors available to her.

It is clear that many of the problems identified in the evolution of participant observation as a research technique are still with us, and have affected our study of family life.

Reliability and validity

We have already commented on the problem of reliability, and the issue of reliability in our own data is considered at length in Chapters 7 and 12. However, we wish to contrast here the concept of reliability in participant observation study with the concept of reliability as evolved in the psychological laboratory. The psychology undergraduate learns that replicability ensures reliability; the same observations should in principle be possible if the experiment is replicated in all its essential features. But as Willems (1967) points out, naturalistic data are not replicable in the strict experimental sense. Against such a strict criterion, one might be tempted to dismiss observational data as quasi-anecdotal and untrustworthy. However, while tight experimental control may be a goal in the sciences it may not always be achieved, and may not always be appropriate. Scientific method can be observational and historical as well as experimental. Ready replicability is not always feasible; single observations, supported by corroboratory sightings, are quite acceptable in astronomy.

However, even within observational methods, some behaviours may be more readily observed than others and some coding schemes may be less ambiguous and less unreliable than others. The possibility that all behaviours, individuals, and interactions cannot be observed with equal reliability has received little attention in the literature on observational reliability. In the context of the home, for example, ease of coding may depend on how many are present (dyads or larger groups), the activity (watching television or eating a meal together), and the mood (unpacking the shopping or having a heated argument). We consider these issues further in Chapters 7 and 12.

Validity presents even greater problems than reliability and is particularly troublesome for observational research. Psychologically speaking, each individual's view of the world is unique and in some respects inconsistent with that of other co-actors. This applies not only in terms of a difference between observer and observed, but also among those who are observed. Consider a committee meeting, where different points of view are exchanged, negotiated, and sometimes not resolved. Will the different participants give an identical account of what was agreed, how agreement was reached, who was influential in determining the outcome, and which contributions were important? The difficulty lies in determining what *is* the reality or in Laing and Esterson (1964) terms, *whose* reality. In Laing's description, the process of interpersonal perception in dyads is overlaid by my notions of what I think, what I think you think, what I think you think of what I think, . . . and so on. When dealing with several points of view simultaneously, particularly when family members are of different ages, have different vested interests in particular events, and have different affiliations with groups external to the family, it is difficult to see how we can achieve a view of reality which captures communality of viewpoint yet does not damage the integrity of the individual viewpoints. We have tried to sample this range of views by employing the Repertory Grid method as a complement to our observational procedures (see Chapter 8).

Participant Observation and Social Psychology

We now turn to concepts and theories in social psychology to illuminate the process of participant observation in the home. Such theories enable us to make predictions about the impact of the observer on the life of the family.

Evaluation apprehension

This will affect the family's perceptions of the researcher and the family members' behaviour. Rosenberg (1969) claims that evaluation apprehension is a systematic source of bias in psychological research. When a person knows they are under observation, an anxiety-toned concern is aroused, and the individual seeks positive appraisal from the investigator, or seeks to avoid negative evaluation. This view has been tested empirically; for example, Chapman (1971) showed that subjects listening to humorous material over earphones behaved differently from those listening to the same material through a loudspeaker. Evaluation apprehension operated more in the latter case because the subject's laughter could be matched against the publicly available humorous material. We have all worried about laughing at the right moment! Similar processes operate with the family. An example from our own research would be the family member who is keen to present their family life to the observer as warm, close, and caring. Thus evaluation apprehension may be one of the filters which contributes to reactivity effects.

Social facilitation

Zajonc (1965) outlined a social facilitation theory to explain why we behave differently in the presence of others. He drew together earlier findings which demonstrated that our perceptions, judgements, attention, and motivation can change in a social context and can be different from when we are alone. He claimed that the mere presence of another affects our behaviour. The theory has generated a great deal of social, psychological, and even physiological research. Motivation is heightened in the presence of others and this increases the probability of occurrence of well-practised behaviour. In learning situations the difficulty of the task interacts with the person's state, so that simple tasks are learned more easily, but difficult tasks are disrupted. The current explanation for these phenomena (e.g., Bond and Titus, 1983) is that the effects are mediated both by increased bodily arousal induced by the presence of others and by cognitive evaluations along the lines of Rosenberg's theory. Thus the mere addition of an observer could arouse individual family members or all the family and increase the probability of occurrence of certain behaviours. For example, a child liable to show tantrums may be more likely to exhibit anti-social behaviour because of the mere additional presence of the observer. This may happen even in the absence of the arousal-inducing effects induced by the novel environment of the clinic. Note that the child's temper tantrum (induced by social facilitation) and the parent's response (constrained by evaluation apprehension) could combine in a variety of ways, not all of which may be representative of parent–child interactions.

Social Exchange Theory

Social Exchange Theory (Homans, 1961, 1974; Edwards, 1980) has been used to understand human interaction and, in particular, family behaviour. People seek to avoid 'costly behaviour' and prefer 'rewarding' interactions, relationships, and emotional states. This active process leads to an optimal outcome, based on the individual's perceptions of rewards and costs. The negotiation between the researcher and the family in order to gain entry, and their subsequent relationships during the observation, may be expressed in terms of rewards and costs for the family. These may be direct or indirect, reflecting the immediate impact of having the researcher in the home, or the less direct effects mediated via friends and relatives. The ratio of reward to cost will be influenced by the perceived trustworthiness and personal acceptability of the observer. Acceptability may be expressed in terms of both reciprocity (which is a positive aspect) and unobtrusiveness (which is a lack of negative interference). The implications for the observer's role are discussed in Chapter 6.

Because the presence of an observer is unlike any previous experience of visitors or guests, the calculation of the benefits and disadvantages of the social exchange will occur as a developmental process over time. For example, help with the washing up is allowed (reciprocity) but interference in disciplining of children is not (unob-trusiveness). Each family member or dyad may evolve a different ratio of reward and cost to themselves. Family members who have a vested interest in resisting change may see the observer's presence and the way it spotlights dysfunctional interaction as too costly.

Attribution Theory

Finally, Attribution Theory (Heider, 1958; Kelley, 1967) and its variants highlight the importance of first impressions during the first encounter with the family. Attribution is one of the processes whereby we filter and interpret the behaviour of ourselves and others. Attributions may be in terms of personal dispositions or situational contexts. Ross (1977) suggests that we are typically guilty of 'the fundamental attribution error' whereby our causal account of events leans too heavily on personal dispositions, particularly those of others, and neglects situational factors. This may affect the family's interaction and the observer's behaviour in three ways: the family may perceive the observer in particular ways, the observer him or herself may use attributional frameworks to select and describe family events, and the family members may commit the fundamental attributional error in accounting for family events. Examples may include family confusion over the observer as individual and as researcher, and scapegoating of an individual family member both by virtue of the observer's account of family events and of the family's interpretations of problems in family life.

Thus we see that social psychological concepts can be focused upon our research strategy, to describe the processes which may occur both in negotiating an entrée into the family and during the period of the observational visit.

References

Barker, R. G. (Ed.) (1963). *The Stream of Behaviour*. New York: Appleton-Century.

Behrens, M. and Sherman, A. (1959). Observation of family interaction in the home. *American Journal of Orthopsychiatry*, **29**, 243–248.

Bond, C. F. and Titus, L. J. (1983). Social facilitation: A meta-analysis of 241 studies. *Psychological Bulletin*, **94**, 265–292.

Chapman, A. J. (1973). An electromyographic study of apprehension about evaluation. *Psychological Reports*, **33**, 811–814.

Darley, J. M. and Latané, B. (1968). Bystander intervention in emergencies: Diffusion of responsibility. *Journal of Personality and Social Psychology*, **8**, 377–383.

Edwards, J. N. (1980). *Coming apart: A model of the marital dissolution decision*. Paper presented at the Midwest Sociological Society, Milwaukee, April, 1980.

Festinger, L., Riecken, H. W. and Schacter, S. (1956). *When Prophecy Fails*. Minneapolis: University of Minnesota Press.

Framo, J. L. (1965). Systematic research on family dynamics. In: I. Boszormenyi-Nagy and J. L. Framo (Eds), *Intensive Family Therapy: Theoretical and Practical Aspects*. New York: Harper and Row.

Gale, A. and Baker, S. (1981). *In vivo* or *in vitro*? Some effects of laboratory environments, with particular reference to the psychophysiology experiment. In: M. J. Christie and P. G. Mellett (Eds), *Foundations of Psychosomatics*. London: Wiley.

Goffman, E. (1961). *Asylums*. New York: Anchor Books.

Gottman, J. M. (1979). *Marital Interaction: Experimental Investigations*. New York: Academic Press.

Hansen, C. (1981). Living in with normal families. *Family Process*, **20**, 53–75.

Heider, F. (1958). *The Psychology of Interpersonal Relations*. New York: Wiley.

Henry, J. (1973). *Pathways to Madness*. New York: Vintage Books.

Homans, G. C. (1961). *Social Behaviour: The Elementary Forms*. New York: Harcourt, Brace, Jovanovich.

Homans, G. C. (1974). *Social Behaviour: The Elementary Forms, Revised Edition*. New York: Harcourt, Brace, Jovanovich.

Hoover, L. K. and Rinehart, H. H. (1968). *The effect of an outside observer on family interaction*. Unpublished Manuscript: University of Oregon.

Johnson, S. M. and Bolstad, O. D. (1973). Methodological issues in naturalistic observation: Some problems and solutions for field research. In: L. A. Hamerlynck, L. C. Handy and E. J. Mash (Eds), *Behaviour Change: Methodology, Concepts and Practice*. Champaign, Illinois: Research Press.

Junker, B. H. (1972). *Fieldwork: An Introduction to the Social Sciences*. Chicago, Illinois: University of Chicago Press.

Kantor, D. and Lehr, W. (1975). *Inside the Family: Towards a Theory of Family Process*. San Francisco, California: Jossey-Bass.

Kelley, E. L. (1967). *Assessment of Human Characteristics*. London: Wadsworth.

Kent, R. N. and Foster, S. L. (1977). Direct observation procedures: Methodological issues in naturalistic settings. In: A. Ciminero, K. Calhoun and H. Adams (Eds), *Handbook of Behavioural Assessment*. New York: Wiley.

Kluckhohn, F. R. (1940). The participant-observer technique in small communities. *American Journal of Sociology*, **46**, 331–343.

Laing, R. D. and Esterson, A. (1964). *Sanity, Madness and the Family*. London: Tavistock.

London, I. D. and Thorngate, W. (1981). Divergent amplification and social behaviour: Some methodological considerations. *Psychological Reports*, **48**, 203–228.

Malinowski, B. (1926). *Crime and Custom in Savage Society*. London: Routledge and Kegan Paul.

Mead, M. (1930). *Growing Up in New Guinea*. Harmondsworth: Penguin.

Moos, R. H. and Moos, B. S. (1976). A typology of family social environments. *Family Process*, **15**, 357–371.

Rosenberg, M. J. (1969). The conditions and consequences of evaluation apprehension. In: R. Rosenthal and R. Rosnow (Eds), *Artifact in Behavioural Research*. New York: Academic Press.

Ross, L. (1977). The intuitive psychologist and his shortcomings: Distortions in the attribution process. In: L. Berkowitz (Ed.), *Advances in Experimental Social Psychology*, vol. 10. New York: Academic Press.

Schutz, A. (1970). *On Phenomenology and Social Relations*. Selected Writings Edited and with an Introduction by H. R. Wagner. Chicago, Illinois: University of Chicago Press.

Schwartz, M. and Schwartz, C. (1955). Problems in participant observation. *American Journal of Sociology*, **60**, 343–353.

Silverman, I. (1977). *The Human Subject in the Psychological Laboratory*. New York: Pergamon.

Stapp, H. (1971). S-matrix interpretation of quantum theory. *Physical Review*, **D3**, 1303–1320.

Steinglass, P. (1979). The home observation assessment method (HOAM): Real time naturalistic observation of families in their homes. *Family Process*, **18**, 337–354.

Tajfel, H. (1981). *Human Groups and Social Categories: Studies in Social Psychology*. Cambridge: Cambridge University Press.

Vidich, A. J. (1955). Participant observation and the collection and interpretation of data. *American Journal of Sociology*, **60**, 354–360.

Watzlawick, P., Beavin, J. and Jackson, D. D. (1967). *Pragmatics of Human Communication*. New York: Norton.

White, G. D. (1973). *Effect of observer presence on family interaction*. Paper presented at meeting of Western Psychological Association, Anaheim, California.

Whyte, W. F. (1955). *Street Corner Society: The Social Structure of an Italian Slum*. Chicago, Illinois: University of Chicago Press.

Willems, E. P. (1967). Toward an explicit rationale for naturalistic research methods. *Human Development*, **10**, 138–154.

Wright, H. F. (1967). *Recording and Analysing Child Behaviour: With Ecological Data from an American Town*. New York: Harper and Row.
Zajonc, R. B. (1965). Social facilitation. *Science, 149*, 269–274.

CHAPTER FIVE
Ethical Issues in the Study of Family Life

Arlene Vetere and Anthony Gale

Introduction

Psychological research creates a number of moral dilemmas. The ethical codes of psychological associations remind researchers that they have professional responsibility for safeguarding confidentiality, securing consent, and treating individuals with dignity and respect. Moral dilemmas arise because there are few examples of psychological research where it is feasible to let subjects know exactly what is being studied and why. If subjects know such things then, it is argued, the research process can become contaminated by expectation, the subject's hypotheses about the questions at issue, the individual's desire to display their better selves in public, and so on. Thus consent to participate in the procedure hardly reflects full knowledge or free choice in the light of that knowledge. Again, because scientists have a professional obligation to publish the results of their research, they need to ensure that confidentiality is maintained, by aggregating data and concealing the identity of subjects. However, there are some sorts of research which of their nature, reveal essential aspects of the individuals which have been the subject of study. There have been many debates about ethical issues involved in laboratory studies; the issues have included problems of consent, deception, manipulation, and debriefing as well as the infliction of discomfort or the promotion of undesirable behaviour in the subject in compliance to the experimenter's senior status. It has also been suggested that the ways in which psychologists treat their subjects can influence the ways in which society as a whole treats people; thus treating individuals as stimulus-response lumps or organisms directed by forces of which they are not aware is alleged to lead to the progressive dehumanization of people (see Shotter, 1975).

Each researcher has to solve a complex equation in which benefits to science and to him/herself need to be matched against the costs to other individuals and the possible erosion of ethical principles which, of their nature, can never be absolute.

Ethics and Participant Observation

Participant observation with family groups involves the researcher with the family members in their own personal surroundings, in a very direct and intimate way. In the laboratory the subject is anonymous, away from his/her own surroundings, performs a specified task, is under study for a brief period, and then departs. In a sense, therefore, the laboratory is a special subculture, in which rather special rules and roles for behaviour are ascribed and understood by participants (Gale and Baker, 1981). Because such arrangements are understood, procedures which would appear unusual in the outside world are accepted. Just as in the theatre one is not asked permission for the actors to stimulate our emotions, so in the laboratory it is understood one will perform tasks, complete questionnaires, allow electrodes to be applied for physiological recording, and so on. In our own research, the formal relationship of experimenter and subject is broken down. The observer comes to know the subjects as *individuals*, rather than numbers on a data sheet. A relationship develops which is more like a friendship than a professional association; friends do not reveal secrets to outsiders, but professional researchers have an obligation to publish information. At the same time, the observer, robbed of the protection of the experimenter's role, is him/herself obliged to disclose personal details. The laboratory is the experimenter's territory, the family's home is its own private castle. In our research, the encounter lasts several days and not a few fleeting minutes. Information is revealed which, of its nature, is more like that disclosed in the intimacy of the consulting room rather than in a test cubicle. The observer can become a confidante. Because the observer is a guest as well as a watcher, the family may feel an obligation to be more cooperative than would an experimental subject. The roles of guest, relative, friend, and confidante become confounded with those of observer, expert, clinician, and stranger. Thus, in some senses the observer is less powerful than the experimenter, but in other senses extremely more powerful.

The data available to our observer are rich in quality and are revealed under three types of circumstance: explicit observation (in line with the agreement made with the family), inadvertent family display, and information given in intimate moments, often in the context of dyadic interaction with the observer by individual family members. Access to so much private information conveys power to the observer and such power, in its turn, also conveys responsibility and accountability. The concept of roles and rules (Harré and Secord, 1972) has associated with it the concept of ascribed rights and responsibilities for all individuals within a specific context. In the case of the observation of families in their homes and natural habitats the principles which guided our actions needed to be developed on the run. In this chapter we discuss some of the ethical problems we were obliged to confront. As in other areas of psychological research, ethical considerations can lead to practical consequences. For example, much of the rich flavour of family life which we have captured cannot be revealed in this book, for fear of hurting those with whom we have lived, and with whom the bonds of friendship and trust outweigh the obligations of science. The moral implications of certain research tactics can make them prohibitive.

Gaining Access: The Clinic

If we were to ask the reader: 'May one of us come and live in your home for a week and make continuous observation of you and your family?', we suspect few would wish to comply with our request. The very intimacy and personal importance of the family home and its association with privacy and personal rights, sets up a boundary between the home and the outside world. We soon realized that only families with a 'problem', who were in distress and had already made themselves open to external intrusion, were likely to make themselves available for our research. To gain contact with our families, therefore, we needed first to make contact with a clinic or child guidance centre. Here again, a similar difficulty arises. Why should the staff of a clinic wish to allow external agents to intrude in the processes of care and therapy? The answer to such a question led us to construct a model of clinic structure and the dynamics of interaction between clinic members, as complex as any model we were to construct of any family (see Shirley Reynolds' discussion in Chapter 6).

It should be remembered that we were *researchers* and not clinicians, that we could promise little of manifest benefit to clinic staff, and that our procedures and methods of analysis were lengthy. However, in living with the families, we would gain access to data of much richer quality and quantity than would ever be available to clinic staff, who may never have visited the family home, or whose contacts with the family were of an hour's duration once per fortnight at the most.

In developing our work we engaged in lengthy negotiations with five clinics. In the event only two offered cooperation which proved valuable. These two clinics had two different reasons for inviting us. One was in a sense organizationally chaotic and had little theoretical basis for treatment, dealing with families by dealing with individuals and on occasion dyads. The therapeutic strategy, if any, seemed to be one of wandering around a darkened room in the hope that one might find the light switch. The invitation to us reflected, on the one hand, the desire of some of the team to help with families who had made little progress, and on the other, the desire of some of the team to draw attention to and highlight the lack of cohesion in the group. Thus, in case discussions with us, the lack of explicit purpose was made more explicit. Yet we were always welcome and were always given full cooperation although, on occasion, agreements were hedged with caution and restraint. The second clinic, with whom we formed our most successful collaboration, was purpose built for family work, was guided by a theoretical view of family process, engaged in family therapy, and saw research activity as a complement to therapeutic activity. Yet here also, we witnessed stress and problems of communication, just as we would with our observations of families.

Thus, in our negotiation with clinics, two sets of roles and purposes became intertwined. Our principal aim was to gain cooperation, so that we could conduct our research. In order to achieve this, we were able to make explicit promises to assist the clinic: making available our transcripts, attending case meetings to discuss our observations and structural analyses. This shift of role from observer to quasi-clinician was acceptable, so long as family members still saw us as essentially observers and researchers. However, hidden behind this explicit agenda were appeals for the formation of alliances with particular clinic members, invitations to observe dysfunctional performances. Just as with families, we resisted the temptation to take sides or make observations about how things might or should be, so with the clinics, we maintained a distance. Having stirred the pot, by the very act of seeking cooperation in research, we felt obliged to leave the stew to burn. There was no doubt in our minds that we could have made sensible suggestions about how things might be improved, but, again, as with our families, we left well alone. Of course, it had been our explicit understanding with the clinics that we would not seek to interfere with families; it became an implicit inhibition for us not to comment on or seek to change, dysfunctional communication patterns in the clinic. However, since we were dealing with professionals, who in turn had responsibility for clients, who in turn we ourselves had come to know well, there was a strong temptation to be critical of the level of competence of the clinicians, i.e., those to whom we owed a debt, by virtue of their cooperation with us.

This situation raised a moral dilemma for us which we had not expected to encounter and which we never resolved. One clinic, having promised cooperation, never delivered the goods. We are absolutely certain that our perception of why things went wrong is very different from that of the clinic members (or some of them!). We must confess that we completed our relationships with families in a more satisfactory fashion than we completed our relationships with some clinicians. Our principal justification must be that we were supplicants seeking help, not organizational change agents or clinicians. Clinics who wished to use our data to assist them with their understanding of particular families made a personal choice to do so. Those who neglected facts which were staring them in the face, in the form of the very special information we had about their families in treatment, also made a free choice in professional terms. We were left with a sense of regret that had these clinicians been more purposeful, the families under their care would have gained a distinct benefit.

Gaining Access to the Private World of the Family

Ethical problems arose in seeking a family's permission to live with them and observe them because three sets of contexts and rules were in conflict: (1) the purposes, rights, and obligations of family life; (2) the objectives and responsibilities of therapy; and (3) the ambitions and intentions of a group of researchers.

According to family theorists such as Murdock (1949), Parsons (1955), and Minuchin (1974), the family has a variety of functions to discharge and is organized in ways which facilitate the achievement of its functions. Thus there is structure, hierarchical power relationships, ascribed roles such as spouse, mother, father, sibling, and the associated relationships between family members. These structures, roles, and relationships enable the family to discharge its economic, expressive, and socialization functions. In our own western society, a boundary has been drawn around the family and privacy is ensured; there is interference from outside agencies only when there is explicit evidence of failure to discharge expected functions. Thus it is not in any sense 'normal' for strangers to enter the family home, observe family members, or interfere with the normal course of family life.

In individual therapeutic contexts, a client seeks assistance from a therapist, because the therapist is a professional with special skills to offer. Since the client is in distress, the client is vulnerable and open to influence. The client may well reveal private thoughts and feelings which would not be revealed in other circumstances. It is understood that a bond of confidentiality holds between therapist and client. It is also understood that the therapist's primary purpose is to help the client, either directly, or by facilitating the client in helping themselves. Thus, the therapist and client share the intention of changing the client's state and removing distress. Similar assumptions are held by families and family therapists in the case of family therapy.

Confidentiality in the Context of Research

The aims of research run in conflict with both the family context and the therapeutic context. Research makes public and explicit that which was private or unrevealed. Researchers have an obligation to disseminate what they have learned because research is never complete until it is available for public scrutiny. The rules of confidentiality which operate in psychological research are not precisely identical with concepts of privacy pertaining to the home or to the clinic. The researcher has a set of purposes which include self-advancement and self-interest as well as loftier ideals concerning the development of knowledge.

Thus we were faced with the problems of juggling the ethical issues which arose from such a conflict of interests. It was important that family members should realize that we were researchers and not clinicians; nevertheless, we had arrived at the home via the route of a therapeutic clinic and had agreed that the material obtained would in principle be available to the clinic, if the family agreed. While we were not clinicians we were likely to be seen as family 'experts' with special insights into family problems.

It was also essential that family members realized that our observations were not mere observations, but would be translated, by a number of procedures, into some form of publication, book, conference presentation or thesis. It would be unrealistic to claim that we succeeded in conveying the full reality of our procedures and their consequences, to families. The majority of the families studied did not read many books or scientific papers, did not attend conferences, and had not read case histories. Thus while consent was obtained it would be difficult to demonstrate that it was a consent based on adequate understanding of the implications of the research process.

The Notion of Consent

The notion of 'consent' raised further problems. First, it is tempting to talk of the family as 'considering our proposals', 'making a decision', 'granting consent'. But such phrases are normally used in relation either to individuals or to committees which have formal decision-making structures. A family is a collection of individuals, and parents, or one parent, often find themselves speaking for the remaining members, for example, the children. It was often the case with the families we approached, that children were not consulted for their views or wishes.

Part of the notion of the family giving 'informed consent' to the presence of an observer in their midst is the implicit assumption that *both* the family and the observer have a clear view in advance of the impact of the visit upon family life. But how does one know what an experience will be like before one has experienced it? Will all family members respond in a similar fashion? As our observers built up their own experiences of visits they became more equipped to spell out the consequences to subsequent families. It was also made clear that the family could discontinue their research involvement at any time. Indeed several families chose to terminate relationships with us very rapidly, and before any visit had been implemented. It is questionable whether any family would have found an acceptable means of removing the observer once a visit had begun; few of us have shown visitors to the door!

Of all the fifteen families we approached, twelve accepted. Of those who refused, one spouse seemed eager to receive us but the other spouse was reluctant. Such conflict of interest is predictable from family therapy theories which claim that different family members have different vested interests in the concealment or revelation of family problems and the maintenance or removal of symptoms. For example, spouses who were apparently keen on the observer's presence were typically 'peripheral' to the rest of the family group and, we believe, sought change. The observer was therefore seen as a potential ally against existing family coalitions. Reluctant spouses, in contrast, seemed 'overinvolved' or 'enmeshed' with the identified patient and, it could be speculated, did not want change at all. Exposure of the whole family to external observation can be seen as a challenge to maintained structures and dynamics, distracting attention from the identified patient and possibly revealing other sources of conflict. Thus refusal to participate and/or withdrawal after initial agreement could in some cases be seen as reflecting the operation of homeostatic mechanisms which protect the family from change (Minuchin, 1974).

The Observer as an Instigator of Change

One possible consequence, therefore, of working with referred families, is that the observer's presence in the home may lead to change in the family system. Reactive effects to observation can include an increased awareness of family behaviour among family members; restructuring of personal experience may lead to change. One particular example is instructive. A clinical psychologist, having heard of our research, sought our assistance. He had achieved little with a couple in marital therapy and sought insights into family relationships which, he felt, could be gained from extended home observation. One spouse welcomed us eagerly, the other was reluctant. By the time we were ready to move into the house, the marriage had dissolved and one partner had moved out. It seemed that the very threat of observation had served to clarify the issues for one of the spouses. Such a demonstration of inadvertent induction of change within a family makes it difficult for us to claim that our research objectives could be seen by family members as neutral and non-intrusive.

In contrast, it is possible for the observer, by virtue of the apparent reasons for their entry, not to create change, but to *inhibit* it. If the ostensible cause is the identified patient, then from the family's point of view, the focus of attention should be the patient and their interactions with other family members, rather than the family as a whole. Much of the family's behaviour during the visit could be designed to confirm the status of the identified patient. Thus, in a sense, the very event of arriving in the home in such unusual circumstances may serve to confirm the role of the identified patient as the primary source of the family's problems.

We can see, therefore, that both theoretical considerations and our experiences of negotiating with families, imply that far from being ethically neutral with families, we were instigating change or serving to inhibit change, merely by seeking their permission to visit.

In terms of Minuchin's theory, which guided much of the work reported in this book, it is inevitable that the observer, by being incorporated into a family system, then becomes an influential factor in determining the behaviour of the system. The observer may not consciously seek to form alliances or to seem to be more favourably disposed to one member than to others. But circumstances can make the formation of such alliances highly probable. An observer alone in the house with one spouse during the day has much greater opportunity for mutual disclosure with that individual than with their partner or children who are at work or at school. In such circumstances, it is impossible to control the perceptions of other family members, who may see the observer-plus-home-based-spouse as a dyad or even an alliance. Also, the technique of participant observation does not allow the opening of discussion about such issues, unless they are raised by the family members themselves. As Chapter 6 indicates, such issues were discussed prior to the visit, but as we have already seen, it is unlikely that family members could fully appreciate the personal consequences of the visit.

One member of the research group, in an attempt to see the world from the other's point of view, invited some medical students into her home for the weekend as observers. The intention was to gain phenomenal experience of being observed. To an extent, this exercise heightened our sensitivities to the consequences for the family of welcoming us into their homes. But it did not help us to solve the problems we have outlined.

Conclusion

We have explored a number of ethical issues arising as a consequence of our research procedures. We have raised these issues because, while they share certain features with other contexts in which psychologists work as researchers or therapists, we consider the technique of participant observation to have unique ethical properties. In our analysis, much of the difficulty we experienced in making decisions about the propriety of our research strategy arose through ambiguity. The ambiguity stemmed from our particular combination of three worlds, each with their own rules for interpersonal behaviour: the clinic, the research laboratory, and the home.

References

Gale, A. and Baker, S. (1981). *In vivo* or *in vitro*? Some effects of laboratory environments, with particular reference to the psychophysiology experiment. In: M. J. Christie and P. G. Mellett (Eds), *Foundations of Psychosomatics*. London: Wiley.

Harré, R. and Secord, P. F. (1972). *The Explanation of Social Behaviour*. Oxford: Basil Blackwell.

Minuchin, S. (1974). *Families and Family Therapy*. London: Tavistock.

Murdock, G. P. (1949). *Social Structure*. New York: Macmillan.

Parsons, T. (1955). Family structure and the socialisation of the child. In: T. Parsons and R. F. Bales (Eds), *Family, Socialisation and Interaction Process*. Glencoe, Illinois: Free Press.

Shotter, J. (1975). *Images of Man in Psychological Research*. London: Methuen.

CHAPTER SIX

The Family Scenario: Observing the Families

Shirley Reynolds

Introduction

Several members of the research group acted as participant observers. The techniques described here were first developed by Arlene Vetere. Subsequently, she was joined by Shirley Reynolds and Claire Jolly. One aim of the research was to develop the method of participant observation in the special context of the family home; another was to examine whether different observers would make similar observations and come to similar conclusions about a particular family. We now consider and describe the method as it was evolved.

Stages in the Process of Participant Observation

There are six identifiable stages in our process of participant observation: setting the stage, gaining family consent, explaining the role, maintaining the role, observation, withdrawal, and keeping in touch.

Setting the stage

Families can be delicate plants and individual family members can be particularly vulnerable. What are the risks of choosing families 'at random'? Might family members seek an outsider as a way of putting family difficulties on a public stage? Or could an outsider be seen as a potential ally in family conflict? Issues such as these made us draw back from approaching 'normal' families and led us to agencies where families were undergoing treatment. This meant that the family was already known, that a judgement could be made as to the family's capacity to absorb the observer, and provided a source of clinical responsibility. Imagine some tragic circumstance in which damage occurred to a family member, either during our stay or after, which might have been attributed to our presence. Such dangers were too great to contemplate when facing a number of unknowns about the method and its viability. Nevertheless, the question remains as to whether families without identified problems would in fact wish to volunteer to be observed.

The involvement of agencies such as social work departments and child guidance clinics raises new problems, however. We have to ask what benefit is gained by their collaboration. At the simplest and most explicit level one might imagine that a psychiatrist or social worker, faced with a family which seems stuck in its problems, might welcome the opportunity to gain knowledge of what happens in the home. This was one of the initial reasons for willingness to cooperate. As it turned out, promises and undertakings did not necessarily become translated into actuality. We had to ask ourselves why this should be so, why some colleagues were able to introduce families for study, while others seemed to hold back.

We realized that we needed to think carefully about the organizational structure and purposes of the agencies with whom we were dealing and the personalities of the staff and their interactions. Some clinics seemed to have a hidden agenda. While involvement in a research project had attractions in terms of status and reflected glory, the hard truth could be that, for example, one was handing over one's possessions (the patient and family) to someone else. Another possibility was that observers, either by observing the family or by listening to the family's explicit comments about the therapist, might thereby undermine the professional amour propre of the therapist. Such fears, if they existed, were real. In a short time each one of us came to know individual families very well and built up a sense of mutual trust and even affection with them. This provided the context for much self-disclosure, including reflections upon relationships with therapists. After all, we were living in their home and sharing their experiences directly.

Such considerations had two effects. Firstly, we had to try to construct a model of each agency in our own discussions and consider the best way to secure cooperation. This involved spending a great deal of time at meetings and on the telephone. Even after observations had taken place, several misunderstandings arose. Secondly, our role gradually shifted from that of the disinterested and almost detached social science researcher to a clinical associate, assisting in the therapeutic process. Therefore, with the family's permission, we attended case conferences and passed on our observational transcripts to therapists. We were also asked, after our visits to the home, to make practical suggestions which might help the therapeutic process. Thus by the time the work was drawing to its end, we were introduced to individual families by their therapists on the understanding that our presence in their homes as observers might assist in throwing light on the problems that beset them. By the end of the research, our transcripts and our analyses of family structure were indeed helpful. In terms of the notion of *exchange*, therefore, we arrived at an arrangement, over a period of years, whereby the benefits to the families and their helpers were clearly apparent.

But such an exchange had its costs for us also. Negotiation took up a great deal of time, it was necessary to form relationships with many people, and the notion that our observations would be available to others (others with whom families had a special relationship) probably contributed to additional reactivity effects.

To gain acceptability, additional roles had to be fulfilled. The first agency to be used was a part-time educational unit associated with a child guidance clinic specializing in school refusal. Arlene Vetere became a member of the unit as a cookery teacher, and became part of the daily organization of the unit, establishing at the same time, links with the children and their parents. But from the outset it was made clear that she was a psychologist researching into family life. When Shirley Reynolds joined the research group relationships were maintained by volunteering to drive children to the unit from their homes.

Gaining family consent

In our culture the family is a private world. Families will vary in their willingness to tolerate intrusion. Moreover, our form of intrusion was to be unusual and unlike that of other visitors (friends, relations, district nurse, salespersons, and so on). Once we had been introduced by the agency, we arranged a visit to the home, to explain our purposes and intentions and secure the family's cooperation. Ethical issues concerning consent and who gives it are discussed in Chapter 5; we focus here on the nature of the negotiation.

In each case the research was presented to all family members as an attempt to discover more about the ways in which families work. We explained why we preferred to study the family in their own home. While hoping that our work would help them with longstanding family problems, many families expressed the view that, as a result, other families might be helped. The likelihood of refusal diminished as a function of our integration with agencies, partially because there had been some preselection, and partially because of our own increase in confidence. From a theoretical point of view, refusal can occur when one family member has a vested interest in resisting therapeutic change; this was apparent when spouses had strong disagreements over the prospect of our presence.

Explaining the role

When the purpose of the study had been explained, we described the demands which participation would entail. It was explained that the observer would live in the home, eat with the family, and join in all other common activities, both inside and outside the home. The difficulty of assessing the reliability of our observations meant that we needed to have two visits by two separate observers. Again, families seemed willing to accept the necessity of two visits.

The role of the observer was then described. In some ways, the role was like that of a family friend and in other ways not. Like a friend, the observer would sleep in the house and share family activity. But unlike a friend, the observer would not be active, she would not make suggestions about what the family might do, nor would she intervene in any family argument or become involved in the disciplining of the children. This latter point was crucial, since we did not wish to be seen to be focusing on the child in question, who typically was the identified patient. We also warned against expectations that we would serve gender-related functions such as washing up or cooking. Arrangements were also made to pay the family for all expenses incurred. Initially, all families refused such arrangements until it was explained that the work was externally funded.

It was stressed that all findings from the research would be confidential and that the identity of the family would be protected when the research was presented to other professional groups. With the family's permission, the transcripts would be made available to their clinician although any particularly sensitive material could be kept strictly confidential if members of the family requested it.

At all times it was emphasized that participation in the study was entirely voluntary and that refusal to participate would in no way jeopardize their relationship with the agency. Families were encouraged to discuss their feelings about participating as fully as possible and to ask questions regarding anything they were unsure about. If necessary, they should discuss our proposal privately and then meet with us again.

Maintaining the role

On the first day of the visit the observer arrived at the family home at a prearranged time, early in the morning. From arrival to departure the way in which we spent our time was almost totally dependent upon the activities of the family. We rose with them in the morning and retired once they had gone to bed. Throughout the day the family was tracked within the house and garden, on shopping trips, outings, religious meetings, and social calls. Wherever possible family activities were shared. This means that over our visits we have been taken shopping, gone down to the pub, drunk much more alcohol than we would normally, visited friends and relatives, attended religious rituals, brass band concerts, ridden horses, swum, and kept fit. Of all activities perhaps the most gruelling and uneventful, was the uninterrupted viewing of the household god, the television, around which, in some families, all life centred, that is, eating, decision-making, bickering, squabbling, entertaining friends, toiletting and socializing the young. Where the family was particularly poor, the room with the television set was the only room to be heated.

Of course, families do not spend all their time together. Parents go to work and children to school, members of the family go out alone to see their own friends, and when at home they are often distributed in rooms all over the house, each engaged in individual activity. As a general rule, we did not go with children into school or with parents to work, as this would be unnecessarily intrusive and probably impractical. During the daytime, we remained at home with the mother or wife, if she was not at work. On occasion, therefore, the observer could be left alone in the house.

Such solitary moments offered a welcome relief. One of the burdens for the observer was the total lack of privacy. During the visit the observer was cut off from usual social contacts, friends, family, and colleagues. Some families were particularly different in atmosphere from the observer's own personal experience. The only moments spent alone were while recording or when asleep. Even so, recording might be difficult because of a listener at the door and, on occasion, we were obliged to share a room with a family member. Thus the role of participant observer intruded not only on the family but on the observer herself.

Most typically, a great deal of time would be spent with the wife. What are the implications of this? Firstly, because it was always the wife who stayed at home, it was necessary for observers to be female, lest there be accusation of sexual impropriety, or in milder terms some alliance-formation to the detriment of the spouse relationship. Of course, female alliances can be equally subject to suspicion, with or without sexual overtones. In a threatened marriage it is presumably daunting for the male to return to a home in which two women have been discussing possibly intimate subject matter. We had to wait for a single male parent family for the male member of the team to undergo the experience of participant observation. A more important issue, in terms of ensuring optimal sampling of key family events, is whom to go with or be with. One principal consideration was the need to sample subsystems during the stay and to ensure that each individual member became equal in their access to the observer. This issue is quite complex. The observer may find some family members easier to be with; going to the shops with a young delinquent could lead to accusations of shop-lifting, and the observer could herself be a toy, plaything or confidante over whom family members might compete. One father, a horsedealer, was able to corner one observer in a stable yard and assault her with his ungelded stallion! It is easy to read such connotations into our transcripts.

It is worth noting that such role ambiguity as our work demanded is unfamiliar to the psychologist. In the laboratory, the experimenter has a well-defined role and status, is in charge of events, and dictates what is to happen. To a large extent the relationship between the observer and each family had to be negotiated anew, since we were entering the family's own domain. Very quickly, we had to learn about the norms and rules which applied in the household, and adapt without question. This imposed additional role strain, since just as we had lost our accustomed position as experimenter, we were also cut off from personal resources which we would normally utilize in our own home or in the home of friends. At the same time few observers can be strong enough not to wish to be liked by others; yet attracting affection is difficult to achieve in a passive fashion. However, the observer had to enable each family member to accept her continual presence, to trust her, and hopefully, to like her.

Observation

The family had been instructed to behave as normally as possible. No notes would be taken in their presence. Each hour, the observer retreated to another room to record observations on a hand-held dictaphone. As far as possible, the report was *descriptive* and not interpretative or evaluative, except that the observer might reflect on their own reaction to events.

This process created great personal pressure, for several reasons. Family life is rich and varied. Individuals move continually from room to room and from house to garden. It is not uncommon for two or three conversations to be held concurrently around a mealtable, and for any one individual to interact with a number of other family members at the same time. The family expected her to interact with them in a natural and friendly manner and to fulfil normal social demands. At the same time, the observer was attempting to track and record mentally an immense amount of complex and sequential information.

The observer is not a tabula rasa. We were always reminding ourselves of biases, selectivity, discrepancies in meaning of even everyday terms, and our professional training and purposes. Intrusions from one's own family life and family values were always likely. Such factors would influence our perception of events, our attention, and of course, our ability to retrieve both events and their true chronological order from memory. To sharpen this awareness, each observer was encouraged to maintain a field diary and to include, in the audio recording, reflections upon bias of which she was aware. Nevertheless, we must concur with the view that as in any other social situation, selectivity inevitably occurred. However, a central feature of training and discussion was to sensitize the observer to the dangers of selectivity. It has been suggested that use of videofilm and microphones around the home (following the approach of Kantor and Lehr, 1975) would have improved upon objectivity. But a camera has to point somewhere and an audio recording, devoid of contextual cues, cannot substitute for the sensitivity of the participant. There is always a balance to be struck between the intrusiveness of technology and additional personnel and the intimacy gained by the formation of relationships with a trusted individual. To suggest that cameras are somehow superior, apart from insulting the profession of film-makers who impose their special meanings on events, is to fail to understand basic perceptual processes. All perception is active and interpretative; like clinicians, however, we attempted to make our observation self-consciously free of bias.

We suspect that some observers are more reliable than others and that some families may generate more stable and unambiguous data. Experience of marriage and childrearing, gender, age, and attitudes towards social relationships, must all have their influence. Strangely enough, audiences which have heard of our work have been more concerned with the experience of observation and maintaining the role, than with the issue of objectivity.

Several authorities on the family have described different family types. Some of the families we stayed with were quiet and reserved, lived their lives at a slow pace and had little to do with the outside world. Other families were noisy and chaotic, lived at a hectic pace, took an active role in the community, and individual members may or may not have shared activities together. In some cases the home was always full of people and the observer seemed to be just another person present. Our sample of families and the number of visits made was not truly sufficient to enable us to disentangle sources of unreliability (these issues are discussed in Chapters 7 and 12).

Withdrawal and keeping in touch

One of the hardest things to do was to say goodbye to the family. Even though in the home for a week or less, great intimacy had been created. This arose as a result of several factors. There had been a need to observe everyone and to watch relationships in action, in other words, to *understand*. There had also been a need to develop the personal contact which the role of participant observer demanded. Even though a bystander and in many senses marginal to the group, one had complied in a passive way to the group's demands. In that sense one was almost a hostage, albeit in self-imposed imprisonment. Departure from the family was therefore a great loss to the observer who would now be bereft of the emotional proximity which had evolved. At the same time, the family itself seemed to be reluctant to say goodbye. In contrast, however, was the sense that a difficult and demanding task had been completed and that one would soon return to one's own social world.

The transition from observer to person was not sudden. On the final day of the visit, once the key material had been obtained, it became progressively harder to resist demands for opinions, advice, and personal revelation. It was inevitable that such exchange was due, in view of the family's generosity in cooperating with the research.

Most families were in fact visited again, for one reason or another. Where two observers were used, the second followed the first within a month. Aware that a colleague was to come, the first observer would be more circumspect in withdrawing. Other further visits to the family included the filming of family activities, administering questionnaires, and repertory grids. As the work evolved, our developing relationship with agencies meant that the observer acquired an additional role as quasi-therapist, working in consultation with the agency team.

The experience of participation is vivid and absorbing. It is hard to forget a family one has been so keen to observe. On several occasions mutual exchanges have occurred (letters, telephone calls, greeting cards) and social events have been shared (meals and family celebrations). Again, the role of the psychologist as objective scientist has been breached.

The Experience of Participant Observation: A Personal View

The following passages have been selected to illustrate my own experience of participant observation. During the course of my own research I stayed with four different families. In choosing these passages I hope to capture my reactions to family life and the role I was required to sustain.

The P Family

This family consisted of Lorraine, aged 14 and her mother Wyn, aged 54. Wyn also had two older children, a son of 26 and a daughter of 31, both married and living away from home. The two older children were the result of Wyn's first marriage. Wyn spoke very little of her first husband and we had almost no information about him. Our role precluded asking searching questions and so her marital experiences remained a mystery to us. It appeared that there was no contact between him and Wyn or their children. Lorraine's father was also something of a mystery. He was not spoken of and again it appeared that neither she nor Wyn had any contact with him. Lorraine and Wyn lived alone together in a council flat on the outskirts of a small town. They depended for their income on Supplementary Benefit and were consequently chronically short of money. They were both members of a fundamental and male-dominated religious sect and played an active part in the local religious community.

We first made contact with this family when Lorraine began to attend the part-time educational unit mentioned earlier. She had been enrolled in a local comprehensive school but her persistent school refusal (which seemed to be supported by her mother) had led to her attendance at the unit. The P family lived about 15 miles from the unit and our first contact with them involved both researchers driving Lorraine to and from the unit during her first few days of attendance. From the outset our relationships with both Wyn and Lorraine were warm and friendly. Both seemed pleased that Lorraine no longer had to attend the comprehensive school and they welcomed the offer of a lift for her first few days. When we returned with Lorraine in the afternoons Wyn invariably offered us tea and seemed genuinely pleased to entertain us. It was made clear to both Wyn and Lorraine that we were research psychologists and that our research concerned families.

After a few weeks it seemed appropriate to approach the family formally in order to discuss the project in more detail with them and to ask them to consider participating. At that time they seemed an ideal family; they were obviously very friendly towards both researchers and, moreover, such a small family would make observing very much easier. As this was the first family I was to observe it seemed sensible to make things as easy as possible.

Although Arlene Vetere my co-observer had already lived with a number of families I felt sure that engaging families in the project would be very difficult. I was therefore extremely surprised when both Wyn and Lorraine were interested in the work we were doing and were immediately keen to participate. Such enthusiasm almost pre-empted our carefully prepared presentation. Nonetheless we stressed that our observations would be confidential, that Wyn and Lorraine would be reimbursed for any expenses incurred and that however keen they were to have us to stay with them, our visit would necessarily involve some degree of inconvenience to both of them. The issue of payment was somewhat difficult as Wyn was concerned that this might jeopardize her Supplementary Benefit payments. She was reluctant to accept any money at all but was finally persuaded to accept a minimal amount which she would calculate on the basis of her expenditure during the observers' visits. Our final task was to arrange a mutually convenient time for both researchers to stay. We arranged to stay for four days each, to include a weekend and two school days. The visits would occur on consecutive weeks. My visit was to be the second, beginning on Saturday morning and finishing on Tuesday evening.

On my arrival I felt very aware that this was my first visit to a family and that I was following a very experienced co-observer. It appeared subsequently that my comparative lack of experience had not gone unrecognized by the family. An extract from the transcript of my co-observer should illustrate this. During the first day of her visit she had become involved in a lengthy conversation with Wyn:

She wanted me to understand the problems, she felt she needed to discuss it with me. An example of strong assymetrical order effects; Shirley will obviously not be subject to the same treatment. She says she won't feel the same need with a second observer. I am informed that she and Lorraine are very conscious of the fact that this is Shirley's first family. Apparently they recognize my experience and consider Shirley to be a 'learner' and want to 'help' her as much as possible. A source of bias but she assures me they will behave as 'normally' as possible to ease Shirley's visit.

Armed then with my own trepidation and curiosity I arrived at the family home at 8.30 on Saturday morning. I was greeted by Wyn; Lorraine was still in bed. Wyn made a cup of tea, took a cup in to Lorraine, and she and I began to chat. Almost immediately my co-observer, Arlene, figured in our conversation:

> . . . she suggested that we could go for a walk on Sunday morning. She asked me if I would like to come with them to the Hall (the local chapel) as Arlene had done. The conversation then turned to a discussion of Arlene's visit: Arlene had sat in this particular chair, would I like to? Arlene's husband must be very understanding mustn't he because otherwise how would she be able to spend so much time away from home? (page 3)

During the first day of my visit I found myself surprised at the ease with which I could both interact with Lorraine and Wyn and at the same time remember accurately enough to record at hourly intervals. My task was of course made easier by the fact that there were only two family members and more so because of the extremely slow and methodical way in which they lived their lives. The first morning was spent in the flat, for most of the time sitting in the lounge chatting to Wyn. Lorraine occupied herself in the corner painting an elaborate picture and took little part in our conversation. During lunch there was an interesting example of reactivity, i.e., where the behaviour of those being observed changes as a result of the presence of an observer.

> Lorraine joined in the conversation and began to tell her mother about a health education lesson that the education unit were to have on Thursday afternoon. Her mother expressed interest and asked Lorraine what it was to be about. Lorraine explained that they were going to discuss V.D. and said to her mother that it might be rather embarrassing discussing this with all the boys there. However, she didn't get any further in her explanation because Wyn interrupted her in mid-sentence very angrily, 'Lorraine, how could you? I don't mind you talking about such things but not at the dinner table while we're eating. If you want to talk about such things we can talk about it later. Whatever will Shirley think of you?' (page 7)

When I first recorded this conversation I noted that Lorraine appeared to be deliberately embarrassing Wyn in front of me, knowing very well that the subject of V.D. would not be acceptable at the dinner table. Even if this was not the case Wyn's reaction was interesting and demonstrated something of her values and her wish to project a 'good' image to the observer.

After lunch Wyn went to bed for about two hours leaving Lorraine and me alone. Lorraine continued with her painting and made intermittent attempts to engage me in conversation. During the latter part of the afternoon Wyn went to the shops and I accompanied her. This was to be the only exercise taken in the entire day. After washing-up the evening was spent in front of the television, chatting and playing board games.

By the end of the day my overwhelming emotion was one of exhaustion. I felt that the lack of exercise had contributed to my tiredness and I was not surprised when I developed backache towards the end of the evening. At this point it was interesting to observe Wyn's caretaking role (usually with Lorraine as the object of affection) now extended to me.

> After we had been playing (board games) for an hour or so Wyn noticed that I was having difficulty crouching at the coffee table and asked me if I was O.K. I explained that my back was hurting a little, she seemed very concerned and insisted that I shouldn't play any more. She told Lorraine to put the game away and told me to sit on the sofa where I would be more comfortable. (page 14)

Hansen (1981) discussed the physical symptoms she experienced during family visits. She saw these as a response to the stress of observing and noted that they were most severe while she stayed with the family in which she observed most distress. My own physical responses to observing this family surprised me. I began to slow down, my movements became more laboured and I began to feel increasingly lethargic. At the same time I experienced feelings of mild claustrophobia particularly when we had spent most of the day sitting in the flat doing nothing. My own feelings of discomfort were exacerbated by Wyn's mood which at times seemed quite depressed. On the third day I recorded the following:

> The atmosphere had become very gloomy and serious and we had eaten in almost complete silence. I helped Lorraine carry the dirty plates out to the kitchen. The flat at this time was a very depressing place. Although it was usually quiet and slow, things now had come to almost a complete standstill. I went out to do some recording and when I returned Lorraine was still in the kitchen washing up. I went in and offered to help. She said that she'd rather do it alone so I went into the living room where Wyn was lying curled up on the sofa. I asked if she was O.K. and she replied, 'Yes, thank you, dear.' She then fell silent again which for her was extremely unusual. The TV was switched on but she didn't seem to be watching it. She looked very childlike and vulnerable somehow and seemed very depressed. (page 38)

I have already referred to Wyn's caretaking role in relation to Lorraine. The relationship between the two women was fascinating and at the end of the second day I recorded the following:

> On the one hand they seem to be very enmeshed; they have 'no secrets' according to Wyn. Lorraine has no front door key, she often finishes off her mother's sentences and finds words for her and seems not to be moving away from the nest as one might expect most 14-year-olds to do. On the other hand, however, mother and daughter seem to spend little time interacting. Lorraine gets on with her homework or drawing while Wyn cooks and washes up. Wyn herself complains that Lorraine is not much as a companion and that she prefers to spend time alone.
>
> Lorraine I find an enigma, she is very poised and self-possessed. She is able to talk to me without embarrassment or difficulty and she is openly hostile to other 14-year-olds who play 'childish' games. She seems very isolated, has no local friends, she does not have a key, and she rarely leaves home. She is still very much Wyn's little girl. Wyn I wonder about; she seems to have an empty life, except for her religion, and I am surprised that she doesn't have a part-time job particularly since they are so obviously hard up. Lorraine is to a certain extent an excuse for her not to work but I think that another reason is that she would be unable to cope with everyday life in

the 'real world'. Life is very sheltered: they have no newspapers or magazines and consciously avoid anything unpleasant on TV. Friends seem to be restricted to those Wyn refers to as 'our people', i.e., fellow members of the religious community. (page 29)

Religion, for me, was an intriguing aspect of this family's life. It appeared that their membership of a religious sect provided a ready made social structure in addition to an unambiguous ethical and moral code. During my visit I attended a prayer meeting held in the family home and a Sunday service in the local Hall in addition to chatting with Wyn about her beliefs and the teachings of her religion. During this time I was impressed by the fact that neither the family nor the rest of the congregation made any attempt to 'convert' me, they accepted that I was there merely to observe and made me feel very welcome. At one point during my visit Wyn outlined to me some of the teachings of her religion.

Wyn went on to explain to me about Christmas and how since it wasn't in the Bible it wasn't something which should be practised. Christianity should, she said, be taken directly from the Bible. Christmas was in fact a pagan ritual; in fact Jesus had been born in October, it couldn't possibly have been in December because the shepherds who were out at night with the sheep couldn't possibly have been out in December as it would be far too cold. The three wise men did not exist at all; they were in fact astrologers who had come to kill Jesus and not in fact to honour him. Christmas in their home was therefore spent quietly as any other day of the year. I asked what happened if they were sent Christmas cards. Wyn said they would thank the person but would not wish them a Happy Christmas. . . Easter she said was also a pagan ritual and could not be found in the Bible. (I began to wonder what kind of a Bible they used!) Sometimes, she admitted there were problems in interpreting the Bible, for example, in one chapter it said that Jesus would come down from heaven on a cloud. This she said was obviously impossible, he would fall through. Other sections of the Bible contradicted one another at first sight but if one was thorough enough it was possible to tie up the contradictions and make sense of them. (pages 31,32)

During the day when Lorraine was at the unit I spent the time with Wyn. Although at times I found the enforced company of only one person difficult, these were times when I felt I got to know Wyn much better. She was one of those rare people who are totally sincere and secure in their beliefs and whose view of other people was untouched by cynicism. The following extracts should illustrate this point.

She began to tell me about the door to door visiting that she does every day for an hour. I asked if people were often rude to her and she said that quite often she had doors slammed in her face. Luckily she had the strength and confidence in what she was doing not to let this upset her. Often she called at large expensive houses whose owners' manners left much to be desired. Riches, she said, weren't very important and the house you lived in was less important than how you lived your life. (page 32)

As we were walking away from the town the houses became larger and more impressive. Wyn said that sometimes she came down here on her visits and she always admired the houses. The thing she envied most was the gardens although she knew that she wouldn't be able to cope with looking after a large garden on her own. Anyway with the forest so near and their bikes she and Lorraine didn't really need a garden. I warmed to her as she said this, she and Lorraine have so little but don't seem to moan about it. (page 47)

On the evening of my last day the weekly prayer meeting was held in the flat. The congregation took it in turns to hold the meeting in their homes and Wyn appeared to enjoy the role of hostess, perhaps in part because it gave her an opportunity to display her caretaking qualities. It was interesting to observe the different ways in which Lorraine reacted to this social occasion.

> During the time when people were chatting casually Lorraine seemed to shrink into the corner. People asked her how she was from time to time and she replied briefly but it looked as if the entire evening was an ordeal for her. Wyn, in contrast, seemed quite at home and circulated much as a hostess at a party would, thanking people for coming on such a cold night and gradually moving people to their seats so that the meeting could begin. Finally everybody was seated. Brother Tom stood up, silence fell and the others followed his lead and rose. He made a short offering of thanks to the god, Jehovah, and asked for his blessing on this meeting. (page 51)

After the congregation had left it was time for me to leave also. As I had to walk to the local railway station Wyn insisted that she accompany me. She borrowed a torch with an alarm from Lorraine who was concerned that her mother shouldn't walk back alone in the dark. Likewise Wyn was concerned that Lorraine would be left alone in the flat. She warned her not to answer the telephone until she returned, nor was she to answer the door to anyone. Wyn had her key with her and would let herself in when she returned. After considerable discussion we finally left and strolled to the station. On the way we discussed the prayer meeting which Wyn had felt to be a great success. The final extract illustrates my unfortunately hasty departure.

> As we arrived at the station I noticed that there was a train standing at the platform I was due to leave from. . . We ran down to the station to see if this was the train, only to find that the door was locked and that the only way onto the platform was to cross the railway bridge and down the other side. At this Wyn said, 'Well, if that's the train I think you've had it. You'll have to wait for the next one.' As we ran up the hill to cross the bridge I noticed the train driver watching us with ill-concealed amusement. I asked him if this was the train to Southshore and if so what time it was due to leave. He said that it was and that he was due to leave in a few seconds.
>   I turned to Wyn and said, 'Well, that's it, I'll just have to wait for the next one.' As I said this we both noticed simultaneously that there was only an embankment and two low fences separating me from the train. She looked at me and said, 'Well, it's worth a try.' I scrambled over the fence with great lack of dignity and she passed my bag over the fence. I said goodbye again and scrambled down the embankment where the train driver helped me over the second fence. I shouted my thanks and she stood there until the train moved off. It seemed like a most unfitting end to what had been a very quiet four days and I regretted not being able to say goodbye more sedately. (page 57)

The T Family

The T family was the second family I lived with. The family consists of Tel and Lesley (father and mother), both in their early thirties, and their two daughters Mary, aged 11 and Gemma, aged 6. Tel worked as a carpenter and handyman restoring old buildings and Lesley worked part-time as a cleaner at the local school. Both girls attend state primary schools. The family live in a small, neat and well-maintained terraced house in a large coastal town. When we stayed with them they were hoping to move to a larger house in the near future.

We were introduced to this family by a clinical psychologist. He had seen the family two years previously when they were having problems with Gemma who was allegedly 'hyperactive'. Since that time the family have had no further difficulties but have remained in contact with the clinician because Lesley works in the school where they were seen. On our behalf the clinician made the first approach to the family and explained very sketchily to Lesley the nature of the research project. An appointment was then made to visit the family one evening in their home so that we could introduce ourselves to them and explain our work further. We met with both parents and with the children briefly before they went to bed. Although we would have preferred to explain the purpose of our research to the whole family it was the parents' decision to see us alone for part of the time and we felt obliged to respect this.

Both Tel and Lesley were happy to participate in the project and we therefore made arrangements for when we would come and stay. There would be two observers, each of whom would stay with the family for four days on consecutive weeks. During our visits we would sleep in the girls' bedroom and in order to accommodate us Gemma would sleep on a camp bed in her parents' room.

On the first day of the visit I arrived just after 8.00 a.m. on Friday. Tel had already left for work and Lesley and the girls were getting ready for school and work. From the outset the atmosphere in this house was quite different from that in the P family. This was not unexpected given a larger family with two lively young children. I was welcomed enthusiastically by Lesley and ushered into the kitchen. Everybody was dressed and last minute preparations were being made before they left for school. At the same time Lesley was in the middle of her washing. The girls left with a friend at about 8.30 and Lesley left a few minutes later. The house was suddenly silent and I was alone until Lesley returned at 12.30. It was a beautiful sunny morning and I sat in the garden. This break from observing so soon after I arrived was very welcome. I had met most of the family and felt welcomed and now I had the opportunity to relax and to adjust to the house in which I would be living for the next four days.

Lesley returned from work on time and we remained in the garden and ate lunch there. In the afternoon we went shopping in town. I was loaned Mary's bicycle and perilously followed Lesley. We spent the remainder of the afternoon chatting as Lesley needed very little encouragement and clearly enjoyed having a captive audience. She told me stories about her own childhood, her meeting and subsequent marriage to Tel, incidents in the life of her children, her opinions of her neighbours, and her relationship with Tel. Her life centred around her family but for all this she had a keen interest in current affairs. On occasions, Lesley's strong opinions differed from mine and it was at these times difficult to remain neutral. The neutrality of the observer is a central aspect of the role we adopted as observers, as we have discussed earlier in this volume. Sometimes this stance can be difficult to maintain particularly in households where it is the norm to offer opinions and to debate. In such situations it is possible that family members interpret silence or acknowledgement as implicit agreement. The following extracts illustrate two instances where I found neutrality a more difficult task than usual. The first occurred on our way home from a family outing.

> As we walked we passed some sailors in uniform, Tel remarked that they looked Pakistani but then Lesley corrected him, saying that they couldn't be because she couldn't smell them. 'Do you know what I mean?' she asked me. What can you say under the circumstances? I think I just smiled. (page 60)

The second incident occurred one afternoon during a prolonged chat between Lesley and me. We had been talking casually about the Isle of Wight and incidentally the subject of Parkhurst prison and the imprisonment of Peter Sutcliffe (the Yorkshire Ripper) arose.

> This brought her on to the subject of rapists. She didn't know whether or not the death penalty should be brought back for such crimes; sometimes she thought it should be brought back and sometimes she didn't. 'But,' she said quite definitely, 'I think that rapists and people who interfere with children should be castrated.' It seemed as if she expected some kind of opinion or support from me but all I felt capable of offering was to say that it would be pretty difficult for whoever was responsible for carrying out the sentence. (page 70)

In larger households there are many more interactions between individuals to observe. The extent to which the observer's presence affects these interactions is as yet unresolved. From the observer's point of view family members appear to adjust remarkably quickly to one's presence. The influence of the observer is unlikely to be consistent in each situation. In some instances interaction patterns may be considerably distorted and in others the presence of the observer serves to exacerbate existing patterns of interaction. The next extract demonstrates how Mary and Gemma used my presence to highlight their competitiveness during a game of cards.

> We began to play. It was a very simple game and therefore we were all fairly evenly matched. Gemma won the first game and I won the second. The two girls seemed much more aware of me than of each other at first and were eager to make sure that I didn't lose. The third game we played was Snap. Gemma was at a disadvantage here because she didn't concentrate on what was happening and kept forgetting that it was her turn and interrupting Mary or me. She lost her cards very quickly. Mary and I carried on and she sat and watched, egging me on and supporting me every time there was a dispute over who had said 'snap' first. . . Mary and I played on. This time Mary was determined to win and became much more sneaky, hiding her cards until the last moment and calling 'snap' before the cards had been played face up. Gemma carried on supporting me and encouraging me every time I won Mary's cards off her. Eventually Mary won. (page 41)

A particularly noticeable difference between the T family and the P family was the range of emotion expressed. In the P family the predominant affect was one of flatness and overall things were quiet and peaceful. In the T family a wide range of affect was expressed from anger and frustration to hilarity. As perhaps one might expect, I experienced no feelings of claustrophobia or lethargy while staying with the T family although I found the experience equally exhausting. With younger children in the house discipline was more of an issue and I often observed the parents' style of discipline. Generally Lesley and Tel were in agreement and were consistent in their handling of Mary and Gemma. Lesley tended to be the primary disciplinarian and was usually successful. A good example occurred on Sunday afternoon as we ate our lunch in the garden.

We sat around the garden eating. Gemma began to play with the laundry basket which Lesley had left on the lawn. She climbed into it and sat in it. Lesley told her to be careful not to break it and then returned to her meal. Gemma fidgeted around for a while. She noticed that Lesley had kicked off her sandals and reached over to pick them up. Lesley looked at her again and Gemma asked if she could wear them. Lesley told her that she couldn't, that she'd break the heels. 'Oh go on mum, please.' No answer. Everyone ignored Gemma. 'Please mum, I promise I won't break them.' Lesley carried on ignoring her. Gemma put the shoes on. Nobody took any notice. She waited. Then she stood up and started walking round the garden, mincing in them. Lesley told her to take them off, adding '. . . if you don't take them off I'm going to be very angry.' Gemma took no notice and carried on walking around in them. Lesley let her carry on for a while. She then announced, 'I'm going to count to three, by the time I count to three I want them off. One, . . .' By the time she had got to two Gemma had taken the shoes off. (page 34)

As in all families there were of course times when not very much happened. This tended to be in the evenings after the children had gone to bed. Lesley told me that she tried to finish her housework during the day so that she would be free in the evenings. Both she and Tel felt, she reported, that evenings were when husband and wife should spend time together. They went out together infrequently and not at all during my visit. The evenings were spent watching television. I found that these times passed very slowly. The TV was switched on from early evening for children's programmes until after midnight when they went to bed. By this time I was usually exhausted and eager to go to bed myself. Before I did so, however, I still had to record my observations. It was often difficult to stifle my yawns late in the evening.

The importance of passivity and neutrality on the part of the observer has already been stressed. While staying with this family, there was one specific occasion where I found passivity, at least, impossible to maintain. We had all gone to the beach for the afternoon and the family had spent the time swimming and sunbathing. At one point Gemma, Lesley, and I went down to the sea where we shivered pitifully for a few minutes. Gemma clung to her mother, shivering and ineffectually attempting to avoid being splashed.

I decided that the water was too cold to enjoy and went to sit at the side of the water on the beach. As I sat there watching Lesley and Gemma and shouting encouragement, Tel crept up behind me, grabbed my arms and dragged me screaming into the water. Under such circumstances it is very difficult to remain a passive observer! My struggles were in vain and I was lifted up and thrown into the water. A water fight then ensued between Tel, Lesley, and myself. Gemma cowered in safety behind Lesley. Eventually we all collapsed in helpless giggles. (page 58)

As in the P family it was impossible to avoid spending a large proportion of my time alone with one person, Lesley. Nonetheless I found that it was possible to establish a positive relationship with each member of the family. The children were keen to include me in their activities and games, and although more reserved than the rest of the family Tel was always eager to discuss his hobby of breeding birds. At the end of my stay I found that I was quite sad to be leaving. On my last day Lesley divulged some information which, while trivial in content, made me feel as if I had gone a long way towards being accepted by this family.

She asked me if I'd had an enjoyable time while I'd been with them. I told her that yesterday while we'd been on the beach that I'd commented to Tel that it was more like a holiday then like being at work. 'Oh yes,' she said, 'you were very honoured yesterday.' I asked why. 'Well, it's not very often that Tel takes his trousers off and shows his legs to anybody, at least not to anybody outside the family!' I couldn't do anything but laugh. (page 71)

Conclusion

In this chapter I have attempted to give some impression of what participant observation is, and in particular what it is like to be a participant observer. As noted earlier there were two other observers engaged in the project and for each of us the experience of observing, even within the same family, was very different. I have presented a personal view of participant observation in the hope that at least to some extent it represents not only my experiences but those of my co-observers. Likewise, all the families we stayed with were very different but the two discussed above represent the others in many ways. I hope that I have not done the other families or my colleagues too great a disservice.

On a personal level participant observation has both costs and benefits. The exercise is exhausting and demanding both physically and emotionally. There is no free time at all and for the period of observation one's personal and home life is effectively suspended. As a result of the passive role, one makes few decisions of a commonplace type: the time you get up, the time you go to bed, what you eat, when you eat, what you watch on television, what direction a conversation will take, and how you spend your leisure time; are all decisions which you cease to make. In such an environment one can imagine how it might be easy to lose one's sense of self-determination. In order to counter this problem and to provide an outlet for any emotional reactions it was customary for the participant observers in this project to keep a personal diary.

On the benefit side of the equation are a number of positive features. As a researcher the experience of being privy to a wealth of confidential and often sensitive information can be thrilling. Moreover, the fact that this access is available as a result of the positive relationship you have established with a family makes it personally rewarding. This positive relationship is mutual in nature and observers have often found that on a social level their relationship with families is maintained long after the period of observation ends. We often send and receive Christmas cards, visit families socially, and on one occasion we were even invited to a family wedding!

In summary, participant observation is unlike the techniques characteristic of most psychological research. It demands personal commitment and a willingness to tolerate a degree of discomfort and inconvenience on the part of the observer and particularly the family. Like any novel situation it can be both tiring and stressful but unlike some novel situations the rewards are plentiful. As a means of taking psychology to the outside world and leaving the protection of laboratories, the distancing of video cameras and observation schedules, it is well suited. Perhaps most importantly the use of participant observation brings the psychologist into close and intimate contact with their subject matter — people!

References

Hansen, C. (1981). Living in with normal families. *Family Process,* **20**, 53–75.
Kantor, D. and Lehr, W. (1975). *Inside the Family: Towards a Theory of Family Process.* San Francisco, California: Jossey-Bass.

CHAPTER SEVEN

The Family Scenario: Systematic Analysis of Family Behaviour

Arlene Vetere and Sue Lewis

Introduction

We have described participant observation as a research technique and our own particular development of the method. In Chapter 6 Shirley Reynolds described the method of gaining access to the family home, the experience of living with the family and the technique of recording observations of family life. We now show how the descriptions of family life were analysed. Each participant observer produced a transcript of the recorded observations of some hundred pages or more: these are called *scenario diaries*. The scenario diaries were read by the participant observer and Minuchin-style structural maps were drawn and short family vignettes were written (these descriptions are to be found in Chapter 9, for all the families we visited). The scenario diaries were marked up into *action sequences*, and the sequences were then coded using our Family Interaction Analyses scheme (FAMINTAN), which describes action sequences in terms of a variety of types of action (including associated affect). This meant that for each family we could describe the behaviour emitted or received by each individual, the behaviour of the family members when in pairs and larger groups, and so on. These were reflected in computer aggregations of acts and sequences, which represented behaviour of individuals, dyads, etc. over the whole visit; positive and negative acts emitted by each individual in a variety of pairings with other family members could then be shown in histogram form. At the same time, we could represent not only what each individual said or did, but *to whom*; therefore, we could draw *sociograms* showing who did what to whom and whether their actions varied as a function of who was present. The question then arises: what *follows* a particular action or statement? *Sequential analysis* was used to estimate the probability of occurrence of particular sequences which characterized family relationships: for example, if Mary says something nice to Bill, what are the probabilities that Bill will respond with a positive or negative action? Finally, we needed to ask whether or not we could trust the observations of a particular observer or accept samples of family behaviour as representative of the family; we therefore set up a research design to explore various aspects of reliability: for example, will the same observer see similar events on different visits, or code the same diary in the same way on two occasions; will two observers see similar family behaviours, and/or code each other's diary in the same way?

Each of these steps in the analysis of family life is set out in the present chapter. Some additional data gathering and analysis occurred for a handful of families and these are discussed in Chapter 8. Before discussing the detail of the analysis of family observations, we need to consider the problems of categorization and classification of group behaviours.

The Advantages and Disadvantages of Category Systems

When the attention of social psychologists shifted from the behaviour of individuals to behavioural exchanges *between* individuals, they quickly realized there was a paucity of methods for describing and analysing such interaction sequences. Social psychologists assumed that social acts and personality cannot be understood apart from the social context in which they are embedded. The person is in constant interchange between self and environment. Only in the examination of such interchanges can one understand the meaning of the individual's actions; the same act in a different context would have a different meaning. Everyday behaviour is organized around recurrent routines; for example, rising in the morning, eating breakfast, travelling to work or school, greeting colleagues, and so on. An essential part of these routines is the context in which they occur. A full understanding comes not only from external observation but from an analysis of the perceptions of the actor. The challenge is to devise methods of analysis which capture the regularity, the range of contexts, and the phenomenal view of the participant or actor.

Early researchers into human interaction described the social experience of individuals by counting the frequency of occurrence of specified behaviours. For example, a focus of interest might be the turn-taking in mother–baby 'conversations' (including smiling, talking, babbling, cooing, attentive listening, face exploring, and so on). Both verbal and non-verbal behaviours would be categorized, enabling the researcher to achieve several objectives, including: making the stream of behaviour amenable to objective analysis; summating and summarizing diverse observations (within or between mother–child pairs); extracting common aspects; reducing complexity within and across situations; enabling comparison between mother–child pairs and situations; and finally, following initial observation, allowing the setting up of hypotheses to test for predictable sequences of interaction.

Categorization alone does not reveal patterns. In our work with families we assumed that interactional sequences and the events which they join together, are crucial to the description of family life. To share a common social environment, these sequences must be predictable for family members, or at least, their occurrence cannot be random. For example, successive statements that family members make to one another are connected by a commonly accepted set of meanings. We cannot gain access to the meaning of a statement without knowing also what preceded it and what follows it. Again, actions and action sequences between family members occur within family contexts, for example, around the dinner table, at bathtime, in front of the TV. One needs to ask therefore whether categorization alone can capture the flow and flavour of family life.

However, the use of any category system for the analysis of family life has a number of associated problems. First, communication among family members involves multiple channels, such as verbal, paralinguistic, and non-verbal behaviour. A description of communication cannot therefore be limited to one channel, since there is constant cross-talk between the channels. Secondly, there is no guarantee that those behaviours which are amenable to straightforward measurement are necessarily the most significant for understanding the *meaning* of communications. For example, an audio tape will not capture facial expressions, gestures or smiles, or indicate the significance of silences. Thirdly, summarizing independent categories of behaviour does not reveal the ways in which those categories are connected or mutually dependent when they are linked in real behaviour, so the crucial elements of meaning can become stripped away. The ideal system will retain both the category events and their antecedents, consequences, and the context. Finally, one needs some guarantee of the reliability of categories; many systems appear to allow for objective analysis but actually involve inference on the part of the observer. However, some category systems have been well developed and standardized and are trustworthy.

The Bales Interaction Process Analysis (IPA) as revised by Borgatta (Interaction Process Scores: IPS)

The IPA and IPS were developed within small group research. They have been used in some of the best family interaction research (Waxler and Mishler, 1970). The IPS forms the basis of all the analyses which follow in this chapter. In deciding whether to devise a system of our own, or take a well-standardized system off the shelf, we chose the IPS as a category system which had proved its value in a variety of contexts, although the Waxler and Mishler study had not provided great encouragement concerning its reliability in family contexts. In retrospect, and in the light of our experience, we would probably wish to develop a more sensitive system (see Chapter 13). Under the time pressures of research funding we decided to focus our efforts on *analysis* rather than devising a new scheme in the absence of extended prior experience of family observation.

The Bales (1950) IPA was based upon the theoretical notion that the essential nature of social interaction is problem-solving. Groups were seen to be instrumentally task-oriented and group processes conceived as means of achieving goals. Task-orientation creates stresses for group members, which are expressed in positive and negative affect. Such affect might distract the group from its tasks and the group needs to reintegrate its activities and return to the task in hand. The IPA focuses on the constant interchange between *instrumental* (goal directed) and *expressive* (integrative, social, emotional) behaviours. The family functions described by

Minuchin (1974) and others (see Chapter 3) can be seen as tasks to be discharged, also in the context of expressed emotion. The difference between formal organizations and families is that the task or goal specifications are much more explicit in the former case.

The IPA uses twelve categories of verbal utterance for observing and classifying interaction. These take into account gestural, postural, and tonal cues. The IPA was derived on the basis of real observation and refined through an iterative process within the context of laboratory research. Family researchers quickly recognized its potential for family observational analysis. We should note, however, that laboratory groups and families are different in several respects: the individual can leave a laboratory group and membership starts and ends with the group; families have a shared history, shared meanings, their own subculture with its lattice of mutual understandings; affect within the family is not just a passing event but reflects past interactions and their associated tensions; and when family groups become laboratory groups they do not leave their history behind them.

Thus, when researchers tried to apply the IPA to family life, they met with several problems. The IPA describes *manifest* or overt behaviour (what is seen) and cannot capture *latent* content (or deep underlying structures); in exploring only those events which are *immediate* the IPA neglects the possibility that the significant *antecedent* event may have occurred some time in the past; finally, in using IPA categories in the family context observers discovered that they were drawing inferences over and above the straightforward application of the categories. Therefore, Borgatta (1962) revised the IPA, with a view to simplifying the categories, extending them, and increasing the chance of systematic and reliable observation. On the basis of factor analytic studies, Borgatta sought to separate out behaviours which, although distinct, had appeared within a single category in the IPA; for example, 'shows solidarity', in the original version, had included greetings and praise and had attributed a similar weighting to them. Borgatta's revisions created a scheme of eighteen categories rather than the original twelve (see Table 1).

Contingency Probability Analysis

A good example of sequential analysis is provided by Gottman and Bakeman (1979) who studied caretaker-baby dyads and calculated contingency probabilities between child and caretaker acts. For example, they were able to ask with what probability can one predict that the mother will respond, within a particular time period, when the baby cries. The analysis depends on events in the immediate vicinity of each other and does not allow for the possibility that an action may occur in response to an event which occurred some time before. *Lag sequential analysis* addresses the time lag problem by allowing variation of the size of the lag between an event and its consequences; it also allows several events to be seen as causal. When dealing with dyads, such a technique generates a considerable computational problem; this has perhaps inhibited its extension to larger groups. A difficulty with conditional probability analysis is that it assumes sequences have stability and are not affected

Table 1. IPS categories. (After E. F. Borgatta, *Genetic Psychological Monographs,* **65,** 219–291, 1962. Reprinted with permission of the Helen Dwight Reid Educational Foundation. Published by Heldref Publications, 2400 Albemarle St., N.W., Washington D.C. Copyright © 1962)

1. Social acknowledgements, joking
2. Shows solidarity through raising the status of others
3. Shows tension release, laughs
4. Acknowledges, understands, recognizes
5. Shows agreement, concurrence, compliance
6. Gives a procedural suggestion
7. Suggests solution
8. Gives opinion, evaluation, analysis, expresses feeling or wish
9. Self-analysis and self-questioning behaviour
10. References to the external situation as redirected aggression
11. Gives orientation, information, passes communication
12. Draws attention, repeats, clarifies
13. Asks for opinion, evaluation, analysis, expression of feeling
14. Disagrees, maintains a contrary position
15. Shows tension, asks for help by virtue of personal inadequacy
16. Shows tension increase
17. Shows antagonism, hostility, is demanding
18. Ego defensiveness

by learning or other sources of temporal change; it also confounds the antecedents of an event with the conditions which maintain it.

In our own analysis of family events we attempted to draw upon the strengths of these techniques and to avoid some of their weaknesses.

Development of Family Interaction Analysis (FAMINTAN)

Identification of sequences

We have already seen examples of extracts from *scenario diaries* (see Chapter 6). These take the form of reported speech, including reconstructed verbal and other exchanges, based upon an hourly recording of events recalled for the previous hour. At this initial stage, there was no communication between observers and coding was carried out independently. However, prior discussions had established the basis for identifying a meaningful sequence. These often began because a natural event initiated them; for example, a mother might enter the room or a family member might make a suggestion which directed the attention of those present to a new focus of activity. Similarly, a sequence would end with a natural boundary or break in activity. Such sequences were stored separately in the computer. Within sequences, individual *acts* were coded, using the IPS. An act was defined as the smallest unit of meaningful behaviour; for example, this could be something like an individual clearing their throat (a single event) to a statement of feeling or intent on the part of an individual (set of words/actions). The acts were the basic unit of analysis but were gathered together within a sequence.

For computer storage purposes the following information was coded for each act:

1.   the *context* (for the first act in a sequence), i.e., family name, visit number, sequence number, date, time of day, location, primary activity (say, eating dinner) and secondary activity (say, discussion about the day's events);
2.   the *persons* present, for example, mother, father, siblings, and/or friends;
3.   the *initiator* of the action;
4.   the *IPS category* (1 through 18);
5.   the *recipient* of the action;
6.   the *family subsystem* involved;
7.   where appropriate, additional categories covering entrance, departure, related and unrelated activities, accompanying the main stream of the sequence but not disrupting it (categories 19 through 22).

In summary, therefore, each sequence was made up of coded acts, set in context, and stored with its own identifying tags. A worked example is given in Table 2.

Table 2.   An example of a Coded Sequence

Partitioning into acts (Family A transcript: Sequence number 35)
'Sal (mother), when she came back in with the tea, sat down on the settee. Tom's (father) back and leg were hurting him but he managed to keep a sense of humour. [He was bantering with his wife and family.][1] [Sal instructed John (younger sibling) to ignore him][2] and [then would smile to herself while reading the paper.][3] [Tom kept telling her that was the first sign][4] and [that she would end up in Wood Mount (local mental hospital) if she wasn't careful.][5] [Sal told him not to be stupid.][6] [Tom made another wisecrack][7] and [he was told not to be stupid.][8] [The children were told to ignore him.][9] [Pete (older sibling) said he thought Tom's behaviour was stupid][10] and [wondered why he did it.][11] (I personally think he has a quick and ready wit and can be quite amusing.)'

Coding. The *context* of each sequence is coded first. Thus, for the above example, the context would be: Friday; 1700 hours; lounge; father, mother, Pete and John present; everyone drinking after-dinner tea.

	Initiator	Act	Recipient	IPS category
1.	father	'bantering'	mother	1 (joking)
2.	mother	'ignore him'	father	17 (hostility)
3.	mother	'smile to self'	father	18 (self-righteous)
4.	father	'first sign'	mother	1 (joking)
5.	father	'Wood Mount'	mother	1 (joking)
6.	mother	'stupid'	father	17 (hostility)
7.	father	'wisecrack'	mother	1 (joking)
8.	mother	'stupid'	father	17 (hostility)
9.	mother	'ignore'	children	2 (alliance formation)
10.	Pete	'stupid'	father	17 (hostility)
11.	Pete	'why he did it'	mother	2 (supportive)

Summation and cross-tabulation of data

For the purpose of the following illustrative examples, we have chosen two families, the A family and the C family. Vignettes for these families appear in Chapter 9 together with information about the number of visits, the observer or observers concerned, and the variety of analyses employed.

The first level of analysis is concerned with summing all categorized acts for each family member. Families A and C are shown in Figures 1 and 2.

Taking Figure 1 we can see that in (a) each member is shown individually with a histogram pair for positive and negative affect, summed over all acts emitted, other than neutral acts (i.e., categories 6 through 13 in Table 1). In (b) these acts (expressed in percentages) are partitioned for context, i.e., for their presence within particular combinations of family grouping. Several points should be noted. It is possible to calculate the probability of particular numbers of acts occurring for particular family combinations, bearing in mind the total number of acts observed for the family as a whole. In the case of family A, a minimum of 40 acts per bar within the histograms is required for us to consider the pattern portrayed to merit formal statistical investigation. Where bars contain fewer than 40 acts, this is indicated in the figure. Secondly, some pairings (for example, Father and John in family A) were never observed; this does not mean of course that there is not an important relationship between the members involved and the absence of pairing may even reflect mutual avoidance. Negative affect was a dominant theme in this family, except for the behaviour of the father, who was rarely present. In the case of the siblings, the ratio of negative to positive affect is persistent. This simple technique, of adding positive and negative affect acts, can tell a great deal about the emotional atmosphere in the family, and particular relationships. It may also reveal asymmetries in power, particularly in the case of parental control. It has promise as a clinical assessment technique.

Figure 2 shows family C as observed and as coded by two different observers (Arlene Vetere and Claire Jolly). The four figures represent: the family as seen by observer 1, the family as seen by observer 2, observer 1's transcript coded by observer 2, and vice versa. This demonstrates a degree of consistency between the two observers, both in their own observations and in their analysis of each other's observations. A consistent observation is that the parents emit a higher ratio of positive to negative affect, while the children show the reverse. Some understanding of the background to these observations may be gained from reading the parents' account of their lives (in Chapter 10) and the vignettes describing the family as observed by us (in Chapter 9). Note that these observations and codings were carried out independently and without discussion of the families. The whole procedure (visit, typing transcript, coding, and computer loading of data) took some eight weeks per family.

Family sociograms: who does what to whom?

Figures 1 and 2 show the summary for all positive and negative acts when members are considered over all situations, in dyads, triads, etc. By drawing sociograms, in

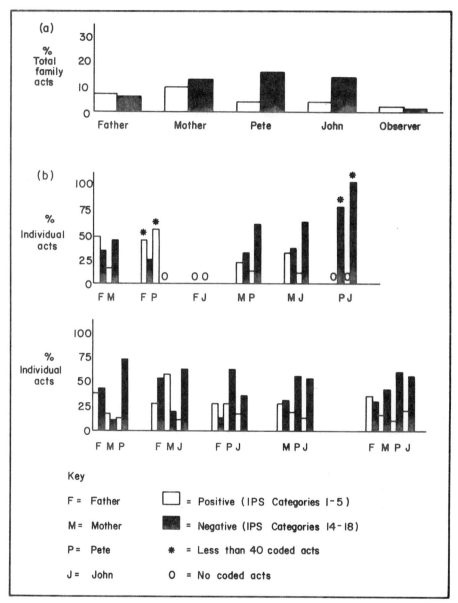

Figure 1(a). Percentage of positive and negative acts initiated by each member of the A family. (b) Percentage of positive and negative acts initiated by A family members within all possible family groupings

which each family member is represented, we can show *to whom* each act is directed. Figure 3 shows groupings of family A, with a separate sociogram for acts within particular categories, for all possible family groupings. The sociograms reveal the relative frequency and character of interactions between family members. Thus the sociograms reveal more of the nature of individual *relationships* than do the

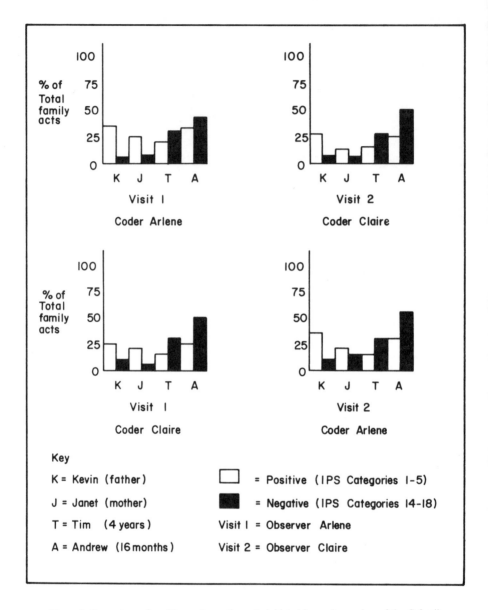

Figure 2. Percentage of positive and negative acts initiated by each member of the C family

histograms. Having drawn the sociograms, the researcher or clinician can then list the more outstanding features. For example, in the case of family C, the observers independently summarized and then agreed upon particular features of the sociograms including the following: parents interact more with children than with each other; much interaction between parents is task-oriented; Andrew (the identified patient)

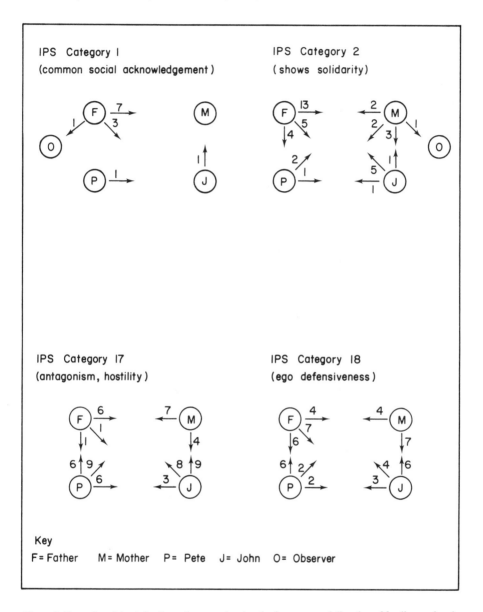

Figure 3. Examples of the A family sociograms showing the frequency and direction of family members'
behaviour

shows more negative affect than anyone else; unlike other families, there were no
cases of destructive hostility (category 17) . . . , and so on. Again, one can see the
power of the technique for clinical analysis and the opportunity such sociograms
provide for comparison of independent judgements by clinicians.

Lag sequential probability analysis

This technique goes beyond the sociograms and asks of the data: what happens next? In other words, what happens after any individual act directed at another person? For example, what happens immediately after the father initiates an affectional overture to his spouse? Does she reciprocate positively, ignore him, or respond in a negative fashion?

Given the large number of acts and sequences (for example, over two weeks of observation, family A generated 140 sequences and 1300 acts) certain combinations of acts within sequences or entire sequences themselves could have occurred by chance. To reduce the number of statistical tests deployed, the Minuchin structural maps drawn for the family were scrutinized in order to make ante hoc predictions. As another precaution against chance outcomes, the level of statistical significance adopted for individual tests was very conservative (at one chance in 1000).

Say our prediction concerns Mother's reaction to overtures from Father. The criterion act in this case is the action emitted by Father in the presence of his spouse. All such sequences are identified, then withdrawn from the computer-stored data. We then compute the conditional probabilities of *all* act types when the couple are together. Following the Father's overture a variety of possible acts could occur (for example, Father speaks again, Mother leaves room, Mother responds affectionately, etc.). The computer then sums all the acts of all different types which follow the criterion act (Father's overture) and including that act (lest it is repeated), giving probability estimates for each act type. This is repeated for each lag following the criterion act, up to six lags. Lag 1 is simply the next act in the observed sequence after the criterion act, lag 2 is the next but one, and so on. This technique can demonstrate the effects of some causal relationships at some temporal distance and is *not* tied to immediately adjacent acts.

Table 3 shows a lag sequential analysis for family A, and such a sequence, when Father and Mother are alone, or are together with the rest of the family. If the reader refers to the grouping where all four family members are together, it can be seen that when father initiates a social overture (category 1) his wife is highly likely to respond (at lags 1, 2 or 4) with a hostile response (17). Where mother and two sons are present, mother can initiate positive overtures to either son. The older child is likely to respond in a hostile fashion; where the younger son is addressed, the mother is likely to repeat her overture.

For family A the observer had made a number of ante hoc predictions, to be tested by formal statistical analysis, based upon the father's peripherality, the failure of parenting strategies, the boundaries which separated the father, and the quality of relationships. The following is an illustration:

> The boundary defining the marital subsystem is diffuse, so that both Pete and John are triangulated into the marital relationship either as allies (vis-à-vis the other spouse) or as a focus of concern. There is little evidence of complementarity of spouse function or teamwork. The father's absence from the home and his peripherality to the group is reflected in a lack of spouse communication. Thus it is predicted that little spouse interaction takes place.

Table 3. Lag sequential analysis of the positive categories (IPS categories 1–5) for the A family.

Family subsystem	Criterion act			Lag 1				Lag 2	Lag 3	Lag 4
	Initiator	Act	Recipient	Initiator	Act	Recipient	Sig.	Sig.	Sig.	Sig.
F-M	M	2	F	F	5	M	**			
M-J	M	2	J	J	17	M	NS			
				M	2	J	*			
M-P-J	M	2	J	M	2	J	*	***		
	M	2	P	P	17	M	**			
	P	2	M	P	17	J	**	**		
				J	14	M	*	*		
F-M-J	F	1	M	M	17	F	***	*	NS	**
	F	2	M	M	8	F	NS			
				M	14	F	NS			
	J	2	F	F	13	M	NS			
				J	8	M	**			

Significance levels: * 0.05, ** 0.01, *** 0.001, NS not significant.
Key: F = Father, M = Mother, P = Pete, J = John.

Thus the lag sequential analysis technique captures *dynamic* aspects of the *process* of family interaction. It captures repetitive sequences which underpin relationships; this is what Minuchin describes as the *rules* of family relationships and boundaries, i.e., the regular patterning which defines the operation of subsystems. Taking Bales' notion of reintegration, the lag sequential analysis can show how positive or negative affect is handled *sequentially*, and which components of group interaction lead to an amplification of negative feelings, or an enhancement of positive atmosphere by tension release or the giving of reward.

Nevertheless, the lag sequential analysis technique has some drawbacks. Like other techniques based on averaging of events and which focus on sequences it does not recognize the potential importance of individual events (see our discussion of the London and Thorngate analysis of amplification in Chapter 1). Clearly, it cannot cope with very remote causes or consequences; we chose lag 6 as our maximum consequential act, but did not move the window backwards for criterion acts.

In summarizing the FAMINTAN techniques we see that they move from descriptive analysis, through structural mapping, to detailed accounts of individual behaviours, through to group interactions and interactional sequences between family members, whether in dyads or in larger family groups. We believe these techniques and their combination to be unique in the family research literature. They capture the flavour of family relationships in a vivid fashion. They also allow for formal comparison of the views of the family as perceived by different observers. In principle, family members could be trained to score transcripts and to compare their differing views of family relationships and the interpretation of events. The basic principle is simple, but the extension of the data to describe the quality of relationships is novel and powerful.

The Assessment of Reliability

Potential sources of error

Participant observation presents problems of reliability, observational reactivity, and the bias of the researcher. Sources of unreliability in participant observer data can be located in at least seven factors: changes in the family and their environment over time; changes in the observer over time; differential perceptions of the family by different observers; differential family responses to different observers; inadequate sampling of family behaviour; poor category definitions; unstable use of the category scheme either within or between coders. Because of the limitations of research funding we were unable to implement a design which could have given answers to questions about reliability in any depth. Within a larger set of families, and with more observers and coders, it would have been logically possible to hold certain factors constant and/or to compute correlation coefficients for retest reliability and inter-judge reliability. Given long enough transcripts, taken over many days of observation, scenario diaries could have been subdivided to test for temporal changes. We should emphasize that the only real constraint for such analysis is a practical one, in which time and resources are crucial.

One of our recommendations in Chapter 13 is for extensive training of observers and coders. Because we were developing a new technique, training occurred by an iterative process and in the light of particular experiences. Nevertheless, we believe we understand what form such training should take in future.

Intra-observer reliability

The initial work, with three families, involved only one observer (Arlene Vetere). Reliability could be tested in two ways: consistency across visits, and consistency in recoding a transcript. In the former case, it is not possible to partial out effects due to change in *family* behaviour.

Table 4 shows the results of two visits to family W1, visited for a week on each of two occasions, some eight weeks apart. The data in the columns represent the percentage within each IPS category of the observed acts (the total acts per category were of course different for the two occasions). The data in the two columns supported the view that the coder was using the categories differently when a chi-squared

Table 4.   Percentage of IPS coded acts for both visits to the W1 Family

IPS category (including Famintan categories 19–22)	W1 visit 1 % acts	W1 visit 2 % acts
1	2.2	6.1
2	7.1	4.5
3	1.8	4.0
4	2.5	5.7
5	6.3	5.7
6	14.4	15.2
7	.6	1.1
8	11.5	15.2
9	.5	.3
10	1.9	1.4
11	4.5	5.8
12	5.5	5.1
13	1.0	1.3
14	7.4	6.8
15	3.7	3.4
16	–	–
17	12.6	6.9
18	5.4	2.7
19	2.7	2.1
20	1.4	1.0
21	6.6	5.8
22	.4	–
Total number of acts	1078	706

test was applied. However, the use of chi-squared tests using 18 categories does weight the procedure against finding consistency across the two visits. But reduction to three collapsed categories of positive, neutral, and negative affect did not serve to improve reliability. Moreover, as Sue Lewis points out in Chapter 12, the identified patient was *not* present for most of the second visit, and from a structural theory point of view, differences in family behaviour would be predicted. Thus the issue of reliability is not resolved with this particular data set, although the procedure employed (albeit a conservative measure) is applicable in future research.

Table 5 shows the results of recoding of the *same* scenario diary by the same observer/coder, some twelve months after the original coding. In this case, positive, negative, and neutral Borgatta categories have been collapsed as a basis for analysis. The chi-squared test showed the columns for the three collapsed categories not to be different for the two occasions; thus the observer/coder was reliable on this measure.

Table 5.   Percentage of positive, neutral, and negative IPS coded acts for family W1 visit 1 and the recoded visit 1

IPS category	W1 visit 1 % acts	W1 recoded visit 1 % acts
1–5	22.4	19.8
6–13	44.8	44.6
14–18	32.7	35.5
Total number of acts	959	801

Inter-observer reliability

Inter-observer reliability was assessed for all family visits where two observers lived in the same family home on two independent occasions. The data for family C will be discussed. The two observers were Arlene Vetere and Claire Jolly, whose visits were four weeks apart. In addition, in the case of this family, a third blind and naive coder was used, to test for the reliability of implementation of the coding system by an outsider who had not lived with a family and had not been trained in the technique of participant observation. The third coder was a psychology graduate and a medical student in training.

Table 6 has six columns showing each observer's coding of their own and the other's transcript, together with the third coder's coding of both observers' transcripts. Percentages are presented for the coded occurrence of each category. It will be seen that there are discrepancies between the paired columns. Such discrepancies were confirmed by significant chi-squared analyses. There appear to be perceptual biases in the selection of particular categories, possibly reflecting willingness to code affective as opposed to neutral acts, the absolute number of acts and sequences identified, and the possible use of categories 19 through 22 as miscellaneous categories. We should also note that any system which involves a level of interpretation is likely to be affected by the fact that one of the coders was the actual observer and witnessed and recorded the events in question. Thus theoretical reliability for the two observers is likely to be different as a function of prior knowledge. Finally, the personality of the observer, and her own habitual attributional frameworks for describing and interpreting the behaviour of others, is likely to intrude into the coding process. For example, Arlene Vetere was typically more inclined than Claire Jolly to employ both negative and positive affect categories and to perceive an overlay of anxiety in the actions of certain family members. Only by the use of reliability studies such as those described, can attention be drawn to systematic biases of this sort. Such exercises should be used in the training of observers. The issues involved are discussed in greater detail in Chapter 12.

Table 6.   Percentage of IPS coded acts for the two visits to the C family
(visit 1 is Arlene's transcript; visit 2 is Claire's transcript)

IPS category	Visit 1 coder Arlene	Visit 1 coder Claire	Visit 1 coder Kerry	Visit 2 coder Claire	Visit 2 coder Arlene	Visit 2 coder Kerry
1	3.1	1.5	1.6	1.7	3.3	2.4
2	8.6	1.8	.6	.7	5.9	3.2
3	1.2	1.3	1.4	4.0	3.6	2.9
4	3.3	1.8	1.4	3.0	4.2	1.1
5	9.0	9.9	6.0	7.1	7.9	6.3
6	21.1	32.4	13.7	20.2	20.4	9.8
7	1.3	2.4	.5	.6	.2	.4
8	13.4	15.4	16.1	18.6	16.4	8.1
9	1.4	.6	.2	.1	.9	.1
10	.7	–	.3	–	.1	.6
11	5.2	1.7	12.2	9.4	6.4	15.9
12	4.9	.3	4.0	2.7	3.2	1.5
13	2.4	.7	4.6	6.0	2.4	7.8
14	4.2	6.0	1.7	5.8	5.4	1.8
15	5.2	.2	4.8	.5	7.0	7.9
16	–	.3	–	.9	–	–
17	4.1	7.1	2.8	4.5	2.9	4.1
18	.5	.3	.1	.1	.8	.3
19	1.9	1.8	3.4	1.8	2.0	2.8
20	.5	1.4	1.3	2.5	.9	1.6
21	7.9	11.0	23.2	7.7	5.3	21.1
22	.1	1.8	–	2.0	–	.7
Total acts	1867	2166	1490	2057	1404	1482

Agreement on units of measurement

The key question here was whether in partitioning scenario diaries into acts and sequences, two coders would agree on the total number of sequences and the total number of acts to be found within a single scenario diary. This is a sort of signal detection analysis in which a sequence might be detected in common (correct detection), or only partially (beginning and/or ending at different points), or identified by only one coder (omission or false positive). The procedure of checking for agreement upon whether sequences existed and where they started and ended was completed for six scenario diaries relating to two visits to three separate families. Coders had worked independently in scoring the original diaries; comparison of two codings was then conducted as a joint effort.

Tables 7(a) and (b) show the results of this procedure. In the case of 7(a) which relates to family P, the observer was for much of the time alone with the mother. Thus the coding of sequences was difficult because much of it was redundant to the understanding of family process. Table 7(b) (the G family) shows superior results when the observation was more representative of family activity and the observer was rarely alone with one family member. However, there is persistent asymmetry in the judgements made, between the two coders. Punctuation of the stream of behaviour has always been a difficult problem for observational work and is a live issue in family therapy where it is not easy to attribute the cause of particular actions to particular family members, bearing in mind the concept of circular causality. The reader should turn to Chapter 12 for a fuller discussion.

Table 7(a). Comparison of two codings of the P Family transcript (Shirley's visit)

	Coder Shirley	Coder Arlene
% of sequences shared	61.6	64.6
% of sequences in common	19.1	17.0
% of sequences unshared	38.3	35.3
Total number of sequences	73	82
Total number of acts	634	623

Table 7(b). Comparison of two codings of the G Family transcript (Claire's visit)

	Coder Claire	Coder Arlene
% of sequences shared	90.0	66.0
% of sequences in common	23.8	25.0
% of sequences unshared	10.0	34.0
Total number of sequences	227	215
Total number of acts	1590	1896

References

Bales, R. F. (1950). *Interaction Process Analysis: A Method for the Study of Small Groups.* Cambridge, Massachusetts: Addison-Wesley.

Borgatta, E. F. (1962). A systematic study of interaction process scores, peer and self-assessments, personality and other variables. *Genetic Psychology Monographs,* **65**, 219–291.

Gottman, J. M. and Bakeman, R. (1979). The sequential analysis of observational data. In: M. Lamb, S. Suomi and G. Stephenson (Eds), *Methodological Problems in the Study of Social Interaction.* Madison, Wisconsin: University of Wisconsin Press.

Minuchin, S. (1974). *Families and Family Therapy.* London: Tavistock.

Waxler, N. E. and Mishler, E. G. (1970). Sequential patterning in family interaction: A methodological note. *Family Process,* **9**, 211–220.

CHAPTER EIGHT
Repertory Grids, Interviews, and Films

Claire Jolly and Arlene Vetere

Introduction

In this chapter and Chapter 11 we report some repertory grid studies of family relationships and family structure. The repertory grid technique was developed out of the personal construct theory of Kelly (1955). The emphasis of the theory and the method used to apply it is upon the individual's phenomenal view of the world. The theory has a number of corollaries, which describe different types of construct and their role within the person's experience. The individual interacts with the world on the basis of his or her *personal constructs*, which discriminate among events and organize the person's experience; thus constructs anticipate events within the world. Constructs were conceived of as bipolar, such as 'warm-cold', 'powerful-weak' or 'kind-cruel', and in the typical repertory grid a person will rank *elements* on the basis of their own constructs. Elements are usually important others and self (father, mother, spouse, child, teacher, friend, etc.) or can be objects, or indeed any item of salience to the person. When a person provides their own constructs (the most theoretically proper procedure) and reveals their own phenomenal view, the constructs are said to be *elicited*. When the constructs are provided by the investigator, they are said to be *supplied*.

While the original notions of personal constructs and the repertory grid were devised for the study of individual patients, it is possible to develop the technique for studying constructions in dyads, for example, to study mutual perceptions, perceived relationships, and discrepancies in construing the self and the other. In a personal relationship two people will perceive each other in terms of their personal constructs, which in turn will be affected by the sharing of common experiences. However, in such cases a difficulty arises: there is no guarantee that two individuals, even those sharing a common and longstanding mutual and social experience, will either use similar constructs or incorporate the same set of elements within the *range of convenience* of a similar construct. Therefore, those who have applied repertory grid methods to the study of family life have been obliged to create sets of constructs by special means, the aim being to create sets which all family members can use with the same degree of personal meanings. Thus, so far in family research with repertory grids, constructs have been supplied rather than elicited; however, as we shall see, in many cases researchers have achieved a compromise between the two. According to Kelly (1955), difficulties can arise for an individual when their anticipations of the world are discrepant with events and when they are unable to revise their constructs.

It is not difficult to see that family conflict could arise because of a discrepancy of anticipations by different family members sharing the same social space. We have discussed such issues in Chapter 3, where we saw that failure to recognize that families are made up of members who have a different phenomenal view, can lead to faulty conclusions. Therefore, a method designed to measure the individual's phenomenal view bears promise for family theory and family research methodology.

A handful of researchers have sought to capture aspects of family life by using repertory grid based techniques (Procter, 1981; Karastergiou-Katsika and Watson, 1985; and Gale and Barker, 1986). Procter (1981) proposed that Personal Construct Theory could be extended for family research purposes to include two new corollaries, the Group Corollary and the Family Corollary. The first, the group corollary, says that an individual can play a part in the activities of a group where he can construe the role relationships which hold within the group. The second, devised for the context of the family, says that for a group of people to remain together over an extended period of time, each member has to make a choice (within the limitations of his construct system) to maintain a common construction of the role relationships in the group. Procter was particularly concerned with families which had a schizophrenic member and also with devising a method for measuring relationships in such families. Initially, he derived constructs from each family member, using family members and persons known to all the family as elements. From these individual grids he then searched for relationship constructs which appeared to be shared; these then formed the basis for a common grid to be completed for all family members. Thus Procter started with standard methods of elicitation in order to derive a set of supplied constructs.

Karastergiou-Katsika and Watson (1982) and Karastergiou-Katsika and Watson (1985) used a text completion method in which subjects were asked to fill in appropriate words in sentences about family relationships and perceptions of the characteristics of family members. Their constructs were: loving, friendly, sad, caring, distant, harmonious, cruel, hostile, full of arguments, understanding, hating, controlling, abusive, dependent, close, happy, good, stable, violent, and bad. These formed the basis for their study of the families of twenty non-psychotic inpatients.

Gale and Barker (1986) derived a set of constructs on the basis of the distance regulation theory of Kantor and Lehr (1975), asking judges who were familiar with the theory to generate statements about family relationships and perceptions of family members. The judges then indicated the extent to which each statement reflected the key theoretical notions of affect, power, and meaning. The statements were then sorted for overlap and a total of 52 derived, which were then incorporated into a questionnaire. Five families (varying between four and six members) then completed the questionnaire, ranking themselves and others on each statement, and also placing family members along a bipolar analogue scale.

Thus the three studies we have mentioned employed different and non-standard methods for producing constructs: combination of family members' constructs, text completion by non-experts, and item creation by experts based on a family process theory.

The study by Karastergiou-Katsika and Watson (1985), the only one to be published as we go to press, has been severely criticized by Bryant (1985). While welcoming the development of the technique for use with families, she regrets their failure to give full details of their methodology. They also fail to exploit fully the dyad grid method in which the element is a relationship (e.g., father and myself; see Ryle and Lunghi, 1970) and from which one may derive differentiated reciprocal roles (e.g., my father's view of father and self, own view of father and self plus a matching set completed by the father). Bryant also criticizes the constructs (as listed above) as failing to capture crucial aspects of family structure such as control, role, and hierarchy; thus while claiming to explore family structure they use the wrong sorts of construct (largely applicable to individuals rather than relationships). Finally, Karastergiou-Katsika and Watson create the impression that they have derived *common* family grids and a common principal component; according to Bryant, they fail to demonstrate that they have actually derived a construct system which is shared within the family.

The findings of Gale and Barker (1986) are relevant to the issue of shared constructs about family structure, since in their study what was particularly striking was the *lack of agreement* between family members on individual behaviours or relationships. Their technique enabled them to see all family relationships from *every* family member's point of view. Even where two members (and others) saw each other as opposed and distant from each other, there was no guarantee that they (or other family members) employed similar constructs or their poles to describe the relationship. Even so, no respondent claimed that the constructs were not meaningful or applicable in the context of family life, nor did any respondent supply additional constructs when invited.

Therefore, we see there are two challenges: to identify individual constructs which have some guarantee of shared meaning, and to devise a method of analysis which samples relationships and discrepant construing of those relationships.

Study of Family Constructs in Association with Participant Observation

As an illustrative case, we have chosen the C family for presentation of our method. The C family appear in several parts of this book. Our vignette and scenario diary extracts for their family appear in Chapter 9; the parents, Janet and Kevin, present their view of their personal history in Chapter 10. Because their children were too young to participate, only the two parents offered grids.

Apart from needing to overcome the problem of shared constructs, we were also concerned to use descriptors which would enable some comparison of *our* participant observers' view of the family and the *family's own view*. Two scenario diaries, from two observers, were scanned to derive a set of descriptors. In addition, a tape-recording of a discussion of family relationships was made by Janet and Kevin when they had observed a videofilm of a family mealtime (see below). Key words, which appeared to be particularly salient, were selected from their discussion. Thus, unlike earlier studies, we supplied constructs on the basis of two sources of information: our descriptions of the family, and the parents' spontaneous descriptions of family members and relationships. We believe such a compromise to be worthy of generaliz-ation to other family studies although, of course, in the present case, the constructs derived depended on a good deal of existing data and prior intimate knowledge of the family's internal life.

The second stage in this process was to ask three judges (other participant observers) to match the parent set of constructs against the Borgatta IPS categories. Sixteen bipolar constructs were then derived to match positive, negative, and neutral groupings, as follows: sociable–reserved, warm–cold, unsure–confident, copes–can't cope, worries–relaxed, helpful–unhelpful, responsive–ignores, sad–happy, understanding–insensitive, moody–even tempered, argumentative–agreeable, dependent–independent, controlling–accepting, aggressive–not aggressive, rational–irrational, and expresses feelings–hides feelings. It will be noted that many of these constructs relate to *personal* dispositions. A further set of *relationship* con-structs were then derived, based on the above list, together with those from the Karastergiou-Watson (1985) study, which the authors claimed discriminated family relationships across their sample of families. Apart from completing the first (personal) grid, therefore, Janet and Kevin completed a *relationships* grid based on the following constructs: close, happy, rational, stable, argumentative, dependent, harmonious, understanding, helpful, responsive, controlling, loving, hostile, caring, distant, and sad. These were not bipolar constructs and they were rated by Janet and Kevin on a five-point scale.

In the personal grid the elements were all the family members and other signific-ant persons, and in the second grid the elements were all the relationships among the four family members.

Janet and Kevin: Their Grids

Family grids: initial analyses

As a preliminary analysis, one can simply determine the degree of agreement between the couple by counting the number of *matching* scores: these are the number of con-structs on which elements are rated the same, and the number of elements whose construct ratings are the same. The total number of elements was eight and the total number of constructs sixteen. One can therefore calculate the probability that two persons will attach identical construct ratings to the same element and vice versa. We could calculate the probability of obtaining agreement as, or more extreme, than that observed when the choice of construct ratings for the elements is made at random.

If this probability is very small, say less than one per cent, then we could conclude that chance alone does not explain the degree of agreement and that the obtained ratings are therefore *similar*. For example, Janet and Kevin achieved very high agreement in the allocation of construct ratings for three of the family members: namely, for Kevin's father, Kevin, and Timothy. They did not reach this level of agreement for Janet, other in-laws or Andrew. Given this pattern of agreement about individuals, the chance that they will allocate similar scores to *pairs* of individuals is reduced. In this analysis agreed similarity occurred only for Kevin and his Father and for Timothy. Finally, one can estimate in how many cases the two respondents see family members as *dissimilar*; here there was no major agreement in assigning constructs to family members. The fact that a couple disagree about their perceptions of self and others would seem to indicate defective development of a group corollary and a basis for mutual understanding. In the present case there is some asymmetry since it appears that views of Kevin and his Father are commonly accepted, but that Janet and Kevin do not share a common view of Janet.

So far as mutual perceptions are concerned Janet and Kevin agreed that they were both rational, confident, helpful, understanding, and able to cope. They agreed that Janet is sociable and expressive, and that Kevin is reserved and hides his feelings. They agree that their elder son is moody and argumentative. Kevin sees Janet as moody, argumentative, dependent, controlling, aggressive, and worried; but she disagrees with him about herself. Both see the two children as similar to Janet in certain ways (sociable, expressive, warm, and happy) but like Kevin in other ways (understanding, independent, and non-aggressive).

Computer analysis of family grids

The grids produced by Janet and Kevin (each rating eight elements on sixteen constructs) were entered into the INGRID P package developed by Slater (1972). This reveals principal components (i.e., factors which organize the constructs) which account for most of the observed variance. The resultant graphical display is shown in Figure 1. This shows two principal components (the ordinate and abcissa) which we have labelled *affect* and *power*. For the purpose of this presentation we display only the data for Janet, Kevin, and their children. The enclosed areas represent the component space occupied by the family as perceived by the two family members. It can be seen that these two spaces do not overlap, although they are adjacent to each other in the same plane. This could reflect perceived differences *or* consistently different styles of use of the scales (for example, Janet is less reluctant than Kevin to use more positive categories). The descriptions of agreement and differences of viewpoint already described can be seen graphically and the computer-based analysis confirms the preliminary analysis while showing evidence of clustering among constructs and elements. Thus the repertory grid technique can be used to explore the following: Janet's view of Janet (J [J]), Janet's view of Kevin (K [J]), Janet's view of other emotionally significant persons, Kevin's view of Kevin . . . , and the discrepancies and similarities between the views of each spouse vis-à-vis each person involved.

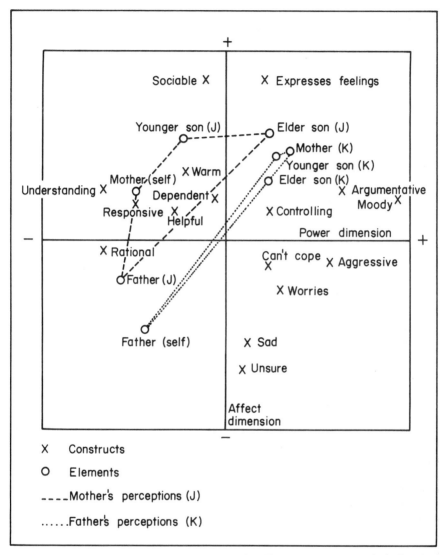

Figure 1. C family grid: graph of constructs and elements plotted in component space. (Analysis of repertory grids courtesy of Dr Patrick Slater, Manchester Regional Computing Service.)

Relationship grids

We now move from persons to relationships between persons. In this case the elements were the relationships which hold between each of the four family members, taken as pairs, giving six relationships (bearing in mind the fact that the children were too young to participate). The sixteen constructs used for the relationships grids have already been listed; these were derived both from our own analysis of Kevin and Janet's life together, their own use of relationship language, the proximity of these constructs to the Borgatta's descriptions, and a handful of constructs shown to be powerful discriminators by Karastergiou-Katsika and Watson (1985).

The *matching* method already described showed that Kevin and Janet agreed with each other on only one construct for their own relationship (rational), while agreeing on five or more constructs about other relationships. They gave inverse ratings for close, loving, happy, understanding, controlling, and dependent; Janet rating these positively and Kevin the reverse. In accordance with our own observations Kevin's relationship with the younger child (the identified patient) was closer than that with the older child; while there was more positive feeling between Janet and the older child than with the identified patient. Here the parents seemed to agree, being able to see each other in relationships with the children with greater concordance than they could see their own relationship. This was confirmed by examining the similar use of constructs to apply to identical elements, i.e., it was the children, their relationship, and the parents' relationships with the children which yielded high agreement. The computer analysis again yielded two principal components which were similar to those identified for the family grid, and the major discrepancy in location on the graph was the spouse relationship, where Kevin sees Janet as distant from him on the affect dimension.

Again, therefore, we can see that repertory grids can supplement our observational data. In this case we obtained information about the spouse relationship and discrepancies in viewpoint. Relatively few of our observations had focused on the spouse relationship given that the children were invariably present during observation and were a constant focus of parental attention. Janet and Kevin, in their own account (see Chapter 10) refer to strained emotional and sexual relationships. It is a matter for conjecture whether these were causal in the creation of symptomatic behaviour on the part of the identified patient. Certainly, the younger child's behaviour served to exacerbate any existing tension, reduced the couple's level of energy, disrupted their sleeping patterns, and intruded physically into their marital bed. Thus they became caught in a pattern of circular causation: marital tension, attention focused on child, child misbehaviour, little time to attend to mutual needs, fatigue, loss of sleep, marital tension . . . Our film study (see below) provided objective evidence of how the couple's time was allocated at important occasions like mealtimes. Our observations and interviews showed how the younger child was treated in ways which (from our viewpoint) rewarded his behaviour rather than controlled it. Janet was reluctant to exercise discipline, which she viewed as a negative way of dealing with children.

The C Family at Lunch

Several of our observations with families revealed that mealtimes were potentially rich in revealing relationships across the spectrum of subsystems, given that they offered an opportunity to see all family members interacting together within a relatively confined space. Janet and Kevin agreed to our request to film them at mealtime and to analyse what we saw; they also agreed to come to our laboratory and view the film with us, sharing and exchanging viewpoints on what could be seen in the film.

Our equipment enabled us to score the film objectively in terms of interactions among family members. We focused on the following variables: number of times Janet talked to Kevin, Andrew or Timothy; number of times Kevin talked to Janet, Andrew or Timothy; the mean durations of these events; number of times Janet looked at each of the others; and the number of times that Kevin looked at each of the others. We also rated the number of times each family member initiated a conversation or an activity (say, a child banging a spoon or leaving his chair).

There was little difficulty in securing agreement on these measures, the onset of events, or their duration. Very clear findings emerged, which revealed two subsystems: Janet and Timothy, and Kevin and Andrew. Janet and Kevin spent no time talking to each other at mealtimes, Janet focused exclusively on Timothy (whom she faced across the table) and Kevin focused on Andrew (who sat immediately on his left, in his highchair). Both parents spent more time feeding both children than enjoying their own food. Indeed, the children were not left to feed themselves, although it appeared to us that they demonstrated a capacity to do so and had most of the skills required for self-feeding. Nevertheless, the children were responsible for the majority of initiated actions and switches of the focus of attention; this further ensured the constant involvement of the parents with their children. The mealtime was not an occasion for pleasantry or exchanges, but a rather serious and anxiety-laden business.

Janet and Kevin Discuss their Film

The parents were asked to watch and make independent notes upon the entire film and then say whether they thought it was representative of their family's mealtimes. Referring to their notes, both agreed that the mealtime had not been unduly disturbed by the presence of the camera; however, they saw the meal as a little quieter and less conflictual than they would have expected. A further spontaneous comment from both parents was that each saw the other as spending more time on the children than in enjoying the meal for themselves. They confirmed the formal event-based analysis which we had conducted earlier: Kevin tended to concentrate on Andrew, trying to amuse him, in an effort to get him to eat, while Janet watched over the older child.

Janet and Kevin were asked to write a description of the meal from the point of view of themselves and all others at the table. While Janet felt able to do this, Kevin could not put himself in the children's shoes. For example, Janet's perception of Andrew was: 'Why do I have to be strapped in — it's tight . . . Why does Daddy keep putting that spoon in while I'm trying to drink . . . That makes a nice mess — I'll do it again — Yes, he (Daddy) smiled'.

Following the showing of the film and the parents' appraisal of its contents, we discussed possible behavioural interventions with a view to making mealtimes more of a cheerful and shared event. These included: allowing the elder son to feed himself; both parents to take turns in supervising the younger son; and, encouraging the parents to talk to each other, rather than using mealtimes just to eat.

In the light of our experience, we believe that the filming of a family meal and an invitation to family members to respond to it, creates opportunities for self-observation, empathy with others, and the consideration of positive changes in behaviour. Systematic re-filming could be used in an objective way to determine whether the agreed changes in behaviour had been implemented or had been successful in bringing about desired change.

Janet and Kevin Describe the Experience of Being Observed

Much of this book focuses on the outsider's view of the family. In this chapter we have emphasized the importance of gaining phenomenal accounts from family members. Earlier, we have discussed the problem of reactivity, and the ways in which our presence in the home might influence the behaviour of family members.

Very shortly after the second observer had completed her visit, we interviewed Janet and Kevin to explore the family members' views and reactions to the novel event of accommodating a participant observer within their home.

An interview schedule was prepared which included the following items (expressed in everyday terms): reactivity to the observer, validity of the observational data, evaluation apprehension, prior expectations, and subsequent changes in expectations. The rationale for these items is to be found in Chapter 4, where we discuss the problem of reactivity in detail.

The couple were interviewed at home when the children were in bed. We have not explored, therefore, the ways in which the interview could be conducted in association with a larger group, including young children. Each item was put to each parent and the conversation was recorded and subsequently transcribed. An informal content analysis revealed several reactions on the part of the observed. The most striking view was an amazement that anyone would wish to live in someone else's home, since such a role would be difficult and make the observer vulnerable. Given the months of consultation with doctors and therapists, they were delighted to have an opportunity to display the 'problem as it was at home'. Initially, the aims of the research were accepted as legitimate, particularly since they too were interested in research as an enterprise. However, there were some misgivings and doubts. Kevin was concerned that 'the problem would not be visible when the observer stayed'; this reflected their experience of disbelief on the part of other professionals. Janet worried about the additional stress of coping with an outsider, as well as their own problems.

There was a degree of emotional and psychological preparation for the visits, such as 'intending to carry on as normal' by continuing to shout at or smack the children. Housekeeping arrangements were organized by Janet (shopping, planning meals, and preparing the observer's sleeping arrangements). Both decided not to alter their social engagements. Both observers turned out to be 'nicer' than anticipated; the observers' behaviour put them at their ease and won their confidence. There was a gradual relaxation of self-consciousness during the first day of each visit; they were not aware of being watched and reported little pressure from being watched. In their view, one day was sufficient to habituate to the presence of the observer.

They were aware of the observer's lack of intervention, and the capacity to keep cool in the face of screaming children and demands or expectations from those people (such as neighbours) who were not aware of the observer's identity and purpose.

While the absence of the observer when recording was seen as a lost opportunity to record 'fraught interactions' it was also appreciated as a welcome 'breathing space' from being observed.

In sum, this couple were pleased at their degree of relaxation during the visits. Janet felt that her proper standards of mothering and housekeeping had been met.

The interview therefore demonstrated that social desirability was low while evaluation apprehension and other reactivity effects were seen to reduce over time. Clearly, such a conclusion cannot be drawn in relation to all families visited. The family structure itself might interact with the degree of reactivity. In the case of Janet and Kevin, we were dealing with reflective and intelligent people, who sought consciously to facilitate the research.

A Conclusion

This chapter has provided evidence of family interaction and response, supplementary to observations made by outsiders. We consider our use of repertory grids to be somewhat more sensitive and successful than in other family studies. One key to the approach was to base the supplied constructs on material already made available by the couple, either during observation or during interview.

The formal analysis of the grids may be used as a means of setting an agenda for discussion among family members. It demonstrates in dramatic and objective terms how much family members agree and disagree. Moreover, it gives each family member an equal status in expressing a view, since each member's viewpoint is represented within tables and graphs. All aspects of the analysis — views of individuals, views of relationships, agreements, and disagreements — bring each individual's thoughts and feelings out into the open. The technique therefore allows for a description of perceived relationships at the outset of treatment and provides a means of estimating the degree of therapeutic change for *all* members, rather than focusing on the pathology and symptoms of the identified patient.

The technique has disadvantages where young children are involved. In the present case, the position of the spouse subsystem within the family's hierarchical structure was crucial; potentially (in our view) the parents had sufficient power to control the behaviour of their child. Indeed, in spite of additional burdens their resilience and creativity in adapting themselves have won through. Their solution was to locate the child's behaviour within his nutritional intake. Our view was that his behaviour was controllable by parental behaviour and that his persistent intractability was a convenient means of distracting attention from a strained spouse subsystem.

The film provides further supplementary information of an objective nature. The results of the analysis of mealtime behaviour would be difficult to challenge even for the most defensive couple. We suspect that films at mealtime might provide a better source of interactional data than the more typical consulting-room film of interaction between families and therapists. Even a mealtable set up in the clinic, because it taps certain well-established habits linked to eating, provides some ecological validity for sampling family life, albeit away from the family home. Further details of this technique may be found in Minuchin, Rosman and Baker (1978). As Dreyer and Dreyer (1973) claim, the family mealtime is a 'unique behavioural habitat'. In our use of the technique, an opportunity is provided for each member to observe themselves and to put themselves in the shoes of the others. Thus the family's film of itself becomes a projective stimulus, in which each member is invited to ask themselves in relation to each other: what is happening, what do I feel, what do others feel, how are others reacting to me?

The reflections on preparation for our arrival and the reaction of Janet and Kevin to our presence throw new light on the problems of reactivity, the suspension of certain aspects of the family agenda during the visits, and gradual adaptation to the experience. Of particular value for future observational research are the comments on the parents' part that prior encounter with the observers created a sense of trust, which, in its turn, reduced reactivity and social desirability effects.

Looked at from a family life-cycle viewpoint, Janet and Kevin, on their own account, were relatively inexperienced adults when they met and married. We believe that a further administration of the grid method would show that their marriage and relationship have now evolved to a later stage. They were learning to live with each other and to bring up young children at one and the same time.

References

Bryant, R. (1985). Families and repertory grids — a brief introduction with comment on Karastergiou-Katsika and Watson. *Journal of Family Therapy,* **7**, 251–257.

Dreyer, C. A. and Dreyer, A. S. (1973). Family dinner time as a unique behaviour habitat. *Family Process,* **12**, 291–301.

Gale, A. and Barker, M. (1986). *A Study of Family Relationships* (manuscript).

Kantor D. and Lehr, W. (1975). *Inside the Family: Towards a Theory of Family Process.* San Francisco, California: Jossey-Bass.

Karastergiou-Katsika, A. and Watson, J. P. (1982). A new approach to construct elicitation for a grid test. *British Journal of Clinical Psychology,* **21**, 67–68.

Karastergiou-Katsika, A. and Watson, J. P. (1985). A comparative study of repertory grid and clinical methods for assessing family structure. *Journal of Family Therapy,* **7**, 231–250.

Kelly, G. A. (1955). *The Psychology of Personal Constructs,* vols. 1 and 2. New York: Norton.

Minuchin, S., Rosman, B. and Baker, L. (1978). *Psychosomatic Families: Anorexia Nervosa in Context.* Cambridge, Massachusetts: Harvard University Press.

Procter, H. G. (1981). Family construct psychology: An approach to understanding and treating families. In: S. Walrond-Skinner (Ed.), *Developments in Family Therapy.* London: Routledge and Kegan Paul.

Ryle, A. and Lunghi, M. (1970). The dyad grid — a modification of repertory grid technique. *British Journal of Psychiatry,* **117**, 323–327.

Slater, P. (1972). *Notes on INGRID '72.* London: Institute of Psychiatry.

CHAPTER NINE
Vignettes of the Nine Families

Arlene Vetere

Introduction

This Chapter describes each family in the study from the point of view of the observer. These descriptions will contrast with the family members' personal accounts as revealed by personal statement and repertory grid analysis (see Chapters 8 and 10). The families are looked at in three ways: background information; an analysis of family process in terms of three key theoretical approaches (structural theory, distance regulation theory, choice-exchange theory); and, finally, illustrative extracts from the scenario diaries.

The A Family

Background

The family lived previously in a rural community. The husband's job provided a tied cottage, and a role in the local community, where the family appear to have been fully integrated. The husband's work allowed him to be near home for most of the day. Because of circumstances beyond the family's control, the job came to an end and the family were obliged to move. His new occupation as lorry driver and occasional horsedealer mean that he is often absent and his presence in the home unpredictable. Mrs A. refers to the past and seems to mourn both loss of the rural environment and its community.

The A family live in a three-bedroom, semi-detached council house on a small estate in a suburb of a large industrial town and port. Mrs A. considers the area to be 'rough' and would prefer to live in a more rural setting.

Members

The father (40) is a lorry driver and horsedealer; the mother (32) a housewife; there are two male children of 13 and 10.

Presenting problem

The elder son was referred to a child guidance clinic because of persistent refusal to attend school.

Observation and analysis

One observer (AV) visited on two occasions, each for seven days. The family was described in terms of structural mapping, positive and negative affect, sociometric relationships, lag sequential analysis, and intra-observer reliability.

Family relationships: Structural Theory

The husband is both physically and emotionally absent from home; he is therefore *peripheral* and his participation in family life excludes direct active parenting. The father's absence has been complemented by the formation of a strong bond between mother and elder son (the identified patient). The mother seems to obtain from this relationship a substitute source of companionship normally expected of spouses; the son also plays a strong role in decision making and parenting the younger son. His school refusal therefore reflects a need for him to sustain his parental roles. The family system keeps him at home. Both children are drawn into the marital conflict; the younger child is described as mischievous and irresponsible by both mother and older son. The younger son expresses concern about becoming overweight; he is slim but the remaining three are clearly overweight. This expressed fear is used as a rationale for his erratic eating behaviour, and he refuses to eat unless his father is present. When father is absent at mealtimes, the younger son departs in a theatrical fashion. He has a strong affiliative bond with his father and they display affection openly. The mother has a long history of overinvolvement with her own mother; on the basis of this model she has made a 'daughter' of her elder son who, apart from other spouse and parenting roles, also discharges some of the mother's traditional caretaking duties. The family forms two conflictual subsystems: mother, elder son, and grandmother, with mother and son sharing many functions, and father and younger son. An illustrative Minuchin-style map is drawn for the A family in Figure 1.

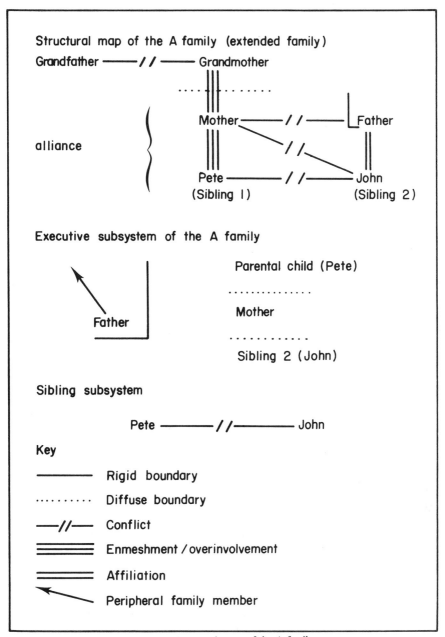

Figure 1. Structural maps of the A family

Family relationships: Distance Regulation Theory

The father's involvement in the external world extends beyond normal working hours. His associates are males and women are not welcome in their company. This distance from the home is complemented by boundaries within the home. Affective tone between husband and wife and elder son is negative. Mother still clings to her own mother and has not freed herself for a full relationship with her spouse. Power is vested in the elder son who makes many day-to-day decisions. The past is particularly important to the mother; she refers often to their former life and takes every opportunity to visit her former associates. The family's activities are asynchronous except where exceptional efforts are made to participate in joint activity. The older son is bounded from his peer community and both children are refused permission to interact with neighbours. Mealtimes are particularly important and much family activity is concerned with shopping, preparing and eating food. Mealtimes are occasions for tension, display of conflict, and the reinforcement of the elder sibling's roles.

Family relationships: Choice-Exchange Theory

The strong bond between mother and elder son is rewarding for both members in terms of positive affection and acquired status. The cost of this relationship is that it reinforces further the father's exclusion; this exclusion allows the father a rich external life and removes the need to act as parent or to communicate with his wife (both of which are potentially effortful). The older son, in exchange for affection and power, has lost access to peers and to education. The younger son has few rewards, other than to refuse to participate at mealtimes (and thus draw attention) or to await his father's homecoming and the affection which ensues. He is subjected to the irrational outbursts and bullying of his elder brother.

Subsequent history

Some four years after the observation, this family split up. The elder son became a successful ladies' hairdresser after a series of boring desk jobs. The mother initiated the breakup by taking a flat back in their original rural community, finding a job as a nursing assistant, and establishing a new relationship with a male friend. The younger son is still living with his father, and finds it hard to maintain contact with his mother, because of his father's violent reaction to her actions. Mother and elder son still keep in touch with her mother.

An Extract from the A Family Transcript (Observer: Arlene Vetere)

Tom (father),went upstairs to have a bath and I went into the kitchen to watch Sal (mother) prepare the evening meal. Pete (elder son) joined us. We were having plaice for tea and Sal was frying it. Pete said he didn't like fish and wanted something done separately. Sal expressed surprise at the fact that he didn't like it but Pete insisted with a very tired air that she knew that he didn't like fish. John (younger son) popped his head round the door and said he would be having fish for tea as he quite liked it. Whilst Sal was cooking, she was told by Pete about an open evening they would be having at the Group next Wednesday evening, when parents would be welcome along with past members of the Group. Pete didn't explain too clearly just who was invited and Sal asked for clarification. He made one or two half-hearted attempts to explain and then flung his hands up in the air, exclaiming that his mother was stupid and that she got on his nerves. He stomped out of the kitchen. Sal looked at me and laughed and said she was only trying to find out what was going on. She is going into hospital for one of her check-ups next Wednesday and tends to get rather 'pulled around' by the various tests and expects to feel tired in consequence. However, as she likes to go out she will try and make the effort and ask Tom to come with her as she doesn't like going out in the evening without him.

Pete came back in and Sal asked him once again if he'd had dinner at his Nan's house. He said he had, but that it was at lunch time and was only a salad and she'd already asked him that before. He was now hungry as it was 6 o'clock and he couldn't understand why she continued to ask him. His lack of patience when dealing with his mother is most noticeable, especially as he demands patience when the interaction is the other way round. Sal began to dish up the peas and potatoes into separate vegetable dishes and asked Pete to carry them through into the dining room where she had laid the table. Pete obliged. Tom came down feeling refreshed after his bath, and commenting that his shirt was fitting rather tightly. He has put on a little weight since I last stayed with them. He leaned on the fridge and started telling me what sort of day he'd had, even though Sal made it obvious she was trying to get us all out of the kitchen and into the dining room to eat our meal. There were only four places laid at the table. I sat in my place and Pete sat next to me. Tom sat at the head of the table leaving one space for Sal. I asked whether John was eating with us and neither Pete nor his father seemed to know. Sal came in, depositing the plates of fish in front of us. The fish was fresh and delicious and looked very appetising. Sal sat down and we helped ourselves to the vegetables. John was not present and no one commented on his absence. John then called out from the living room, asking Sal if she'd prepared his tea. She called back, saying he'd said he didn't want any. I was surprised, not having heard John say this. John insisted that he'd asked for fish. Tom had two plaice on his plate and offered to give him one. No, John didn't want his food. Tom again called him, telling him to fetch a plate. John didn't want his father's fish, asserting that he'd asked for some, whereas Sal maintained he hadn't asked and must therefore go without.

While we ate, Tom entertained us with stories of his flights to Italy, made during his sheep selling days; telling of the food and wine and the people. He has led a varied life. When we'd finished eating, Sal got up to fetch the apple pie and ice cream for dessert. John saw the ice cream and called out for some. Sal told him he would have to come and get it. John took a plateful back into the lounge. A lot of banter at the dinner table revolved around the subject of fattening food as Tom and Sal mustn't eat this or that. The sugar on top of the pie attracted Tom's attention. John poked his head round the door while we were eating to see how we were getting on, then went back into the lounge. Sal said it was wrong that John was not eating with them; it was rude. Tom felt he ought to sit up at the table even though not eating. Pete said we'd been there for 27 minutes and John would have to sit at the table for the same amount of time. The parents felt he shouldn't be allowed to get away with not sitting with them.

I helped Sal clear the table and wash up. Pete and Tom came to chat while we did this. There was a large brown envelope on the kitchen table. It was lying under some dirty dishes. Pete noticed this and picked it up, commenting that it was all greasy. John came in and was cross because the envelope contained one of his school folders. Pete picked it up gingerly by the corner, held it up and then thrust it at John telling him to throw it away. John wasn't going to because he hadn't made it greasy. Pete denied having done it and peremptorily told him to dispose of it.

John then wanted his mother to cook him some scrambled eggs. She raised her voice and told him quite loudly that as he hadn't wanted to eat his dinner, he certainly wasn't going to have any scrambled eggs now. Tom said he'd cook them. John raised his voice and said, 'I don't want your scrambled eggs!' His mother said he must learn to come to the table and eat with them if he wants food. John became very agitated, shouting, and then left the room.

The B Family

Background

The family live in a three-bedroom, semi-detached, privately owned house on a pleasant estate, in a semi-rural setting. Previously, they had emigrated abroad in order to make a new start. They returned because emigration itself did not work. They then set up a business, which, in its turn, failed. Thus when the observer met the family there was an air of failure which permeated their lives.

Members

The father (38) is a long-distance lorry driver; the mother (36) a part-time shop assistant and housewife; there are three male children (ages 15, 12, and 9) and a female child (8).

Presenting problem

The eldest son was referred to a child guidance clinic for refusal to attend school.

Observation and analysis

One observer (AV) visited on one occasion, for seven days. The family was described in terms of structural mapping, positive and negative affect, sociometric relation-ships, lag sequential analysis, and intra-observer reliability.

Family relationships: Structural Theory

This is a flat, bland family group, with little emotional expressiveness. The sense of failure lies like a depressive blanket on the parents. The mother has no self-esteem and appears inadequate and undermined. She had an unhappy love affair before meeting her husband which has led to 'open' unresolved secrets. The father accuses the mother of marrying him on the rebound; this is the family 'dance', whereby the father is asking: 'Do you want me for myself?'

The oldest son has a long history of referral for school refusal, but now he is 15, his interests are work-oriented. One reason for his absences from school is the informal work experience he gets by going on long trips with his father. In structural terms, it is the daughter who carries the emotional expression for the group and discharges it. Her tempestuous behaviour is a focus of concern for the mother, away from the troubled marital relationship. The mother is affiliated with the second child more than any other; he and his mother are somewhat separate from the strong male group of father, eldest and youngest son. The daughter is indulged in by everyone.

Family relationships: Distance Regulation Theory

The size of the family did not allow for personal privacy. But although apparently overcrowded, frustration as a result of proximity is seldom realized, let alone expressed. Temporal focus is in the past, which is facilitated by reference to the family photographic album, while the future holds uncertainties and threats of further failure. The identified patient's problems go back ten years. Many activities underline the family's synchrony of action. Games of a wide variety are shared by everybody and provide the opportunity for energy release including quite riotous emotional expression, and frank invasion of personal space. Such bouts would end through fun turning into hurt. The daughter's explosive behaviour controlled the relationship of the parents; this power was sustained by virtue of its ability to draw attention away from the parents' own problems. Having a 'good family' was an important theme, particularly because both spouses saw their own parents as having become estranged.

Family relationships: Choice-Exchange Theory

The daughter has taken over from the eldest son, whose 'pathology' originally offered the mother a chance to show affection and support. The tempestuous outbursts of the daughter, apart from being beneficial in uniting the parents on an external issue, are more tolerable than the effort involved in facing up to marital conflict. The male grouping allows opportunities for gender role identification at the cost of keeping the father away from the mother; this grouping is balanced by the mother's relationship with the second son. The daughter is the link between the groupings.

Subsequent history

The eldest son has now married. He and his father have a successful lorry business. The parents also have a thriving small shop which the mother manages. The other children help in the shop in their spare time. The parents' relationship now seems more stable. Three years ago the mother left to escape from the family; when she returned, she and the husband were able to discuss their problems. This reconciliation was brought about when the father contacted one of the observers and asked her to help the family.

Two Extracts from the B Family Transcript (Observer: Arlene Vetere)

Extract 1

When Jimmy (youngest son) came down we all sat around the board and started to play. Linda (daughter) and Paul (second son) explained the rules to me, asking if I'd understood and I vaguely thought I did. The game proceeded smoothly at first but then an argument broke out between Linda and Jimmy, inevitably. They argued about a particular move and Jimmy said he wouldn't play so Linda grabbed his playing piece and said, alright, don't play. Vera (mother) put it back, saying it was up to Jimmy whether he played or not. Linda took it again and threw one of the playing pieces at Jimmy. He left in a huff. He disappeared for about half an hour. Meanwhile, back at the New Faces board, Linda and Paul were getting quite hysterical. I had them both subjecting me to a verbal and physical onslaught. I tolerated it as best I could but it reached a pitch where I had to ignore Linda's overtures and physically remove her from my lap and set her on the floor. Vera eventually noticed and told Linda to move away from me and leave me alone. The game seemed to drag on interminably, with no one able to win. Linda eventually cheated and she was declared the winner. At one stage in the game, Linda had to pay some of her money to her mother. She called Vera a pig, pouted and hid her face behind a pillow, fell all over me, fell over the board scattering the pieces, etc. This game was based on a TV talent show and required the players to sing, mime, impersonate, tell jokes, etc. and was quite funny when conducted in an orderly manner. Linda would carry her act to extremes, getting in people's way and knocking things over, etc. Vera made no comment. Paul spent most of the time giggling hysterically. He has started to touch me, putting his head in my lap or his arm on my shoulder. When Vera was penalized, Paul would feel sorry for her and want her to cheat to get ahead. This annoyed her. She said she wouldn't play if he insisted on doing it, it was only a game, she didn't mind losing and wanted to play properly. Jimmy came back with his lorries and climbed on to the coffee table and started to drive them over our playing cards, telling Paul to move out of the way. The game was abandoned because it degenerated. Linda continued to show off. Vera told them it was time for bed.

Extract 2

Linda came in. She spotted me first and gave me a quick smile, then opened the French window, leaned round to where Vera was at the sink and shouted, pig, sticking out her tongue and 'blowing a raspberry'. You forgot to meet me from school, she shouted. Oh dear, replied Vera, in a conciliatory tone, I'm so sorry, I forgot. You're a pig, shouted Linda, you're horrible. I hate you, you don't like me. She dumped her school bag on the floor and sat opposite me. As she undid her coat she continued to call Vera a pig and a cow. Vera twice approached her in appeasement by apologising or trying to laugh her out of it. As she touched her, Linda screamed, get off, I don't care, I don't want you. The tirade of verbal abuse continued. Jimmy came in from school, told Linda to shut up, and went to hang his coat in the closet. Vera mainly ignored Linda, occasionally interjecting with, I know, I'm sorry. Linda then went into the lounge where the abuse still reached us in the kitchen. Jimmy came down with two pairs of old jeans that needed patching at the knees. He was going to attempt it himself. He started to cut up one pair as patchwork for the second pair. Jimmy didn't seem much disturbed by Linda's behaviour, grinning at me and saying, she's noisy isn't she? He told me she's always like this, though not in front of her father. The abuse continued and Vera became increasingly distressed. Linda appeared in the doorway and threw a pack of playing cards over the floor. Her tear stained face was twisted and angry. She demanded a drink, calling, missus, come here, I want you.

The W1 Family

Background

The family lived in a small, crowded, three-bedroom, semi-detached council house, on a run-down estate, in a semi-rural setting. This has been their home for all their married life. They have no means of independent transport; their life is focused on their own life and their immediate community. Little interest is expressed in events in the outside world; when the TV is watched, the programmes do not include current affairs or news.

Members

The father (42) is a bar manager in a local hotel; the mother (42) sells door to door cosmetics and is a housewife; there are five boys (14, 13, 12, 8, and 5).

Presenting problem

The child of 13 was referred to a child guidance clinic for refusal to attend school.

Observation and analysis

One observer (AV) visited on two occasions, for seven days on each occasion. The family was described in terms of structural mapping, positive and negative affect, sociometric relationships, lag sequential analysis, and intra-observer reliability.

Family relationships: Structural Theory

The father is peripheral and unable to maintain effective control and discipline within the family. His job makes him unavailable as a male model for the children, and he is often denigrated by the mother to the children. The identified patient is a powerful child who dominates his brothers. He is a companion to his mother, helps with shopping and housework, and assists in selling cosmetics. The alliance between him and his mother helps to maintain distance between the parents. The mother is overweight and unfit to the extent that she cannot climb the stairs without great exertion, and thus she welcomes any assistance her son provides, given the domestic burdens of raising a large family.

Family relationships: Distance Regulation Theory

Space is a crucial concept for this family, which is chaotic and unregulated. Several people live in a small house, but only one, the identified patient, has his own bedroom. He barricades himself in the room with the aid of the furniture whenever he is asked to attend school. The appeals are made by his father, standing in the hallway, who, in vain, shifts between entreaty and demands. The 8-year-old child has no space and no recognition; he follows other family members like a lost spaniel, to no avail. Cupboards and freezer are inaccessible because possessions are stacked everywhere. The family is asynchronous in some respects; for example, food is eaten at any time and anywhere. In other respects, in spite of large age differences, bedtime and rising are common, except for the father who arrives home from work when others are asleep. The 5-year-old sleeps in the marital bed. All affection is channelled toward this child, described as 'the baby', and 'the gift from heaven', who is still in nappies at night and still drinks from a bottle. His nocturnal enuresis wets the marital bed. The mother supports her second son's power and refuses to follow the father's demands. Her rationale is that any interference by her in the process of discipline would lead to her losing her temper. The family's goals or ambitions for the future are never discussed; they are frozen in space and time, keeping all the children as near as possible to childhood.

Family relationships: Choice-Exchange Theory

The key beneficiaries in this family are the identified patient and the 'baby'. The former is powerful and bullying, abusing others (including his mother) both verbally and physically. The latter is the focus for affection in the family. There is little cost to the identified patient except in two ways: the negative affect and distance he provokes in his siblings and peer group in school, and his physical condition. In identifying with his overweight mother he too is well above his appropriate weight by some 80 per cent. The father and the 8-year-old son sacrifice most and for little return; the father's sadness and despair is moderated by the love and affection he shares with the 'baby'. No doubt, when this child goes to school, there will be advantage in a further pregnancy.

Two Extracts from the W1 Family Transcript (Observer: Arlene Vetere)

Extract 1

I arrived at 7.15 a.m. . . . Philip (second eldest son) had locked himself in his bedroom, something he has been doing for a year, according to his parents. He pushes a small bureau behind the door, which Graham (father) tells me effectively prevents him from entering. I surmised that the performance was for my benefit. Monday is Graham's day off and he was to spend it in an effort to encourage Philip out of his room. . . . Graham came down after 8.00 a.m.; Susan (mother) had said he was having a lie-in. However, he informed us that Philip's behaviour had spoiled that and he must deal with Philip. All the while Graham tried to cajole Philip out of his room, alternating between this and an attempt at firmness, Susan calmly continued with the washing, seemingly unaware. She did not overtly indicate that she supported her husband's attempts, telling me that she would lose her temper if she went upstairs and hence stayed down. Graham's cajolery continued to the tune of: why are you in there? why are you playing up? what's wrong with you today? don't you like school? you're going to miss tennis. When Graham realized that Philip would not emerge, he and Susan decided he should ring the Group (special education unit) and inform James (teacher). However, James was the sole teacher at the Group that day and was unable to come and help the W1 family. James wanted to encourage the parents to deal with Philip alone as it is preferable that they learn to manage their own child rather than always relying on outside intervention. Graham went back upstairs and stood outside Philip's door continuing his lone dance of entreaty interspersed with moments of quasi-firmness, you come out now, enough of this nonsense. Unsuccessful, Graham came down. He openly expresses his worry and concern. Susan carried on with the washing. . . . I have not seen Philip this morning, I have been here a few hours and am already aware that Philip is a powerful child; his father stands powerless outside his bedroom door. The door that gives Philip space in this crowded home, so that three brothers share a cramped room and the youngest sleeps in the parents' room. . . . Susan remarked that it was inconvenient that Philip acted up today as she was hoping to make her cosmetic deliveries this evening and needed Philip's help. Further, Graham has been prevented from visiting his old and ailing mother. He usually takes Peter (youngest son) with him but doesn't feel he can leave just yet. . . . Graham went up to see if Philip was ready to emerge but was rebuffed with a cry of: shut-up, go away, I don't want to know you, leave me alone. . . . Graham went into the kitchen to wash and combed his hair down. He got Peter ready for a visit to his grandmother. . . . We heard some movement upstairs as Philip went into the bathroom. Susan wondered whether he would come down. Graham had known that Philip would come out as soon as he left for his mother's. He came downstairs and leaned against the lounge door. I acknowledged him. His mother asked him how he was, to which he responded, leave me alone, and went off into the kitchen. Susan looked at me and shrugged and commented that she hadn't said anything yet. He came back, wanting to know who had been touching the football cards. Susan explained that Donald (third eldest son) had sorted them out and Simon (fourth child) had taken some to school. Philip watched TV for half an hour before coming over to take an interest in Susan's activity. He had made her a stamp from his printing set so that she could stamp the back of each order form with her name and address. (On the way to the shops I noticed that he'd mended the front gate.) Philip has eased into a conversation with his mother. Neither of them has mentioned or alluded to his earlier behaviour.

Extract 2

Philip then had the notion of taking the paddling pool into the garden. Peter was ecstatic. . . . While in the kitchen, Philip discovered there was a leak in the pool. Susan reckoned she was unable to mend it because the plastic was wet. Oh, blimin' Hell, was his frustrated reply. Susan tried to seal the crack using some old glue. Philip watered the garden while he waited. Susan informed him that he was watering at the wrong time and ought to wait for the cool of the evening and that Graham would 'moan like mad' when he realized what he'd done. Philip said, oh, I'll kill him. I'll kill you if you get my washing wet, she replied. Her effort at mending was futile because she had run out of glue. You better not had, he shouted, go and buy some more, it's only 95p. No, she wouldn't and if he wanted any glue he would have to buy it with his own money. I'll kill you, I'll get you wet and I'll get your washing wet. He sprayed the water closer and closer to her. She got up and angrily replied, if you get me wet, you won't get any dinner. Use your own money to buy the glue. He didn't want to do that.

Martin (eldest son) came home and wanted a cup of tea but the hose was still attached to the cold water tap. He told Philip he was going to turn it off so that he could fill the kettle. Philip allowed it, albeit grudgingly. Martin and Susan watched through the window for Philip to turn the nozzle towards his face so that they could switch the water on. They waited but he didn't oblige. He grew impatient of waiting and picked up a stick and started banging on an old spin dryer. He demanded they turn the water on, threatening to soak the washing if they didn't and kill Peter if they didn't. Philip screamed that they could fill the kettle from the bathroom tap. Susan yelled back that he could put his hose through the bathroom window. She decided it would be prudent to gather in the washing. Martin was trying to reconnect the hosepipe to the tap and when the water flowed, Philip sprayed it in our direction, soaking us as he shouted. This was a childish display, over which Susan had no control and in fact, exacerbated. After receiving a drenching, she screamed at Martin to turn the water off, she'd had enough. The flow of water hesitated a moment then resumed with greater force. Philip was soaked now, Martin had drenched him. A woman from across the path was leaning on the fence, instructing Philip to shed his wet shirt. Oh, shut up you old bag, he told her. She continued to offer advice in spite of the insults. The hose had been disconnected so Philip picked up a container of water and threatened to tip it over Martin's shoes. Martin defended himself by holding the washing basket containing the clothes in front of him, but Philip still managed to soak his boots. Martin then threatened Philip with an equally dirty container of water. Susan intervened and stopped him. Martin protested his boots were wet and was told to go in and change.

Susan was talking to the woman about the ambulance that had called over the road earlier that day. Philip picked up a stick and banged it against the spin dryer, causing the two women to shout in order to be heard. Peter was hanging on the gate and the woman said, you're a good boy, aren't you?

Susan tried again, unsuccessfully, to mend the tear in the pool but the patch kept curling at the edges. Martin, Philip, and Peter who were crowded round, didn't help by jogging it. Martin was playing with Peter, Oh, I saved you from falling in, didn't I? and pretending to throw him in. Philip was resting his foot on the edge. Susan was screaming at them to stop and get out of the way. They were all screaming by now.

The P Family

Background

The family live in a two-bedroom, third-floor flat in a council housing complex in a small town. Only glimpses of the past have been revealed. The family at present consists of two members.

Members

The mother (52) is a housewife. The older two children are married and living away from home. The youngest child (14) is female.

Presenting problem

The daughter was referred to a child guidance clinic for refusal to attend school.

Observation and analysis

Two observers (AV and SR) visited on two occasions, each for five days, including weekends. The family was described in terms of structural mapping, positive and negative affect, sociometric relationships, lag sequential analysis, and inter-observer reliability.

Family relationships: Structural Theory

This is now a single parent family. Both members gain satisfaction largely from each other. Although an elder daughter lives elsewhere, she seeks constant support from her mother, as a result of a string of miscarriages and other misfortunes; regular contact is maintained by telephone. The younger daughter's dependency is context specific; away from her mother, at a special day centre for school refusers, she seems competent and socially poised, speaking for herself. But at home, the diffuse boundary between them is reflected in several ways: the mother 'knows' what she is thinking and feeling and speaks on her behalf; the mother does all her cleaning and tidying, monitors her health, toiletting, and all else.

Family relationships: Distance Regulation Theory

This family is isolated from the outside world. The daughter is not allowed to go out alone, for fear of meeting men. Journeys to and from school are by taxi, and the daughter is accompanied to the taxi or met at the taxi. The only contact with men is through a fundamentalist religious sect, which itself is well-bounded from the community at large. Within the home, there are few boundaries; there is no lock on the daughter's bedroom, which contains the only mirror in the home, and to which her mother must go to adjust her clothes and hair. The past is rarely mentioned (particularly aspects of marriage) and the future carries the threat that the daughter will grow up and leave. Religion is a powerful force in their lives; it determines what is watched on the TV and the church governs their entire social life. At home the daughter is locked into a particular mode of emotional expression, which includes whining, complaints about health and finnickiness about food and hygiene; negative affect that is not seen at school. The mother has the power in the home.

Family relationships: Choice-Exchange Theory

The mother's power is not total since it is manipulated by the daughter to gain attention and nurturance. Her mother is a doting servant as well as an emotional master. The cost to the daughter is separation from her peer group and outer society. Her independence is the price she pays to secure her mother's emotional security. By maintaining her daughter young and virginal (by separation from peers and by adhering to strong religious beliefs and practices) the mother ensures that sexual themes are kept well below the surface. Men and sex are distasteful.

An Extract from the P Family Transcript (Observer: Arlene Vetere)

Wyn (mother) woke me up at 7.10 a.m. with a cup of tea. I came into the kitchen to drink it. Lorraine (daughter) emerged from her bedroom in a pink nightie and headed off down towards the toilet. I shouted good morning Lorraine and received no answer. Her mother said oh that's very rude Lorraine. Lorraine shut the bathroom door. I went back into the lounge. Wyn popped her head round the door a few minutes later to say that Lorraine sent her apologies but her voice had gone. Apparently she wanted her mother to say good morning for her.

Wyn then went into the kitchen to make Lorraine's lunch box. She cut four slices of white bread and buttered them very carefully and meticulously. She ended up with four upturned bright yellow smiling faces. She grated some cheese over them, telling me that she mustn't put a lot as Lorraine would not eat it. She packed them. She put a rubber band around the box to secure it. She said she did try to think ahead on Saturday to have something but it just didn't seem to work out. She shouted out to Lorraine, do you want an apple dear? No. Do you want a banana? No. There was nothing wrong with the voice then.

A few minutes later, Lorraine entered the kitchen and I again said good morning. She kept her back to me and didn't answer. As she went out the door, Wyn commented that she was rude, Arlene (observer) had spoken to her. My voice has gone, she said, and I'm in too much of a hurry. She doesn't mean to be rude, Wyn assured me. I was somewhat puzzled then as to her change in behaviour. She remained closeted in her room for nearly three quarters of an hour and then emerged, dressed. She then went back into her room. Wyn asked what she wanted for breakfast. No reply. Do you want some toast, Lorraine? No. Do you want some beans? Yes. Wyn stooped into the fridge. She said it was like Old Mother Hubbard's cupboard. She took out a bowl of beans and heated them. She prepared some brown bread and butter. By now it was 7.50 a.m.

Lorraine entered the kitchen, perched on a stool near me. She took the bowl of beans in her hands and her mother put the plate of bread on her lap. There was a small teaspoon with the beans. This is no good. I can't manage with this. Wyn said she thought it would be alright. Lorraine nodded her head in dissent. Wyn opened the cutlery drawer and took out a dessert spoon. She took away the tea spoon. While dressing, Lorraine had been unable to find any underpants. Apparently she has six pairs and Wyn hasn't done any washing. Wyn looked at me and commented there was nothing to stop her rinsing a pair or a pair of tights. In the next breath she excused the girl, saying she hasn't been up to it, she hasn't been feeling well. While Lorraine ate her breakfast, Wyn packed her school bag. She separated the books and put the flask and the lunch box in. Lorraine wanted some clean hankies as there was no more toilet roll. She did wish to take the remainder of the toilet roll but Wyn would not allow it. Wyn went off and returned with two clean rags. She explained, if you fold them like this, no one will know what they are. She packed those into the bag and then took one out, thinking Lorraine ought to have one on her person. She suggested she put it up her sleeve. Lorraine wasn't keen. She thought it looked ugly. Her mother urged her to do it for now, dear, so she did.

She was struggling to eat the bread and butter and her mother encouraged her to finish it. She eventually managed. Laura (a schoolfriend) is coming to tea. Lorraine had not managed to tidy her room. She asked Wyn if she could sweep in there as there were bits on the floor. Could she please also rearrange the ornaments, putting them in their allotted places. She said she didn't have enough time last night and she didn't have enough time this morning. Oh, I also haven't made my bed, can you do that for me? Don't worry, Lorraine, I won't let you down. By now it was 8.00 a.m. Lorraine went into the hallway and picked up the toilet roll and dropped it. It unrolled like the Andrex dog commercial. She laughed. Her mother came out and laughed, tore off a bit and rolled up the rest. Lorraine disappeared into the bathroom with the hot water kettle to 'do' her face and brush her hair. At 8.10 a.m. she was still in there. Before entering the bathroom, Wyn suggested she hurry as the taxi was arriving at 8.15 a.m. Lorraine disagreed, no, it doesn't arrive until 8.20 a.m. Wyn insisted that it was 8.15 a.m. Lorraine protested that it was always late. Wyn said that doesn't matter. If they say 8.15 a.m. you must be ready for that time. Don't be obstinate, Lorraine, it just makes it awkward for me. Lorraine walked out with the kettle.

At 8.10 a.m. she was still in the bathroom. Wyn shouted out that she had five minutes left. At one point Lorraine coughed and this arrested Wyn in full conversational flow. She then continued talking. The time crept onwards and still Lorraine had not emerged from the bathroom. Two minutes, said her mother. One minute, said her mother. Lorraine came out at 8.15 a.m. They had a look out the window and realized the taxi was there. Lorraine hadn't combed her hair which was very tangled. She rushed into the kitchen, pushing past her mother quite brusquely and threw a tissue away. She picked up her bag and her anorak and panicked. She had had an hour and a quarter in which to get ready. Wyn, who was still in her dressing gown, accompanied her downstairs. Will you come with me, mum, she said. Oh, you can't, realizing Wyn wasn't dressed. Wyn reassured her, it's alright dear, I'll come down with you. Lorraine took a hair brush with her, intending to brush her hair at school.

The T Family

Background

The family live in an old but modernized, two-bedroom, terraced house on a busy street, in a large port. There is an attractive and sunny rear garden with an aviary. At the time we stayed with them, there was no presenting problem. Previously, nocturnal enuresis in the younger child had brought the family to a child guidance clinic.

Members

The father (34) is a craftsman; the mother (32) is a part-time domestic cleaner and housewife; there are two daughters of 11 and 6.

Observation and analysis

Two observers (AV and SR) visited on one occasion each, for five days, including a weekend. The family was described in terms of structural mapping, positive and negative affect, sociometric relationships, lag sequential analysis, and inter-observer reliability.

Family relationships: Structural Theory

The spouses have a strong affectional bond, characterized by much playfulness. But the mother's constant need to demonstrate their love to the observer, seemed to reflect some possible fragility in the relationship. The executive subsystem conducted its business well away from the children, in a way which reflected a clear boundary. The siblings interacted well and showed mutual affection; they shared common interests and were well bounded. However, the mother was inclined to intrude on their relationship, to seek to protect them from the responsibilities of adulthood, frequently saying that she wished them to enjoy their childhood and remain young as long as possible. While the father expressed a different view, his behaviour was tolerant of his wife's beliefs. Conflict was generally avoided by following the mother's wishes. All the family expressed affection openly and freely.

Family relationships: Distance Regulation Theory

The boundaries in this family were clear and functional. The children mixed freely with their peers, and their friends were welcome visitors. The family's lifestyle was structured, well-ordered, and predictable, without being stifling. The mother had strong views about parenthood, motherhood, childrearing, and conforming to social norms about family and personal behaviour. This was a synchronous family in which each member, nevertheless, had freedom and autonomy in their relationships with the outside world. The mother attended church sometimes with the children but never with her husband, who was tolerant of her religious views.

Family relationships: Choice-Exchange Theory

This was a balanced system in which costs and benefits were evenly distributed among family members. Positive affect was a major source of exchange. The only member to experience cost was the younger child who was labelled (in our view inappropriately) as hyperactive.

Four Extracts from the T Family Transcript (Observer: Arlene Vetere)

Extract 1

Gemma (younger daughter) was still playing with the dolls. She showed me her legs and told me she didn't have to go to the hospital to have her knees straightened any more. She was jumping around a lot so I asked her if she was warm. No, I sometimes get cold hands but that's because I'm hyperactive, she said. It was said so matter-of-factly that I wanted to laugh.

Extract 2

When he'd finished, Tel (father) climbed down and went in to spin the next lot of clothes. He put his hands into the sink and flicked water over Lesley (mother), then over the girls (daughters). They ran back into the bathroom and retaliated by flicking it over him. There was much laughter. When Tel leaned over the spin drier, Lesley bit his backside. He yelped and ran out into the kitchen, saying, ooh, she bit me, she bit me! He then ran back in to claim a penalty of a kiss. Money dropped out of one of the jeans and he said, finders keepers. That's mine protested Lesley. She pinched his leg to get it back, all the while watching me to see if I was looking.

Extract 3

Lesley asked Gemma how she wanted her hair done. Gemma wished to have it down today. Alright said Lesley and proceeded to comb it out for her. She then started to clip it back behind her ears. Gemma protested, no, I want it down. I want it like this, she reaffirmed. Lesley insisted she have it clipped back and continued. She held the piece of hair up as she said it. Gemma twisted round and round, repeating, no mummy, no mummy, I don't want it, I don't want it. She began to cry. Lesley persisted and clipped the hair back. I'll run away, wailed Gemma. No you won't, stand still, repeated her mother. She then started to clip back the other side. Gemma continued to moan and cry, insisting she didn't want it done like that. After giving the child a choice, Lesley insisted she conform to her wishes. Then Lesley suggested, do you want it up in a pony's tail? By this time, Gemma was quite tearful. She had been sulking previously because she wanted a whole orange and had been told she could only have half. Mary (older daughter) walked in with an apple. Gemma said that's not fair, that's the one I wanted. Her mother told her not to sulk. Mary walked over to the work top and cut the apple in half. Lesley came over and commented, you haven't cut that properly, that's not a proper half. She proceeded to make amends and offered half to Gemma. She hung her head and didn't answer. Lesley proffered it again. Gemma still didn't answer. Alright she said, I'll have it. She looked at me (observer) and grinned before putting it on the work top. A few minutes later, Gemma got up and came over. She poked her hand through the trellis and took the apple. Lesley was still asking her how she wanted her hair done. In a pony's tail? Gemma would not answer. She would just go, mmm, twisting her head and gathering her hair in her hands to indicate her wishes. Lesley said that unless you ask me properly, I won't do it. This interchange continued, with Gemma holding her hair up in a pony's tail and Lesley refusing to do anything unless she was asked properly. Gemma stamped out of the room and went upstairs crying. Lesley turned to me and predicted, you wait, in ten minutes she'll be down and apologizing.

Mary had taken a catalogue out of the cupboard and was leafing through it. She seemed relatively unconcerned by what was happening. Gemma came down a few minutes later still somewhat tearful and still refusing to ask properly. She continued to hold her hair and offer it to her mum. Lesley stood her ground and said no. Gemma sat down and hung her head. A few minutes later she got up, walked over to Lesley and whispered in her ear. And then what do you say, queried Lesley. Please, I heard her mumble. Then what do you say? Mummy. Alright. So Lesley calmly combed her hair and tied it up in a pony tail, with the ribbon that Mary had previously fetched when asked. Then Gemma gave her mother a cuddle, burying her head in Lesley's breasts, who smacked her playfully on the bottom. You're a naughty girl, she said, you know you are. No I'm not, said Gemma, smacking her in reply. Lesley threateningly held her hand over Gemma's bottom, but didn't smack her. Mary said you should smack her, you smack me. Gemma wandered off to finish eating her apple. I always win, Lesley said to me, I always win, don't I Mary? Mary continued to leaf through the catalogue.

Extract 4

Gemma was getting irritable and kept making demands on Mary. When Mary didn't comply, she screeched in a high pitch. Lesley commented that she was getting irritable because she was tired. Then Gemma picked up her magic stick and demonstrated how to use it. Mary wanted a turn and Gemma irritably refused, it's my turn. Lesley looked at Mary sternly, saying, it's hers. Mary then said, alright, I'm going in, asserting herself. She stomped off. You do that, said Lesley, you go in and sulk alone. Gemma calmed down and demonstrated to her mother the working of the magic stick. Gemma then said, alright, now it's Mary's turn and went indoors to find her. Mary had esconsed herself in the lavatory and refused to come out. Gemma coaxed, come on Mary, you can play, come on you can play, it's your turn. Lesley followed her in, leave her to sulk on her own, she went in on her own and she'll come out on her own. Gemma wouldn't accept that, insisting in an irritable voice that Mary come and play with her, it was her turn to use the stick. Gemma's rate of crying increased. Lesley said she had to go to bed, she was tired, she'd had a long hard day. Why does she have to go to bed, asked Mary, who had emerged, she doesn't have Sunday school tomorrow. It doesn't matter, replied Lesley, she's miserable and she needs to go to bed early. I won't be miserable, persuaded Gemma, mummy, I won't be miserable, please let me stay up, she pleaded. No, firmly, you're going to bed early, both of you. Why me? Mary was astonished. There was no reply from Lesley. Mary fetched her doll and started to feed it. Gemma fetched hers and sat over in the corner sniffling quietly.

The R Family

Background

The family live in an old, dilapidated and damp rented house, with three bedrooms, in a town where unemployment is high. This is the mother's second marriage and the husband's first; there are four children and he is the father of the youngest. The first marriage ended because of marital violence. The wife is still preoccupied with fear of physical attack. This fear is accentuated by uncertainty as to whether the eldest daughter will return to live with her father, the encounters which this entails, and the family's ambivalence over the outcome.

Members

Mrs R is a housewife (34) and her husband (28) unskilled and unemployed. There are four daughters (14, 12, 8, and 4).

Presenting problem

The family were referred to a family guidance clinic because of their complaints about the unmanageable behaviour of the eldest daughter who runs away from home.

Observation and analysis

Two observers (AV and CJ) visited on two occasions, each for five days, including weekends. The family was described in terms of structural mapping, positive and negative affect, sociometric relationships, lag sequential analysis, inter-observer reliability, and family repertory grids.

Family relationships: Structural Theory

The spouse subsystem is rigidly bounded and the children have little access to their parents. This rigid boundary is reinforced because while the children are at school both parents are together. The two youngest children live in a world of their own and are strongly affiliated; parenting of this pair is shared between the mother and the second eldest daughter, who has many household duties. The oldest daughter is peripheral and isolated; she identifies with her original father and this helps to create antagonism towards her from her mother. The clinic wish to retain this child in the home, although the parents join in wanting her to be placed in care; in discussion of such issues the mother is the spokesperson. There is conflict between the oldest child and her mother, and she accuses her younger sister of currying favour ('mother's pet'), although she refuses to win such favours by doing housework.

Family relationships: Distance Regulation Theory

The family is poor. Observation was carried out in the winter. Only one room is heated. All the family spend most of their time in the living room; the TV is constantly switched on. In the house, therefore, the family is always in close proximity. But the parents do go out for social occasions, and treat themselves to special dishes which are not shared by the children. Because the TV is a focus of attention, little overt energy is expressed. Meals are not always taken together. Mrs R makes most of the executive decisions; the father expresses his power by switching between TV channels whether others wish it or not. The husband looks younger than his age and his wife looks older than her age. There are several items in the house with sexual connotations, such as porno films and playing cards with nudes. Survival is an important goal. Parenting is not a priority. The future revolves around decisions relating to the identified patient's future; the past and the earlier marriage are a major theme or concern in the mother's reminiscences.

Family relationships: Choice-Exchange Theory

All the children pay a cost in terms of their mother's preoccupation with her husband. But the largest cost is borne by the oldest child who is a scapegoat; she represents her father and the past, has been labelled with his unpleasant characteristics, and has an ambiguous relationship with her stepfather. All these factors make the eldest daughter an object of her mother's dislike. The youngest siblings provide each other with mutual support. The second daughter gains her mother's affection and approval by her role of housewife and mother (to the younger children). While the mother gains some reward from her relationship with a younger man, she has to put great effort into it and is not wholly secure. The husband is a key beneficiary in the group because he gains a great deal for very little effort.

Five Extracts from the R Family Transcript (Observer: Arlene Vetere)

Extract 1

Yvette (mother) spotted Marilyn (eldest daughter) coming home from school. Look at her, walking with her coat unbuttoned. She doesn't feel the cold. Dilly Daydream she called her. Bet she'll come in the back door predicted Yvette. Marilyn then came into the room and sat down. She smiled at me (observer) and we introduced ourselves. She handed her parents a letter from school saying that it was of a trip to Belgium and she wanted to be allowed to go. She said it only cost £15. Her mum looked surprised and Keith (stepfather) opened the letter. Fifteen pounds was the deposit, £85 was the correct amount of money. They said there was no way they could afford it given that they needed £95 a week to survive and they only received £65 a week in Social Security. Marilyn's response was to hang her head and say nothing. Keith didn't explain this to the girl but angrily told her and his response was that she was crazy to think they could afford to support this. Yvette had some sympathy for the child and her wish to go on a school trip. Mary (second eldest daughter) who had come in by now said, well I couldn't go to Devon so therefore I don't see why she should go to Belgium. Marilyn kept her head down. Yvette tried to smooth waters by saying that perhaps not all the children would be able to afford to go, and it was silly of school to expect parents to be able to afford so much money so that she wouldn't be the only one, anyway she laughed, if you are they might take you anyway for free. Keith was still angry and said to me, look at her. Look at the hate on her face. I didn't see any such thing on her face. I just saw a disappointed child with her head down, embarrassed in front of a visitor. Marilyn repacked her school bag. She had unpacked her tape recorder which was a Christmas present and her stepfather, Keith, had checked out if it worked, because apparently they think that when kids take things to school they sometimes come back broken. He checked it out and it worked, and so she repacked her bag and got up and left the room. When she left, Yvette said to Keith, well she'll be like that for the rest of the evening now. . . . We then went upstairs and I was given a tour of all the bedrooms. . . . We then went into the second bedroom where there are four bunk beds, with Marilyn sitting in her school uniform between them with her head virtually between her knees. Look at this, said Yvette. What are you doing up here getting cold, it's daft; and Keith again interjected with, you know we can't give you £100 to go on holiday, £85 to go plus £15 spending money. You know we can't afford it. Marilyn said nothing.

Extract 2

Mary spent the rest of her evening in the living room curled up next to her mother on the settee with Marilyn remaining in the other chair. Marilyn has an endearing way of looking at her mother slightly open-mouthed as if from underneath her fringe. She's always looking for approval and she initiates conversations constantly with her mother who responds to her. At one stage Marilyn said that Mary was her mother's pet. Yvette immediately denied this saying, that's not true, is it Mary? Mary said, that's right. It's not true. She said, I have to do all the work, put the girls to bed, and I make the coffee, and you don't do anything Marilyn. Well, I still think it's true, said Marilyn. Well it's not, said Yvette.

Extract 3

Yvette told Marilyn to hurry up as the neighbours were waiting. At this point they rang the bell. Marilyn started flapping around looking for her coat and left the neighbours at the door. Yvette commented on this saying, you know, she hasn't got a clue. She leaves people on the doorstep. Keith said she was ignorant. They often make very negative comments about her. Earlier this morning her mother described her as spiteful, and said that she used to threaten to beat up the younger children if they didn't do as she said, but she only found out about this second hand a few weeks after it had apparently occurred. The neighbours breezed in full of health and vigour. They had a dog with them. I was introduced to Jane and Derek. Jane vigorously shook my hand. Derek smiled at me. They didn't look surprised at my presence. They discussed the weather and the fact that they were going for a walk. As they left Keith shouted, and don't forget to dump Marilyn. What? said Jane. Dump Marilyn, shouted Keith.

Extract 4

Mary spotted Marilyn walking up the road. Here she comes, she said. Keith leaned round and looked out the window. Dilly Drip, he commented. Here, said Yvette, I forgot to tell you what she did this morning. She swopped bags with Mary and she was going to go to school with a huge carrier bag. Keith looked again. Well, she hasn't got Mary's bag now, he said. No, no. I told them to swop back, said Yvette. Marilyn came in. She was not greeted. She stood in the doorway. Look at her socks, said Becky (third daughter). They were covered in mud. How did you do that, asked her mother? Well, if you had to walk home the way I did you'd get covered in mud. Don't walk that way, said Keith sharply. Go and take them off, advised Yvette, and make yourself some toast, she said, as Marilyn disappeared through the door.

Extract 5

When I got back into the lounge Keith and Marilyn were engaged in a particularly rough version of rough and tumble play. Yvette warned Marilyn, stop it now, she said, because you'll end up getting hurt like you always do. Marilyn continued to aggravate Keith by pushing up against him, and he grabbed her by the hair and leaned forward into her face, and said, stop it now. Are you going to stop it? She continued *to giggle and he pulled her hair harder and eventually she submitted and said she'd stop, and then sat on the carpet.*

Three Extracts from the R Family Transcript (Observer: Claire Jolly)

Extract 1

Mary asked Keith for the paper and he said she'd have to wait. When he finished reading it he handed it over his shoulder and she took it saying, thank you. She then proceeded to read the newspaper quietly. Keith had looked up the programme timetable for television, and he changed channels. But the programme's only half finished, said Becky. Yes, said Jilly (youngest daughter), Daddy's always doing that. Yvette agreed with her that Daddy would always change the programme over when he felt like it, regardless of what anyone else wanted. Keith said nothing.

Extract 2

Marilyn put her head round the door and said she was going out. Yvette screamed at her, but your hair's wet. You're not going out like that. Marilyn said she'd put her hood on. Yvette then screamed at her again, and do your blouse up before you go anywhere. She stared at her. I (observer) couldn't see Marilyn who was in the hall. Yvette then screamed at her again, and if I get any back from you, you'll get a punch, OK? Marilyn said, yes and disappeared.

Extract 3

Mary came into the room. She looked round the door to see who was in and started to go out saying it was OK. Keith said, oi! what do you want? She came in and said, I wish you hadn't given Marilyn the 'Captain Beaky' record. She keeps playing it all the time. He said, and what else? She said, nothing, and went out. He shouted, oi! come back here. She put her head back round the door. He said, what did you want? She said, just to tell you that. Oh no you didn't, he said. There was something else. You're always looking round to see who's here first. No I'm not, said Mary, and she went back out. Keith called her back again. Come right here, he said. She went up to him. He grabbed her by the arm, twisted it behind her back, and pulled her down across his lap. He grabbed her hair with his other hand, and pulled it back. Now you tell me what you wanted, he said. She squealed and protested that she didn't want anything. He pulled her hair harder, and she said, ouch! you're hurting me. Yvette said, Keith, let her go. He held on for a few more moments and then let her go. Yvette said, now off you go upstairs, to Mary, and thump him first. Mary made to thump Keith, and he made to thump her back. They both giggled, and she squealed and ran to the door.

The G Family

Background

The family live in a privately owned, three-bedroom, semi-detached house, in a quiet cul-de-sac in a small town. The mother has been married before, but there were no children from the first marriage. Her first husband had a severe illness and a tendency to violent behaviour. Her courtship with her second husband was clandestine; Mr G was already 40 when they met and had lived with his parents.

Members

Mr G (50) is a self-employed craftsman; Mrs G (44) is a housewife, and works in bars on a freelance basis. There are two boys (10 and 8).

Presenting problem

Referral was made to the family guidance clinic because of the elder son's disruptive behaviour in the home and the parents' inability to control or manage his behaviour.

Observation and analysis

Two observers (AV and CJ) visited on two occasions, each for five days, including weekends. The family was described in terms of structural mapping, positive and negative affect, sociometric relationships, lag sequential analysis, inter-observer reliability, and repertory grids.

Family relationships: Structural Theory

The spouses behave warmly to one another, without open expression of affection. The father was facing middle age when the children were born, and neither parent had prior experience of children. The first child was born under conditions of medical mismanagement and the parents report his behaviour as being difficult from the outset. Their general practitioner informed them that difficult births lead to difficult children. Parental behaviour in the context of discipline is erratic. Most decisions in the home are made by the mother. Mrs G admits to the observers that she dislikes her elder son and shows him no affection; he has an affiliation with his father because they share a love of carpentry. The younger son is favoured by both parents. The siblings do not cooperate, their relationship is fraught and conflictual, and they tend to live independently.

Family relationships: Distance Regulation Theory

The elder child is for most contexts branded as a source of problems and held at a distance. Father threatens to distance himself from the family by leaving home, unless his son makes amends for his behaviour. However, the mother has a fear of physical anger and in her turn threatens to leave should the father seek to use physical correction of their son. The family are not bounded by time and each member has his/her autonomous activity both in work and play. While the elder child is a focus for negative affect, there is plenty of positive energy within the home. Mother and elder son are a focus of power.

Family relationships: Choice-Exchange Theory

The younger son is the winner, and he can do no wrong. For little effort he achieves considerable reward. The older son, conversely, can do no right and his only source of reward is to achieve the creation of distress in others. However, both boys seem to perform adequately in school, although the older boy has poor relationships with peers. The scapegoating mechanisms are difficult to locate in rewards in the form of the avoidance of deeper concerns. The parents seem to have a functional relationship (albeit not overtly affectionate), and have considerable autonomy; however, their child's poor behaviour is sustained through inadequate and inconsistent parenting. Nevertheless, it is clear that Mr G had no prior relationships before marriage and that Mrs G has had some unfortunate relationships.

Two Extracts from the G Family Transcript (Observer: Arlene Vetere)

Extract 1

Bob (younger son) fetched his mini pocket game, putting it on the dining table between Barbara (mother) and Paul (father), and emptied out the batteries. He asked Paul if he could go into his treasure box to get the new batteries. Paul consented and Bob tipped the batteries onto the worktop. They're mine, said John (elder son). No, they're not, said Barbara. They are mine, said John. I found them. No you didn't, said Barbara. I bought them. I found them in that bag, she continued. You liar, he said. They were packed away when we moved, said Barbara. They were in some lampshades, said John. It doesn't matter, said Barbara. We packed everything away, and I bought them for your game that you broke. Accidentally, John shouted. Well, Barbara looked unconvinced. Anyway, John said, Bob's broken three digital watches. The last time, said Barbara, he got in the bath with it, looking at me (observer). That was an accident, John said. We all do that. It was an accident when I broke the game, said John. Well, I don't know, said Barbara. It was liquid, and you could see all the liquid inside it. You shouldn't have told them that at the Clinic (Child Guidance Clinic), said John. It caused a lot of trouble. Paul looked at him then, and John stomped off into the kitchen. He came back in and said, it's stealing, referring again to the batteries. He was ignored.

Extract 2

When we pulled into the driveway John produced a live match from his pocket, saying, I found a match. Is it dead, asked Barbara? No, said John. It's mine. Finders keepers. Let me have it, said Barbara. No, finders keepers. Let me have it, and she grabbed hold of his wrist. He twisted away from her, but she wrenched the match away from him. The rest of us got out of the car. There was no attempt at explaining why he wasn't allowed to have the match.

We filed into the living room. Paul switched on the fire because it was somewhat chilly. John went straight to the armchair and picked up his embroidery, and began to concentrate on it. Paul sat next to him on the other armchair. Barbara went into the kitchen to prepare the dinner. John addressed his father. She nicked my match. She didn't, said Paul. She nicked my match, affirmed John. You're not supposed to have matches, said Paul. I'll go and buy my own then, said John. That's right, said his father, you'll set alight to yourself. I'll set alight to you, said John. I'll put a match in your petrol tank and burn the car with you in it. Don't be cheeky, said his father, quietly, tapping him softly on the knee. Bob came out of the kitchen. What's that miserable Bob doing, said John, and got up to have a look. He kicked his cardboard cut-out across the floor. Throw that away, said Paul. No, you throw away the rubbish, said John. He was defiant and hostile. Put it away, said Paul. No, you do it, said John. He would continue to tell his father to do it as he picked it up. His father opened the cupboard door for him and they put it away in the cupboard.

An Extract from the G Family Transcript (Observer: Claire Jolly)

John crept up on Barbara to try to give her a surprise, but she saw him just in time. He giggled and said that Bob's watch said twelve o'clock. What do you mean, said Barbara. Have you been touching it? He laughed and said that he'd set it to twelve o'clock. Barbara was very upset. She told him he was very silly; that he should not touch other people's things, especially at the swimming pool, and he had no business to touch Bob's watch. She told him this several times. John kept laughing. In the end, she told him to go back downstairs and get the watch, and bring it to her. He went off downstairs and came back a few minutes later. He handed Barbara the watch. He'd put it back to the right time. Oh, you've put it back, have you, said Barbara? She told him off again, repeating the things that she'd said before. She told him he was lucky he wasn't getting a hiding in front of everyone. She was absolutely furious with him. He was chastened and sat down on the floor.

We watched the swimming again, watching Bob have his lesson. I noticed that John was leaning against Barbara with his head on her arm, but she was still very annoyed with him. Now and again Barbara would point someone out to me, one of the children, and tell me the family's life history. When Bob had finished, we went downstairs to the waiting area. Barbara went off to call to Bob through the changing room that she'd got his watch. I heard her shout to him, and him reply. She told him that she'd got his watch. She came back over to the waiting area downstairs, and met one of the coaches on the way out. She chatted to him for a few minutes, while John wandered around reading notices. When Bob came out, we went outside. It was still pouring with rain. When we got out Barbara turned to Bob and said, a certain person, meaning him, nodding towards John, thought it was very funny to change your watch time to twelve o'clock. That's why I've got it. I made him go and get it. He still thinks it was very funny, but it was a very silly thing to do, and he shouldn't have gone to anyone else's things at the pool. She turned to me and said, if you hadn't been here, Claire (observer), I'd have given him a good hiding in front of everyone. She turned round. He was still grinning. This infuriated her even more. We walked on and John started scraping his shoes on the ground. Yes, that's right John, your new shoes. You'll rub the sole straight off, won't you? We walked on, and got to the house. When we got in, Barbara turned to John and said, you're going to bed at the same time as Bob tonight. You can have a packet of crisps to eat, and a drink, and then you're going straight up at the same time as Bob. John didn't say anything, but went off to get his crisps.

The W2 Family

Background

The W2 family live in a rented, three-bedroom, semi-detached house on a quiet estate in a small town. The family has been established in the house for many years, the father has held the same job for many years, and his second eldest daughter has joined the same employer, in a senior staff position to her father, elsewhere in the company. The family are very involved in the local community: church, youth clubs, and guides.

Members

Mr W2 (54) is skilled, Mrs W2 is a housewife and home pieceworker and they have four children. The oldest child (a daughter of 24) has left home, is unmarried, and has a son of 4. The remaining three children are two girls (19 and 14) and a boy (10).

Presenting problem

The family were referred to a family guidance clinic for help in the management of their relationships, and in particular, the relationship between parents and the eldest daughter (who live elsewhere and has a son).

Observation and analysis

Two observers (AV and CJ) visited on two occasions, each for five days, including weekends. The family was described in terms of structural mapping, positive and negative affect, sociometric relationships, lag sequential analysis, and inter-observer reliability.

Family relationships: Structural Theory

All the relationships in this family are triangular. The early years of childrearing were uneventful. With the onset of adolescence, however, parenting was not adapted to meet new challenges. Escape from home, and individual autonomy, were important aspirations for the two eldest children. The circumstances in which this occurred were traumatic, and placed the parent–child subsystem under great stress. Pregnancy and living rough were strategies deployed by the elder children. The stress led to therapy which resulted in a stronger spouse subsystem and greater flexibility in attitudes to the problems of adolescent autonomy. The mother is overweight and has low self-esteem although she is well integrated and accepted in the community. After her return to the home, the second daughter adopted many housewifely and parenting roles and is the key source of discipline for the son, whose behaviour is deliberately attention-seeking. She has revised her former role in several respects; she is allowed considerable freedom in her personal life and is allowed to entertain her boyfriend in her bedroom. All the siblings are mutually affiliative and cooperative. Individuals are not clearly bounded because everyone is interested in everyone else's business.

Family relationships: Distance Regulation Theory

Of all the families we observed, the W2 family probably changed character most during the various stages of its evolution. Earlier, parenting was a strong theme and individuality was apparently denied sufficiently to provoke dramatic break-out. Now, while the elder children are treated more appropriately, the younger child lacks discipline. It is hard in the present circumstances to understand the causes of earlier rebellion. The parents have become accustomed to questioning their relationship and their ideals. While family members come back and forth independently there is nevertheless a lack of distance. Although chaotic, the family is not overcrowded and there is a separate bedroom for the offspring; a dining room was converted for the returning daughter. The general level of energy discharge is high. Power is distributed and it is hard to identify a hierarchy. When the son or the grandson misbehave, there is general approval and encouragement in the form of appreciative laughter.

Family relationships: Choice-Exchange Theory

There is a complex pattern of rewards and costs. The elder daughters had to pay in an extreme fashion for their freedom. The younger son is maintained as a child and has little chance to mature. He does gain reward by being the centre of attention and by manipulating the feelings of his parents and other family members; he resents the presence of his nephew, as a rival for adult attention. When alone together their relationship is sound and he nurtures his nephew; however, in the company of adults, the ten-year-old uncle sulks, hides in the corner and sucks his thumb. Little reference has been made so far to the second youngest child, who appears to be developing in a normal and happy fashion; she pays little costs for the benefits she receives. So far as the outside world is concerned, the eldest three children seem set to have a successful working life.

Two Extracts from the W2 Family Transcript (Observer: Arlene Vetere)

Extract 1

Earlier when Anne (third eldest daughter) was laying the table, she asked Richard (son) where he was going to sit. You know where I sit, he replied rudely. She said, all right, I'm only asking. Are you going to sit on a chair? What do you think I'm going to do, sit on the floor? he asked. She laughed and said again that she was only asking. We sat down to our meal. We had a plate of rice with some sweet and sour pork placed in the centre. We all picked up our knives and forks and started to eat. Richard had refused to sit down when urged, saying he didn't like rice and wasn't going to eat it. He eventually came to the table and sat there not moving. Everyone continued to eat, ignoring him. Geoff (father) commented that it was quite tasty. Jane (second eldest daughter) was pleased. She looked up and then said to Hilary (mother) that she was going off rice a bit. I've gone off it altogether, said Richard.

Geoff was asking Jane about her work today and what she'd been doing, and she told him that they didn't have a lot of work so she'd cleaned out someone's office. When the family started discussing this among themselves, Richard was not receiving any attention. He picked up his knife and stabbed at the stodgy, jellied mass of rice, and continued to insist that he didn't like rice. He said it was Irish food. This occasioned some laughter. Well, it's not English food, he said. He continued to say that he didn't like it. He was somewhat ignored. He then picked up his fork and hid it behind his back and asked his mother if she noticed anything about the table. No, she said. Richard indicated near his plate. Do you notice anything about the table? No, repeated Hilary. Look, I'm giving you a clue, he said exasperatedly. He's picked up his fork and hidden it, said Jane in a tired voice. He then picked up his knife and fork and said that it could go back in the cutlery drawer. No it can't, said Jane. Not since your grubby fingers have been touching it. He carried on saying that he didn't like the rice, and Jane, who had been looking away in a pointed fashion now turned to him and irritably told him he didn't have to eat it. He gladly sat back. He picked up his cup and drank his milk. Ugh, he said. This milk's warm. I don't like warm milk. It's not warm, said Hilary. The cup's warm because I washed it, but the milk isn't warm. He put the milk down. A few minutes later he picked it up and drank it all.

Geoff was looking quite weary. Once Richard was apparently cleared of eating his meal, he started to liven up, and the second session became frenetic as of yesterday evening. He started off by asking Anne to play 'Mastermind'. He'd ask her, what was her name, and said that she had two minutes on this subject, and he'd ask her who were certain TV programme characters, and she had to identify the programme. Everyone else had finished eating by this time, and Hilary got up to go and make the tea and coffee. She asked me what I (observer) wanted, and I said tea. Don't you remember? said Anne. She's already told you she wants tea with her meal. You're not taking things in. I'm just checking, laughed Hilary as she went out the door. She came back a few minutes later. In the meantime Richard had been playing with his knife on the edge of the table and was told to stop it a few times by his father. He continued to do it. He'd picked at his meal a bit and Anne proceeded to tell him off and to tell him to eat his meal. She did this a few more times before Hilary interceded and told her to mind her own business. Then Richard started to ask Hilary the 'Mastermind' questions and the two girls helped her out with the answers. He then sang tunes for everyone to identify. His voice became louder. He would sing a tune, and there was one in particular that Jane liked, and she would ask him to repeat it, and as he repeated it Anne would sing along with it. This annoyed Richard because he wasn't the sole centre of attention and he'd shout, shut up! at Anne. He did this quite frequently. Unfortunately, I was sitting next to him, and it continually resonated in my right ear. This continued for fifteen minutes while we drank our tea and coffee. If Anne continued to sing along with him, he'd shout, shut up! at her, and then he'd say to his mum, mum, tell her to shut up, in an equally loud voice. Eventually Hilary asked Anne to be quiet so that Richard could sing the song, and Jane would laugh and egg him on and say how much she enjoyed it. Now you shut up, said Anne, hitting Jane.

Jane started to pick at a scab on her father's hand. What are you doing? he said, irritably shaking her off. I'm just picking, she said. Well don't, he said. He had his head in his hands at this stage and eventually turned to Richard and told him to shut up. Richard was asked to clear away the cups. He had been asked to clear the plates as this was his job, but had refused to do it saying he hadn't finished his meal, and started to eat his food again. Anne said, that's all right, that she'd do it, and he could do her job of clearing away the cups later. When asked to clear the cups, he didn't want to and screamed that he didn't want to. His father had now retired to his armchair, and from his position yelled at him to shut up and do what he was told. Richard stomped over to the living room window and sat in the dog's chair, staring out of the window. By this time Hilary said that she'd had enough and she was going to go into the kitchen and sort out the washing up.

Extract 2

Jane was playing with Luke (grandson). She was holding him and standing in front of the hall mirror, and they were making faces at their reflections. She brought him into the lounge and asked where he was sitting. She then sat down at the laid and prepared tea table to wait for everyone else. Luke didn't want to sit still and needed a lot of encouragement. Esther (eldest daughter, Luke's mother) came in with a cup of tea and put it on the tea table, and Hilary followed her with plates of sandwiches. Richard went upstairs in a very loud sulk and locked himself in the bathroom. Where's Richard? asked Geoff, as we all sat at the tea table. Oh, I don't know, said Hilary. He's upstairs. Leave him. I've called him down to tea. If he doesn't come it's up to him. Geoff went upstairs to look and came back down and reported that he was locked in the bathroom. Not for long, predicted Hilary. He hadn't come down a few minutes later and his absence was again commented on by Hilary. Shall I go upstairs and get him? offered Anne. No, Hilary advised. Leave him to come down. Richard entered a few minutes later, two fingers in his mouth, and sat in an arm-chair with his back to the assembled company.

Luke was sitting next to Esther. He pushed his plate away from him exclaiming that he didn't want his tea. He fidgeted and fussed until Esther was obliged to let him get down. She asked the people at the table, particularly Hilary, if they minded. Of course not, they said. The eating of the sandwiches was quite uneventful. Richard came and sat up when we'd nearly finished. Hilary asked him if he wanted a sand-wich, and he squealed and wriggled in his chair and refused to answer. She asked him again and elicited the same response. She then ignored him. She gathered up the plates and asked if we wanted trifle. Luke said he wanted some trifle, and so it was pass the parcel across three daughters into his position. Hilary asked Richard if he wanted some, and he refused to answer. She came back in with the ready served portions. Luke began to tuck into his. He appeared quite concerned at Richard's silent behaviour. What's the matter? he kept asking. What's the matter? Richard told him to shut up. What's the matter? Shut up you! mimicked Luke. Richard now had his forehead in his hands and his elbows on the table. Come on Richard, sit up straight, Hilary admonished, and attempted to pry his elbow from the table, but Richard remained firmly in position. Luke was now poking his tongue out at Richard and calling him naughty. He's sulking, explained Hilary, to Luke. Richard's naughty, Luke repeated, poking his tongue out at him. Esther told him not to do that, and laughed. This is characteristic of her disciplining of Luke. She will tell him not to do something and then look at everyone else and laugh, and everyone else will laugh too, and, of course, so will Luke who will then repeat the behaviour. There is no sense of who is a parent in this family. They're all big kids together.

Luke ate very little of his trifle and wanted to get down again. Hilary then offered the rest of the cake and another cup of tea and coffee to whoever wanted it. As Hilary passed Luke back along the line of daughters to put him on the floor, Esther asked him if he wanted to go to the toilet. Yes, he replied. Ask Auntie Jane. She'll take you to the toilet. So Luke stopped at Jane and sat on her lap while she asked him if he wanted to go to the toilet. No, he said, and hugged her, and snuggled his face into the side of her neck. Don't you want to go to the toilet? repeated Jane, forcing his body away from her to look him in the face. No, he laughed, and snuggled back into her neck. By now, the rest of the family were laughing at his antics. She forced him to face her again and repeated the question. Boobs! he said, screaming with laughter, Boobs! and attempted to clutch her breasts. Jane was laughing uncontrollably at this stage, and was therefore unable to adequately control Luke who wriggled and squirmed in his attempts to get his hands down the front of her sweater and clutch her breasts. He succeeded, much to the amusement of the assembled company. Jane was laughingly fending him off, and he started repeating, Bugger! Bugger! Bugger! to her. This occasioned more laughter. I sat there and thought, just what are they teaching that little boy. They seemed to have no sense of what he was learning, or more particularly, what he was not learning.

Geoff, I thought, would inappropriately laugh whenever Luke performed this kind of behaviour, and he was over-stimulated and egged on by the three girls. Hilary would sit with a somewhat disapproving look on her face while all this was going on, but would not intervene. Richard wanted a piece of cake and Hilary asked him to ask for it nicely. He refused to do so, and was told that he wouldn't get any until he did. This occasioned more sulking. After a further ten minutes of this raucousness, Geoff quietly turned to Hilary and said, shall we get away from all this. What about the washing up? asked Hilary. Well, the girls can do it, said Geoff.

Two Extracts from the W2 Family Transcript (Observer: Claire Jolly)

Extract 1

We all sat down to our meal. Richard was making disparaging remarks about it and Jane became quite annoyed with him, and kept poking him with her elbow. He said it made him feel sick and he wasn't going to eat all of it. He wasn't going to eat those bits, pointing at the meat. Hilary asked him if he'd tried it, and he said yes, he'd tried one bit. He went on making comments about feeling sick. Hilary and Geoff were laughing at him but Jane was getting quite annoyed with him and told him not to speak like that and to eat up his meal. A little later on, Richard asked Hilary if he could have a biscuit later on. She said she'd see. Jane said, only if you finish your meal, pointing to it. Richard said he didn't like it, it made him feel sick. He sat back, put his fingers in his mouth, and wasn't going to eat any more.

Extract 2

Richard's behaviour throughout the meal was absolutely appalling, and as usual the rest of the family watched him intently, smiling and laughing indulgently at his antics. First he spat cracker crumbs around and Hilary told him not to, but he didn't take any notice. He only ate one and a half and then said he wasn't eating any more. Hilary stood up to go out to the kitchen to get the trifle. Jane came in with a plate of cheese scones. She offered one to her father, who took one, and to Richard, who said he didn't want one. Then she offered one to me (observer), and I took one. She put the plate on the table. She asked Richard if he was going to eat his crackers as she wanted to take the plate out, but he wouldn't answer her. Then he said he wasn't having them, and she went to pick his plate up, and then he said yes, he would have them. She was exasperated with him and walked over to the door. She said over her shoulder, now you know why I don't want any, and went out. Geoff looked puzzled for a minute, and then realized what she meant, and laughed.

While they were out of the room, Richard was kicking the chairs and stools around. He got down from the table. Geoff called him back, but Richard said, I'm just going down again for a minute. Eventually, he returned to the table. He picked up the cutlery and started banging the table with a spoon. He banged Hilary's stool with the spoon. He was clanking it against the crockery. Geoff told him not to. He carried on. Geoff told him again, sharply, not to do that. He didn't take any notice.

Hilary came back in with the trifle and gave one to each of us and sat down. Richard then said he didn't want it. He'd only wanted jelly. Hilary said it was the best she could do. She couldn't pick all the jelly out of the trifle. He stirred it around, and decided not to eat it. He stretched over and got a cheese scone. He took one bite out of it and wanted to put it back on the plate, but Hilary wouldn't let him. Hilary was beginning to get irritated at him and told him not to mess about, several times. She said if he did mess about, he'd have to go straight to bed, but he carried right on. Again, both Jane and Anne were amused by his antics, as was Geoff, who smiled indulgently, looking at me every time he did so.

The C Family

Background

The couple have not been married very long and have two children. Mrs C had to give up work as a computer programmer to stay at home and rear the children. They live in a spacious, three-bedroom, detached house in a semi-rural setting, within easy reach of a large town. One reason for choosing this house was the large garden, which provides room for the children to play. The family belongs to the local community; Mrs C attends coffee mornings, and their elder child attends a playgroup. Their neighbour is willing to look after the younger child when necessary, but Mrs C is reluctant to take advantage of this offer because she fears he will misbehave.

Members

The parents are 28 and both are computer programmers. There are two male children of 4 years and 15 months.

Presenting problem

The family was referred by a paediatrician to a child guidance clinic, because of the incessant crying and 'miserableness' of the younger child.

Observation and analysis

Two observers (AV and CJ) visited on two occasions, each for five days, including weekends. The family was described in terms of structural mapping, positive and negative affect, sociometric relationships, lag sequential analysis, and inter-observer reliability. In addition the parents completed repertory grids, the family was filmed at a mealtime, and the parents underwent two interviews, one concerned with the analysis of the mealtime film, and the other with subjective responses to participant observation. Mr and Mrs C also prepared Chapter 10.

Family relationships: Structural Theory

There is a diffuse boundary around the spouse subsystem, which by virtue of the couple's lack of experience prior to marriage is still evolving. In Chapter 10 the couple admit to physical problems in marriage. The parental subsystem is the most prominent, and the majority of the parents' time and energy is devoted to it. However, it does not work effectively, because the mother regards most discipline as punishing and unacceptable. Her response to misbehaviour is to divert the child's attention and express affection. Unfortunately, this leads to a spiral which leads to further attention-seeking behaviour. When the younger child wakes in the night, often in the early hours of the morning, one of the parents will take him downstairs and play with him when attempts to comfort or console him have failed. In the early morning both children join their parents in bed. The older child uses his younger sibling as a model and imitates his disruptive behaviour in order to gain attention. The mother is overweight and says she is depressed and reports that she has little time or space for her own interests. Given the nature of her training, the observers felt she could have sustained extra-familial interests by carrying out work at home. To the observers, the younger child did not seem unmanageable; rather he seemed to be a scapegoat whose behaviour was sustained through lack of appropriate discipline. The parents' view was that his diet contributed to hyperactivity; after changes in diet (which themselves meant additional work in the preparation of food) his behaviour was seen to be more manageable. This is an intelligent couple who see rational decision-making and rational childrearing as desirable goals; there is disagreement as to whether both can be achieved and the father expresses some reservations about his wife's childrearing practices.

Family relationships: Distance Regulation Theory

There are few boundaries in this family, although the siblings are developing their own relationships. Energy is devoted to childrearing to the exclusion of all else. Lack of sleep and preoccupation with the younger child leaves both parents exhausted. Meals illustrate the timing of family behaviour: the children have first priority and the parents allow their own food to get cold while concentrating on feeding the children. Food is also important because it provides an explanation for the child's hyperactive behaviour. This explanation is physical, and involves biochemistry rather than the behaviour of the parents or their interactions with the children. In contrast, suggestions for changing the mother's behaviour, made by the family therapist, are seen to involve a rejection of the principles of good motherhood. Each week the parents make formal lists of what they have to do, but so much time is devoted to the younger child that their plans are rarely achieved. Power is clearly vested in the younger child whose behaviour is the major determinant of the behaviour of others. Positive affection, caring for others, and being a good mother are dominant themes. The couple recognize differences in their emotional expression, the husband being seen as more rational and less expressive.

Family relationships: Choice-Exchange Theory

The family is characterized by few rewards, many costs, and the expression of continual effort. The father has a set of rewards: work, jobs around the house, and escape to woodworking tools. The younger child does not enjoy his power; his sibling does not appear to suffer from his brother's domination of the family's social space. Most of the cost is borne by the mother who appears to have few rewards; this is reflected in her mild depression and lack of emotional support.

The family have written about their more recent history in Chapter 10.

Three Extracts from the C Family Transcript (Observer: Arlene Vetere)

Extract 1

Andrew (younger son, 15 months) went to bed at 8 o'clock yesterday evening and was awake at 11.30 p.m., and had a drink of milk prepared by Kevin (father). He was apparently awake at 3.30 a.m. when his nappy was changed and finally woke up at 4 o'clock. Kevin knocked on my door (observer) at 4.50 a.m. telling me that everyone was up, so I also got up, blearily stumbled into the kitchen in my dressing gown to find Kevin making a cup of tea for Janet (mother) and myself. He was holding Andrew in his arms as he did so. He needed to seat Andrew on the worktop whilst he put the teabags in the pot. When he did so Andrew immediately burst into tears and clung on tighter. Janet came down in her dressing gown and asked, do you want me to take him up with me? Andrew cuddled tighter still. He seemed to understand what his mother was saying. Tim (older son, 4 years) came down in his dressing gown and wanted to know where his slippers were. His father pointed them out in the hall and Tim put them on by himself. Janet, who had gone upstairs while Kevin finished making the tea, came down and held out her arms to Andrew, who ran across the floor to her crying as he passed me. Kevin was thus able to make the tea. Kevin handed me my tea and I followed him upstairs. Janet had gone up with Andrew and Tim followed her. Janet was in bed with Andrew climbing on top of her. I was invited into the bedroom and I sat down on a stool with my back facing the wardrobe. Tim was somewhat irritable and asked for his drink. He'd already had a cheesy biscuit earlier on. His father said what did he want, and he said a milk shake and his father offered to go downstairs and make it. Tim was behaving somewhat irritably. He asked his mother for a dummy, his mother said she didn't know where it was, probably in his bedroom. He asked her to get it. She said that, no, he would have to do that. He wasn't content with that and scrambled fidgetingly in the bed. Why don't you cuddle down beside me, his mother suggested. So slippers and all, he tucked himself up under the continental quilt and snuggled against her, fidgeting all the while. Kevin returned with Tim's milk shake and offered it to him. Tim said that it wasn't enough; complained in an irritable tone that it wouldn't be enough, which goes against what I have observed before when he is usually polite and thanks his father for his drink. He finished his drink and decided that he had had enough and got out of bed and put the cup up on the ironing board. I had finished my tea by now and so had Kevin. Kevin took Andrew downstairs to get Andrew a drink of water. Tim then decided that he would go and fetch his dummies, and then did so, but found that he couldn't shut the door. Janet told him not to worry, that his dad could do it on the way back up. He was concerned that Andrew would get into his bedroom and mess around with his toys. Andrew appeared in the door-way with his drink, finished it off and then flung the cup on the floor and promptly began to cry. Kevin got up and picked up the cup, realized it was empty, crouched down in front of Andrew and took the lid off and said, oh look it's empty, and drew his attention to it. Tim came across and said that he wanted to look and stuck his finger inside to check and said it was dry. His father told him not to put his finger in the cup. Tim then got back into bed beside his mother. Andrew then began climb-ing over his mother towards Tim and wanted to take the dummy from Tim's mouth. Oh look, said Janet, he's telling you that you shouldn't be having a dummy in your mouth, it's too late in the morning for that. Kevin fetched Andrew another drink of water, which he drank. He was quite cheerful, running around all the while climbing over people, being tickled and making a nuisance of himself with Tim, e.g., by climbing on his face. Tim constantly complained that the sleeves on his dressing gown rolled up and his father or mother would tell him to pull them down again. He eventually took the dummy out of his mouth and put it into his pocket and then complained that the dummies hurt him, so his mother took them from him and put them on the window sill, out of the reach of Andrew. Tim then wanted his space shuttle toy that he had bought yesterday, from downstairs, and said quite con-fidently that he knew where it was and he would go and fetch it. His father did it for him as the gate was up to protect Andrew. Janet offered to let Kevin have a lie-in if he so wished, but he declined saying it wasn't necessary. Janet explained that they thought they had had a reasonably good night with Andrew, i.e., going from 8 o'clock to 4 o'clock in the morning, but because they had gone to bed so late at half past eleven, they hadn't taken full advantage of it.

Kevin was in the kitchen making up some of Andrew's soya milk, whilst holding him in his arms. He made a few attempts to put the boy onto the floor so that he could get on with things like filling kettles and boiling them, but Andrew refused to be put down. The slightest murmur and Kevin would accede to the child's demands, and keep him in his arms. However, at one stage he did need to put the boy down to fill the kettle, and whilst he did that Andrew screamed and clutched at his legs, until he was picked up again.

Extract 2

Tim was sitting on the worktop and Janet gave him a cuddle after having given one to Andrew. Tim demanded his cuddle because he'd seen his mother cuddle Andrew who was being held by Kevin. As I've said before Tim and Andrew call for affection by screaming for it. So Janet continued to cuddle Tim while he buried his head in her shoulder, while Andrew squealed in his father's arms for a cuddle from his mother. Janet ignored Andrew's demands and continued to cuddle Tim, which in my opinion was necessary. She then left off cuddling Tim and stood between the two of them, turning from one to the other with her hand out saying, which one next. Me, me said Tim. So she picked him up off the worktop, then picked up Andrew in her other arm. Can you manage, inquired Kevin. Yes, how do you think I do when you're not here, she said. She then put Tim back down on the worktop so that she could continue with her meal and put Andrew on the floor after having given him a tin to play with.

Extract 3

At 9 o'clock, when supper was finished, Jan decided that it was time for Andrew to go to bed, so she picked him up, cuddled him in her arms and danced around to the Mike Oldfield music. He scowled and protested but she continued to hold him firmly and to jog up and down. He was trying to struggle to get his hand out towards his father, straining towards him, and Kevin who was sitting down said, he loves his daddy, and Jan said, that's only because he knows you'll play with him, and continued to hold him firmly and jog him. She then jogged her way out of the lounge and into the hallway where we could hear her moving up and down for a few minutes. Kevin went outside and said he'd take over, and she said, oh he's nearly dropped off. That's all right, he said, I'll finish it off, and took the boy upstairs and finally settled him down. When he came back he gave Jan credit saying she'd done most of the hard work.

Three Extracts from the C Family Transcript (Observer: Claire Jolly)

Extract 1

I (observer) went into the kitchen for a few moments and chatted to Janet (mother). She was making some cakes. She was telling me that the diet they had put Andrew (younger son) on involves her in a lot of baking and hard work but she felt that it was worth it as there had been some improvement. She went on to tell me that although there was still room for a great deal of improvement, he was sleeping a little better and was happier during the daytime and not hanging round her miserably, quite as much as he had been before. She seemed quite positive and happy that this was the case, although she was very careful to point out there was still a great deal of room for improvement. She commented that baking was something that she had been used to doing occasionally as a treat and now that her whole life was taken up with it.

Extract 2

Andrew was grizzling and moaning and throwing himself about a lot in Kevin's (father) arms. Tim (elder son) said, I think he wants to get down. Kevin said, does he? and attempted to put him down. But Andrew very clearly didn't want to, he screamed and grizzled and tried to climb back up so Kevin lifted him back up onto his lap. Tim was not watching the television at this point, but was watching to see what Andrew was doing. He said, what's the matter with him? and Kevin said, I think he's very tired. Then Tim said, I think he wants a biscuit. Kevin said, I offered him a biscuit but he didn't want one. Tim settled back in his armchair. Kevin lay Andrew down in his arms and rocked and soothed him, attempting to get him to sleep.

Extract 3

Tim suddenly started to grizzle and throw himself about, saying I want my dinner, I want it right now. Jan said, yes Tim. She put his dinner on a plate and took it into the dining room and put it on the table. She sat down with Andrew on her lap, and attempted to feed him again. He still rejected it and didn't want any. Tim said, what's the matter with Andrew? Jan said, he doesn't want his dinner today. Tim took a spoonful of his and said, I don't like it either. Then he suddenly started to shriek and grizzle and yell and say that it hurt his mouth, did it have any cheese in it. Jan said no it didn't. He then moaned and cried and grizzled and said that his mouth hurt and he wouldn't eat it. Jan went to get the torch to have a look in his mouth. He opened it wide and she looked in. She said that she couldn't see anything. Tim continued to make a fuss and Jan asked him if he would like it chopped up. She chopped it up with a spoon and asked if he would like her to feed him. She fed him a spoonful or two, then he calmed down and ate for a few minutes, just a very few spoonfuls. Then he said he didn't want it and could he have a sandwich instead. Yes Tim, said Jan. Tim held up his hand and said, this many. Jan said, yes Tim, what would you like in them. Tim said ham and pickle, so Jan took his dinner and Andrew's dinner out to the kitchen and made him his sandwiches and brought them back.

CHAPTER TEN
Family Life as Viewed from the Inside

Janet and Kevin C.

Introductory Statement by the Researchers

One of the problems of being both a participant observer and a scientist is that two conflicting ethical codes need to be resolved: the requirement to publish and add to knowledge, and the requirement to maintain confidentiality and respect privacy. When selecting material for this volume we therefore had several difficult decisions to make: the choice of good illustrative examples (without revealing the families' identity), trying to gauge a family's response to the public display of information about them, and not trying to present a one-sided view (ours rather than that of the family). One family were particularly interested in the research and always cooperative; they participated in several modes of measurement. We invited them to describe the impact which participant observation had on their lives (see Chapter 8) and their own view of the state of their relationship and family. In this chapter the parents of family C describe how they met, how their relationship evolved, and how they responded to the problems which beset them. The reader may wish to contrast the different views of family C reflected here and elsewhere.

Introduction

We met as a couple (Janet and Kevin), when doing a day release course for HNC. I worked for a group of consultants and Kevin worked for a large computer firm, both of us computer programmers. Both of us were still living with parents, older sisters having married. We were married 18 months later (both 25 years old), and moved into a new semi-detached house with two salaries to pay the mortgage. Tim was born 18 months after (not planned). We were now down to one salary. We both found the demands of a baby hard but life settled down and about one year later we looked for another house with more garden, which we felt we needed for the children. As soon as we'd moved we tried for and succeeded in having another child.

173

We both felt that another child couldn't be any harder than the first. Andrew was born and we soon found out how difficult a 'crying baby' made life.

As we had just moved our financial state at that time was pretty grim. The older house needed decorating at the very least, there were no savings to draw on, but we ticked over, and kept an old car on the road. The house was a good size (3 bed semi, with large frontage and a 200 ft back garden). The neighbours were pleasant and I joined in a coffee morning where every Wednesday morning about seven mums would take turns to have the others in. I and Tim quickly made friends and felt part of the village. We were glad we had moved.

Our expectations at the time were to establish a happy family home for the children. To make the home a comfortable and relaxed place. We wanted to do a lot to the garden and grow our own vegetables. As a couple we both felt that we had been plunged into parenthood rather early in our married life, there was a lot of room for improvement in the physical side of our relationship. We both expected life to go on a slow but nevertheless uphill route.

We can't remember exactly when Andrew started crying. He had a dummy before he was three weeks old so it must have been about then. This wasn't a normal baby cry that would stop when he was fed or comforted. Andrew would cry regardless of what we did. He didn't like sleeping either, during the day he never slept longer than 15 minutes, he would always wake up screaming. Night times were a little better but it didn't seem to improve with time. We thought this was 'colic', lots of young babies cry a lot. I was breastfeeding and although this generally went well, and Andrew sometimes appeared to be satisfied, he would always wake screaming again after a short time. When Andrew was five months old we stopped breastfeeding and went onto formula milk. If anything this seemed to make him worse. At this point Andrew slept for a total of only five hours in 24. The GP suggested trying soya milk. This seemed to make a slight improvement, he didn't cry quite so often and his sleep was more settled. We were referred to a paediatrician. This we found very disappointing because he suggested that there was nothing wrong with Andrew. It was us as parents who were too 'soft'. We were referred to a psychologist. At around this time our GP gave us some literature on food allergies and hyperactivity. Having seen the positive effect of taking Andrew off dairy produce we decided to follow this up and wrote off for an additive free diet. Within a week of following this diet Andrew became quieter and calmer and his sleep pattern started getting better.

The research team visited us just after we had started the new diet. Before the research team visited us we felt as though the whole household was disrupted by Andrew. We shared night times. I would go to bed early and Kevin would sleep downstairs with Andrew. I then got up in the early hours to let Kevin have some uninterrupted sleep. We have difficulty in remembering exactly how we felt as individuals at the time. We felt that people couldn't understand and we also seemed isolated — it was unreal, nightmarish, we felt so tired we had difficulty thinking even simple things out.

Relationships

Relationships (as we remember them) *at the time of the visits* between Janet and Kevin were very strained. There was no time to discuss anything in detail and decisions were hastily made. This was acceptable to both of us given the circumstances. The physical side of our marriage was reduced to a minimum, we were hardly in bed together! We both felt resentment, Janet with a lack of physical affection, Kevin with the effect the children would have on the future.

As I Janet Saw Things

At this point I felt a complete failure as a woman, wife, and a mother, I felt more like a robot. Children always respond to their mother's 'tender loving care'. Andrew didn't. I am usually an optimistic sort, always looking on the bright side. At this time I felt very negative. Tim at this time I regarded as generally happy, obviously frustrated with us and himself at times (he was then nearly 4). I have always kept discipline to a minimum. Obedience has been more important to me than lots of 'dos' and don'ts'. Tim usually did as requested, eventually, so this didn't seem to be a problem. Despite the seemingly full-time demands made by Andrew, I felt I managed to meet Tim's needs. Tim was assertive enough in his demands for me to give him a share of attention. My feelings of love, affection, etc. for Tim were consistent from day to day unlike the emotional see-saw I felt for Andrew. Tim tried to play alongside Andrew. Andrew was then 15 months old, and very active so Tim found this difficult. We would try to give Tim time to play by one of us taking Andrew into another room for a while. Tim couldn't understand why Andrew was unhappy but he often tried to involve Andrew in what he was doing.

My feelings for Andrew varied all the time, sometimes I would want to cuddle him, to comfort him, the love I felt at times like this could reduce me to tears. At other times I almost hated him and resentment was strong. Andrew was very active, he walked well at 10 months, he was always climbing, and striving to do more than he was capable, he didn't see danger and would not be put off. He needed constant watching. This made me very aware of his movements and I became neurotic about checking what he was doing. It got to the point where I didn't trust anyone else to look after him because no one else seemed to understand what Andrew was capable of.

Kevin at this time was the steady one, which looking back, was marvellous in the circumstances. However, at the time, I would sometimes resent this and accuse him of showing no emotion. I used to get 'steamed up' often. I also felt strongly that my treatment of Andrew was correct. Kevin isn't impulsive like me so at the time he was a steadying influence. I was worried about our relationship but we usually managed to show each other some affection. I also worried about Kevin's work. At one stage his boss let him work more flexible hours to allow one of us to have more sleep in the morning for example. This helped but it must have been very hard switching from the demands of work to the more demanding home environment and vice versa.

As I Kevin saw things

There seemed to be little happiness in the early (2) years of Andrew's life. This made me wonder when, if ever, he would give us the enjoyment and satisfaction of parenthood that a normal child would bring. Andrew's unusual drive to walk and climb earlier than was normal seemed a cruel trick of nature leading to frustration, pain, and danger for him and anxiety for us. On the positive side, I could see that his skill and intelligence would benefit from his wider experience and greater number of wakeful hours compared to other children.

However, it seemed that this was at our expense and while we expect to give a high proportion of our attention and efforts towards the children, it was difficult to accept that *all* our efforts were needed and even then, this was not enough. Timothy provided some much-needed relief from the constant demands of Andrew. Meeting his needs was somehow more satisfying as I could watch him learning and exploring on his own.

Towards Janet, I felt concern for the degree of stress she was under. This showed itself in no uncertain terms. I was concerned on two counts. Firstly, I had never seen my wife under such stress and didn't know how much she could take. Secondly, how long would it last? Both were unknowns which only time would reveal. I always maintained a degree of admiration for Janet's ability to strive to make things better, never giving up — continually searching for improvements in Andrew's diet, looking for ways to break the daily and weekly routines in order to provide stimulation and variety for the two of us and for the children.

What Came After

With his change in diet, Andrew slowly settled down, the crying spells came less often, he became easier to control and even started playing quietly. His sleep pattern slowly improved as well. We continued our visits to the psychologist and eventually he reached the conclusions that Andrew had become much calmer, we were more in control, and although he couldn't prove that diet had played a part in this change, he was prepared to admit that we had certainly achieved something.

As We Are Now

A few months later we discovered that Janet was again pregnant. This time we had a little girl, Hannah. Hannah is a happy, easy-going little girl, now just 2. She has shown us the pleasures a normal baby can bring. We feel she has done all of us good in different ways. Tim and Andrew both love her and she has fitted in well.

Andrew is now 4, he is a happy child, who plays and sings like the others. Sleep still doesn't come easy to Andrew and he rarely sleeps through the night, he usually creeps in with us at some point. We don't mind this, at least he's doing it quietly! Andrew is always awake by 5 o'clock in the morning, but usually plays quietly and we can still doze. He goes to playschool two mornings a week and plays well with other children.

Tim, now nearly 7, is at school, and thoroughly enjoys himself. He has got on well, has lots of friends and is usually happy with life. He is always busy doing something. Tim and Andrew play well together most of the time and it's music to our ears to hear them enjoying each other's company.

Janet and Kevin's relationship has also improved dramatically. We now have time to talk and do things that we want to do, not as much time as we'd like at times but at last we are heading in the right direction.

CHAPTER ELEVEN

Classification of the Nine Families by a Repertory Grid Method

Arlene Vetere

Introduction

Much of the data reported so far is about single families. An attempt has been made to translate qualitative observational data into quantitative terms. Throughout our studies we have used Minuchin's (1974) structural theory as a guide and imposed his systemic/structural analysis upon the families whom we observed. We have been concerned about reliability and the extent to which observers are consistent, agree with each other, and can use the methods we have developed in a meaningful and consensual fashion. Arlene Vetere, our principal observer, and the person who was most responsible for the development of the technique, had lived with nine families. The question therefore arose whether those nine families could be classified in a consistent fashion and using a common framework. Given a particular dimension derived from family theory, for example, enmeshment-disengagement, could families be ranked along this dimension in a meaningful way? Again, given concepts like *boundaries* and *relationships* would these be used in a consistent fashion across families and in a way which captured the different qualities of the family atmospheres which had been experienced? The one common factor which connected these families, was of course, Arlene. We therefore decided to tap into Arlene's construct system to see if it could be deployed to provide *general categorizations* of the families and provide additional confirmation of the applicability of our method and its utility or validity in describing family life. Therefore, in addition to the observational data, and the sampling of the family view, we sought to explore our own perception of families. In addition, the drawing together of all families within one analytic framework, offered the opportunity to explore the observer's relationships with families and the degree to which the observer as participant role had been realized within different family contexts.

The Grids

Each of four family subsystems (spouse, parental, parent-child and sibling) was taken first and a grid constructed, covering all the nine families. A fifth grid related to family/extended family networks. Included were subsystem boundaries, relationships, and functional rules. Boundaries were considered for clarity, rigidity, and diffuseness; relationships for affiliation and conflict; and functions were characterized as effective or noneffective.

Thus the elements within the grids were the families, and the constructs were boundaries, relationships, and rules. The nature of the constructs was varied for each subsystem, given their different functional requirements, as is shown in Table 1. Thus it was not feasible or theoretically acceptable to apply an identical set of constructs to all elements.

Table 1. Constructs employed for each of the six grids (following Minuchin 1974)

Grid 1. *Marital Subsystem*
   Boundary (diffuse, clear, rigid)
   Relationships (affiliation, conflict)
   Rules (complementarity of function, teamwork, mutual support)

Grid 2. *Parental Subsystem*
   Boundary (diffuse, clear, rigid)
   Relationships (affiliation, conflict)
   Rules (guidance/control, flexible authority, consistent discipline, age-appropriate
      parenting)

Grid 3. *Parent–child Subsystem*
   Boundary (diffuse, clear, rigid)
   Relationships (affiliation, over-involvement, alliances, conflict)
   Rules (sex-role identification, modelling adult behaviour)

Grid 4. *Sibling Subsystem*
   Boundary (diffuse, clear, rigid)
   Relationships (affiliation, alliances, conflict)
   Rules (cooperation, negotiation, competition)

Grid 5. *Nuclear Family/Extended Family System*
   Boundary (diffuse, clear, rigid)
   Relationships (affiliation, over-involvement, conflict)

Grid 6. *Observer Plus Family System*
   Boundary (diffuse, clear)
   Relationships (affiliation, alliances, conflict)
   Rules (reactivity, active intervention, neutrality/emotional involvement, role
      confusion)

To explore the relationship of observer to observed, a sixth grid was created, to examine the observer's perceptions of her professional and intimate relationships with families, within the newly created family-plus-observer system. For example, was the perceived boundary between the observer and each family equally clear?

Had the degree of affiliation been constant for all families? Had the observer been able in all cases to remain equally uninvolved at an emotional level and equally passive as an observer?

Thus within the first five grid sets the observer acts as the generator of constructs about others, in the sixth set constructs are elicited about self and others.

The essence of the Kelly (1955) technique is to tap the person's own constructs and not to impose a 'right' way of looking at events and relationships. In the case of the C family, we saw how family statements and observations were used to derive a set of supplied constructs. This enabled us to use common constructs for husband and wife rather than elicit constructs which may not have had common content. In the present case, the constructs came directly from Minuchin's structural theory (1974). However, the observer was not only familiar with the theory but had used it to guide and focus her family observations; to that extent, therefore, structural concepts were part and parcel of the observer's construing of family relationships and occupy a half-way house between being supplied and elicited.

The Procedure

Initially, the families were ranked on each of the six grids shown in Table 1. The observer forced herself to rank the families without using tied ranks. This process helped her to clarify her range of convenience in using the constructs in her thinking about the families, and to clarify the ways in which Minuchin's theoretical concepts were defined for her in terms of specific family events. Even so, forced ranking proved to be unsatisfactory since it did not necessarily distinguish families in terms of their absolute position on a continuum; on occasion, several families clustered at one pole, and others at other points, rather than being continuously distributed. Thus each family was rated on a scale of 1 through 7 for each construct across the six grids. This allowed ties but allocated an actual score in so doing. Indeed, such graded or rated grids are easier to analyse and they give fuller results; the ranking process, in contrast, artificially equates the variance on all constructs.

We have already pointed out that the construct set was not appropriate to all elements. A further difficulty arose. While relationship and family rule constructs could be treated as bipolar, the structural theory distinguishes three types of boundary, albeit on a continuous scale. Thus the boundary construct was partitioned into three single dimensions; the observer then rated each family system for clarity of boundaries (diffuse, clear, rigid). Again, while the family grids were based on Minuchin's theory, the observer role constructs were derived from the participant observation literature, as discussed in Chapter 4. So, for example, the construct *reactivity* assesses the observer's perception of the degree to which the family has reacted to her presence by altering some patterns of normal responding (for example, physical punishment of children may be restrained). *Active intervention* assesses role passivity; *neutrality/emotional involvement* describes her capacity to distance herself from family members while maintaining cordial relations; and *role confusion* expresses the observer's view of the family's understanding of the observer's role, whether the family had unrealistic expectations of her, and so on. An example of the data constructed for the observer-plus-family grid is given in Table 2.

Table 2. Ratings of the nine elements (families) on the nine constructs for the observer-plus-family system grid

Grid 6: Observer-plus-Family System

| Constructs | Elements (families) | | | | | | | | |
	A	B	W1	P	T	C	R	G	W2
Diffuse boundary	6	6	1	2	2	2	2	2	3
Clear boundary	2	3	6	6	6	6	6	6	5
Relationships:									
Affiliation	6	6	3	3	5	5	4	5	6
Alliances	4	3	2	1	1	1	1	1	2
Conflict	1	1	1	1	1	1	1	1	1
Rules:									
Reactivity	6	5	2	3	4	4	3	3	4
Active intervention	4	3	2	2	2	2	3	2	2
Neutrality/emotional involvement	4	4	2	1	3	2	1	2	4
Role confusion	4	3	3	2	2	1	1	2	2

Rating: 1 = least, 7 = most.

The Grid Analyses

The ranked and rated grids were analysed using the programme developed by Higginbotham and Bannister (1983). This analysis provides a tabulation of constructs (showing the degree of relationship among constructs in terms of correlations), a table for elements (also based on correlations), an indication of the variance accounted for by constructs and elements, and graphical descriptions in two-dimensional space, showing elements or constructs plotted in terms of proximity, in relation to two components which account for most of the variance. One can thus explore, for both elements and constructs, which items cluster together or are negatively correlated. Where elements (families) are seen to be significantly different from each other, one can return to the original data (as shown in Table 2) to determine which constructs account for such differences.

Family Subsystem Constructs

The marital subsystem

Two principal constructs emerged, teamwork and rigid boundary. The former was positively associated with affiliation, mutual support, clear boundary and complementarity of function ($p < 0.01$) and negatively correlated ($p < 0.01$) with conflict and diffuse boundary ($p < 0.05$). The latter principal construct had no related constructs. These results mean that the observer has been consistent in her application of structural theory concepts to the marital subsystem which is, of course, the highest subsystem within the family's hierarchical structure.

If we explore the position of elements (families) within this construct space, two clusters emerge, with positive relationships between C, T, and B families (cluster 1) and P, A, and W1 families (cluster 2). Reference to the vignettes in Chapter 9 show that P, A, and W1 families had peripheral or absent husbands and conflictual relationships. In contrast, the C, B, and T families had clear boundaries around the marital subsystems; despite some dissatisfactions, relationships were seen by the observer to be affiliative.

The parental subsystem

This demonstrated a similar degree of consistency. Two principal constructs emerged: clear boundary (related positively to consistent discipline and flexible authority and negatively with diffuse boundary, $p < 0.01$); and conflict (negatively correlated with affiliation and consistent discipline, $p < 0.05$). Here P, A, and W1 families shared the characteristics of over-involvement with children, cross-generational alliances, and higher levels of conflict (see Chapter 9). Families A, W2, and C formed a second cluster around the construct of affiliation, while, finally, family W2 was negatively correlated with a third cluster, the R and G families, whose parental relationships were characterized by rigid boundaries and little affiliation.

The parent-child subsystem

Three constructs were identified: alliances (positively correlated with diffuse boundary and over-involvement, $p < 0.01$; and negatively correlated with modelling and sex role identification, $p < 0.05$); clear boundary (positively correlated with affiliation, $p < 0.05$; and negatively correlated with conflict, $p < 0.01$); and, rigid boundary (negatively correlated with over-involvement, $p < 0.05$). The first major cluster of families to emerge were families P, A, and W1 who shared the extreme scores on the alliances construct; they were also negatively correlated with the G family, who together with the R family formed a second cluster. Both these latter families were characterized by rigid parent-child boundaries. These relationships are demonstrated in the vignettes and abstracts in Chapter 9, which for family G and R demonstrate scapegoating and exclusion of individual children.

The sibling subsystem

The data here are unusual as sibling relationships are rarely a focus of concern in the family therapy literature (Bank and Kahn, 1975), although they appear as a specific subsystem within Minuchin's theory. More typically, the focus is on spouse, or parent–child relationships. Two principal constructs were identified: affiliation (positively correlated with negotiation and cooperation, $p < 0.01$; and negatively correlated with conflict, $p < 0.01$); and, clear boundary (negatively correlated with conflict and diffuse boundary, $p < 0.05$). The families which were rated highly for sibling conflict and competition were noticeably characterized by parental intrusion into the children's social world and an absence of independent activity by the children (families P, A, G, and W1). Another correlated group of families were T and C, where sibling subsystem relationships were seen to be affiliative.

The nuclear family/extended family subsystem

This analysis depended on a more limited data base since observations were both rare for individual families and differed between families. The principal construct which emerged was over-involvement which was positively correlated with affiliation ($p < 0.01$) and diffuse boundary ($p < 0.05$) on the one hand, and negatively correlated with rigid boundary ($p < 0.05$). Only one cluster of families emerged, who were seen to have severed links with the extended family: P, G and W1.

The observer-plus-family subsystem

This provides us with an insight into the observer's perceptions of her role relationships with each family. Two principal constructs emerged, clear boundary and affiliation. The first was negatively correlated with diffuse boundary, alliances, reactivity, and active intervention ($p < 0.01$) and role confusion ($p < 0.05$) and positively correlated with neutrality ($p < 0.05$). Affiliation was positively associated with reactivity and emotional involvement ($p < 0.01$) and diffuse boundary ($p < 0.05$). If we turn to Table 2 we can see how it was that two clusters of family emerged in the elements grid (A, B, and W2; G, C, T, R, P, W1, and W2). Thus the observer perceived her relationships with the A, B, and W2 families to be strongly affiliative; she also finds them to have higher ratings for diffuse boundary, reactivity, active intervention, and emotional involvement than for her relationships with other families. We should note that families A and B were the first to be visited by the observer. Her perception of the relationship is unlikely to have been affected by the passage of time, since the diaries were available during the repertory grid process. Rather, it seems that at the time of the visits, the observer was still in the process of clarifying her role of participant observer and had not achieved the degree of neutrality finally intended.

Conclusions

From the analyses, it emerges that the most discriminating constructs for family subsystems are as follows: *clear boundary* (for all subsystems), *teamwork* (within the marital subsystem), *alliances* (within the parent–child subsystem), *affiliation* (sibling subsystem), and *over-involvement* (family/extended family). These were the key constructs which organized the remainder, i.e., which accounted for most of the variance while correlating with other constructs. Among constructs which accounted for little variance were *rigid boundary* (in marital subsystems), *age appropriate parenting*, and *conflict* (in the family–observer system). It is appreciated that the latter two effects might reflect the observer's desire to portray herself as value and bias free. The particular sample selected, and the need to secure the permission of both parents to enable access, could account for the absence of observed rigidity in relationships between spouses.

It is well recognized that the repertory grid technique has clinical and diagnostic value for individual clients (see Ryle and Lunghi, 1970). Constructs can provide axes for plotting changes in therapy as well as helping to map out future directions for change. Constructs also have an anticipatory function since they can be used to predict future behaviour and/or the impact of therapy.

We have demonstrated that repertory grids have potential utility in the case of families as well as individuals. Moreover, the technique, as developed in this chapter, can be used during the training of family therapists. The looseness or tightness of their family constructs can be explored, not only at one point in time, but across the duration of training. The method can also be used to increase the therapist's awareness of his or her use of theoretical concepts and their exemplification in different families. The act of ranking or grading families brings into consciousness the need for objective analysis and description as a basis for discrimination.

The range of convenience of Minuchin's structural theory constructs is wide for the therapist. The clinical value for therapeutic practice lies in the opportunity for examining the therapist's *consistency* in the use of the constructs. From our analysis it appears that the Minuchin method does lend itself to such an approach. Consistency in the use of theoretical constructs is important both in terms of dealings with different families but with the same family over a series of therapeutic sessions. We should note that the Higginbotham and Bannister programme is available for use on standard microprocessors.

References

Bank, S. and Kahn, M. D. (1975). Sisterhood–Brotherhood is powerful: Sibling subsystems and family therapy. *Family Process*, **14**, 311–337.

Higginbotham, P. G. and Bannister, D. (1983). *The GAB computer program for the analyses of repertory grid data*. University of Leeds.

Kelly, G. A. (1955). *The Psychology of Personal Constructs*, vols. 1 and 2. New York: Norton.

Minuchin, S. (1974). *Families and Family Therapy*. London: Tavistock.

Ryle, A. and Lunghi, M. (1970). The dyad grid — a modification of repertory grid technique. *British Journal of Psychiatry*, **117**, 323–327.

CHAPTER TWELVE
Issues of Validity and Reliability

Sue Lewis

Introduction

A major aim of the research was to answer the question: 'To what extent can the method of participant observation be used to reveal patterns of social interaction in families in their own homes?' In this chapter we assess the usefulness of the data generated by the observation technique as a descriptive tool for exploring interactions. The data have many shortcomings and pitfalls which are examined and illustrated using results from the study. Many of the problems are common to all observational studies and arise from the investigator's lack of control over the process under observation. Some of the difficulties are made acute in this study by the demands imposed by the observation technique and the high judgemental element in recording the observations and coding the variable values. Confronting these issues provides guidance on interpreting the results from this particular study and planning future research.

We begin by outlining sensible objectives and sound practice for observing interactions in natural settings. We then discuss how the demands of participant observation limit, and in some cases prevent, the achievement of these objectives. In most previous participant observation studies no attempt has been made to assess the validity and reliability of results, for example Mead (1930), Whyte (1955). Much can be learned from the attempts to tackle these issues in the present study of family life.

Observing Interactions in Natural Settings

Many authors have presented sound cases for studying the behaviour within groups of individuals in natural, rather than laboratory, settings. A detailed argument and long list of references is given in Lincoln and Guba (1985).

First we consider studies based on *non-participating* observers. This approach has been used in a wide variety of investigations which differ in many features. An example, given by Johnson and Bolstad (1973), is a study of families in the home under the restrictions that all family members should remain in two adjoining rooms; there should be no interactions between the unconcealed observers and the family members; and no visitors, television or lengthy telephone calls. Observation sessions lasted forty-five minutes and preceded dinner on each of five consecutive days. Brinker and Goldbart (1981) describe a study of early communication skills in groups of young children at play, some of whom were developmentally delayed. Video and audio recording and concealed observation were used. Each child was observed for fifteen minutes and categories of social behaviour, non-verbal communication, intentional vocalizations, and verbalizations were recorded each time they occurred. In addition, play codes were noted every fifteen seconds. The observational system aimed to provide a description of a child's social and communicative strategies which could be used to guide intervention, and to provide a macro-analysis of the relationship between semantic and pragmatic communication. An important feature of the study is its emphasis on reliability attainment and assessment.

These two examples illustrate some of the features which may differ within naturalistic studies. Important factors are: the environment and restrictions placed upon it, whether or not the observer is seen by the group under observation and the length of the observation period. In addition, the type of information recorded may range from the occurrence or non-occurrence of a small number of predetermined events to a detailed summary of actions and their durations. A useful discussion of different types of information is given by Bakeman and Dabbs (1976) who classify information according to two criteria: whether it is event- or time-based and whether it is observed concurrently or sequentially. These authors give a concise account of simple methods of analysing and displaying the different data types. Studies also differ in their methods of recording information and the time when coding takes place. If video or audio cassettes are used then coding may take place a long time after observation. When data acquisition machines or simply pencil and paper are used then coding follows immediately after observation. These factors are decided at the planning or design stage of the study and are determined by the nature of the group under observation, the objectives of the investigation, the available resources, and other constraints on the study.

A concern common to all observational studies is the reliability of the data collected. We should aim for high agreement between observers on three key issues. Firstly, it is important that observers should agree on the successive subintervals of observation which are to be separately recorded. As an example, suppose an observer has a clock and is required to note the presence or absence of particular kinds of behaviour during successive fifteen-second periods. In this case the subintervals (fifteen-second periods) are easily identified and high agreement between observers is achievable. More difficult are studies in which observers record sequences of non-overlapping events in a stream of behaviour without time measurement. Then the subintervals are identified by the events which occur; for example, A speaks to B, B laughs, B speaks to A. Agreement between observers on what constitutes an event and the occurrence of an event becomes less likely with increasing numbers of behavioural features to be recorded and individuals to be simultaneously observed.

A second important requirement is that observers should agree on what is observed, in other words the team of observers should form a reliable recorder. This does not guarantee that observers are recording accurately the actual events which take place, since the observers may have biases in common. For example, suppose one member of the observed group has an unappealing manner, then all observers may unwittingly misinterpret aspects of this behaviour. A further difficulty here is that there may be no objective description of the events which took place against which accuracy can be assessed. The issue is then 'Whose truth?'. Behaviour viewed by one person as supportive may be judged quite differently by an observer or by another member of the group with different relationships and experiences of group members. Individual preconceptions can be overcome in part by training observers to use a common theoretical window, as in the present study. To assess observer accuracy we are forced to examine the similarity between observations on variables designed to measure the same feature of behaviour. In the present study Minuchin maps were used for this purpose (see Chapter 9). In addition, adults within a family gave their personal view of the relationships within the family; a repertory grid analysis was performed (described in Chapter 8) and a video film of a family mealtime was studied (see Chapter 8).

In order for the coded data to be useful we should aim for as high agreement as possible on the coding of observations. The level of agreement which can be achieved is limited by the simplicity and ease of identification of the categories in the code. There is a much greater chance of agreement on the coding of behaviour into the two categories 'a shout occurs' and 'a shout does not occur' than into the much finer categories of the present study shown in Chapter 7 which involve a high degree of judgement in the identification of the appropriate code.

Usually observation takes place on several different occasions. The study should then aim for consistency of method over time. In particular there should be strict adherence to the unit of behaviour to be observed. Also agreement between observers and use of the coding scheme should be maintained over time.

In order to achieve these reliability aims it is sound practice to organize training sessions in which observers simultaneously observe the same group of individuals in the natural setting. A comparison of the observers' performances and discussion of how differences arise can lead to improved levels of agreement. As performance can change over time, reinforcement monitoring sessions during a study are also advocated to maintain high agreement. Similarly, programmes to achieve and maintain high coding agreement are also necessary when coding and observation are not conjoined. A review of the use of agreement indices and correlation methods in assessing the level of agreement is given by Hartmann (1977) and used, for example, in the study of Brinker and Goldbart (1981) described earlier. In some investigations the pursuit of high levels of agreement is considered an unacceptable constraint on the study design and on the information which can be gathered, an approach expounded by Lincoln and Guba (1985). Thus the priority attached to the goal of high reliability covers a wide spectrum in current research.

Limitations of Participant Observation

In the range of naturalistic studies participant observation allows the greatest freedom to the group of individuals under study. The group is not restrained to stay in shot for a video camera or confined to a single room equipped with one-way observation mirrors. The observer is free to become a member of the group, although confined to a passive role. The price of these freedoms is that several of the standard methods of assessing and achieving reliability and validity cannot be employed.

A comparison of observations made simultaneously by two observers was considered infeasible in the present family study. The presence of two participating observers in a home would be too great an imposition on the families. Further, two observers would be likely to completely distort the family interactions and to create a situation totally different from the single-observer case. For these reasons the training and monitoring of observers through participant observation of the same events was not possible.

Participant observation restricts the ways in which observations can be recorded. The observer must be free to participate in activities, as and when requested. There are few activities which can be performed while clutching a data acquisition machine! The method of recording observations in the family study described in Chapter 6 is open to criticism on several points. There may be a delay of as much as two hours between the occurrence and recording of events. Some events are likely to be forgotten by the observer. More dangerous is the opportunity for covert evaluation of the events. At a conscious level the observer's attention is taken by tracking members of the group and retaining knowledge of the events. At the subconscious level some filtering may take place, influenced by earlier or later events, personal biases, and prior knowledge of the family members. This is an important issue for both the reliability and validity of the data.

A weakness of the present study is that there is no provision for monitoring observer agreement on recorded events. Although it is infeasible to assess observer agreement in the field, some guidance for training and monitoring performance could be obtained by asking observers to view, and later record, interactions amongst family members shown on video film. A similar approach could be used to investigate how the time lapse between observing and recording events affects observer agreement. This might lead to a compromise time-lapse length which gives a tolerable level of agreement, and yet is feasible in the context of participant observation. This is a challenge for future research.

We now describe an attempt made in the present family study to gain some insight into observer agreement by allowing two different people to be participant observers of the same family on two different occasions. Some difficulties in interpreting the results will be described. These seriously restrict the usefulness of the results for studying observer agreement. Table 1 refers to two visits made to the C family on separate occasions by Arlene and Claire. It shows the percentages of all the identified acts which were allocated to each of the twenty-two categories described in Chapter 7. In each case the coding was performed by the person who observed the session.

Table 1. Percentages of acts within each category for two C family visits

Category	Visit 1 Arlene	Visit 2 Claire
01	3.1	1.7
02	8.6	0.7
03	1.2	4.0
04	3.3	3.0
05	9.0	7.1
06	21.1	20.2
07	1.3	0.6
08	13.4	18.6
09	1.4	0.1
10	0.7	0.0
11	5.2	9.4
12	4.9	2.7
13	2.4	6.0
14	4.2	5.8
15	5.2	0.5
16	0.0	0.9
17	4.1	4.5
18	0.5	0.1
19	1.9	1.8
20	0.5	2.5
21	7.9	7.7
22	0.1	2.0
Total no. of acts	1867	2057

A comparison of these two sets of percentages measures not only discrepancies between Arlene and Claire in the use of the observation and coding techniques, but also changes which may have occurred in the family's interactions between the two visits. These two features are confounded and cannot be disentangled from these data. We cannot conclude with certainty that, for example, the absence of acts of category 10 was due to Claire's different interpretation of this category. Studies of this kind, however, can prompt a useful re-examination and discussion of the meaning of the categories which would lead to improvements in observer agreement.

The same problem arises in attempts made to assess the consistency over time of an observer's recordings using repeat visits to a family. A clear illustration is provided by Arlene's two visits to the W1 family which were four weeks apart. This family consists of Father, Mother, and five children, one of whom refuses to attend school, and is described fully in Chapter 9.

In order to examine intra-observer reliability, comparisons were made between the proportions of acts assigned to the various categories for each visit. In Table 2 a summary is presented for the sets of codes corresponding to positive, neutral, and negative categories of behaviour. For both visits the coder was the participant observer.

Table 2. Percentages of positive, neutral, and negative acts on two visits to the W1 family by the same observer

	Visit 1 %	Visit 2 %
Positive	22	29
Neutral	45	50
Negative	33	22
Total no. of acts	959	643

A comparison of the percentages for the first and second visits shows a clear drift from the first visit to the second away from the negative forms of behaviour towards the positive and neutral categories. This is confirmed to be of very high statistical significance, beyond the 0.1 per cent significance level, by a chi-squared test. What interpretation should we put on these results? Could they be regarded as evidence of inconsistency by the observer/coder? Perhaps more charitable assessments of the family interactions are being taken at the second visit as a result of familiarity with family members.

An alternative explanation can be found by examining the differences in family circumstances at the two visits. On the first occasion all seven family members were present. However, on the second occasion the referred child was away from home on a school trip for most of the visit.

The method of recording observations in the family study has considerable impact on the identification of the subintervals of observation. Observers describe a stream of events which are not partitioned into sequences and acts within sequences until the transcript of the recording is coded. A comparison can be made of different coders' identifications of sequences and acts within sequences by examining their independent codings of the same transcript. Table 7(b) in Chapter 7 gives a summary and explanation of the relation between the sequences separately identified in the same transcript by the two coders.

The two coders identified similar *numbers* of sequences, namely 227 and 215, but only about one-quarter of the sequences coincided exactly. The percentage of sequences of the first coder which were not shared by the second coder was 10 per cent. The corresponding figure for the second coder was 34 per cent. This indicates that in order to support the most detailed level of analysis in which individual acts are examined, reliability in identifying and coding the individual sequences of acts needs to be improved. Ways of achieving this include increased training of coders, and simplification and selectivity in the recording made by the observer. The latter course presents a dilemma since in improving reliability we would restrict the observational material which could be collected, a restriction that may not be tolerable because meaning is lost from the data.

How should our recognition of this reliability problem affect our interpretation of the results presented in Chapter 7? The greatest impact is on the results of the lag-sequential analyses. If the observer/coder had been shown to be a very reliable recording system at the level of ordered individual acts then we could have divorced the results of the analysis from the actual observer/coder whose data produced them. This is often possible in non-participating observation studies in which easily identified activities are recorded. However, in the present study we must recognize that the observer/coder may affect the stream of acts recorded. Hence the lag-sequential analysis gives conclusions dependent on that particular observer/coder. We can think of the results as a detailed record, assembled over time, of the observer/coder's view of the sequence of different types of behaviour.

The problem has much less impact on the conclusions from the sociograms and frequency counts for the positive and negative affect initiated by each family member, as discussed in Chapter 7. As these are based on whole sessions it is whole-session reliability measures which must be used to assess their worth. Examples of these are presented in Chapter 7 on pages 111 and 112. Although there are statistically significant differences for the frequency counts between observers and between coders, there are substantial common trends giving a useful description of the quality of the interactions within the family.

The third important reliability question is the extent to which coders agree in their use of the coding scheme. In the present study, the performance of coders is likely to be affected by a number of factors. If the coder is also the observer whose recording produced the transcript then she is likely to bring extra information and clarification to the coding procedure. If the coder has previous knowledge of the family, from a clinic or another observation session, then she may unintentionally draw on this in her coding. In contrast, a coder with no prior information on the family may show marked differences in coding the same transcript. Some evidence of this variation in the use of codes is presented in Table 6, data columns 1–3, in Chapter 7. Arlene was the person who observed the session, Claire had observed the family in a previous session but had less experience of participant observation and coding than Arlene, and Kerry had neither experience of participant observation nor prior knowledge of the family. A revealing feature is the variability in the use of category 21, 'activity related to the ongoing interaction' by the three coders. This appears to be used as a refuge for acts which coders cannot allocate to other categories. Almost 23 per cent of the acts coded by the least experienced coder, Kerry, were assigned to this category. The corresponding figures for the most informed coder, Arlene, and less experienced, Claire, were 7.9 per cent and 11 per cent, respectively. The second part of the table shows codings of the transcript obtained from the observation session of Claire. Again the least experienced Kerry resorts to using category 21 far more often than the other two coders. Coders Claire and Arlene have percentages of 7.7 and 5.3 with the more informed but less experienced coder Claire making greater use of the category. There are marked differences in the use of other codes, for example category 2 which corresponds to an action 'showing solidarity through raising the status of others', and category 15 indicating 'shows tension, asks for help by virtue of personal inadequacy'.

Greater agreement was achieved on the identification of initiators of acts across an observation session. Figure 1 illustrates the agreement between two coders of the same transcript of a visit to the P family consisting of one parent and one child (described in Chapter 9). It shows the percentages of all acts for which the various people were coded as initiators by each of the observers. The main difference is that coder 1, who was also the observer, attributes 5 per cent fewer acts to the observer. The small percentages of acts identified as being initiated by the observer in both codings indicates the success of the observers in adopting a passive role in the family. Coder 1 identified 686 acts while coder 2 identified 713 acts.

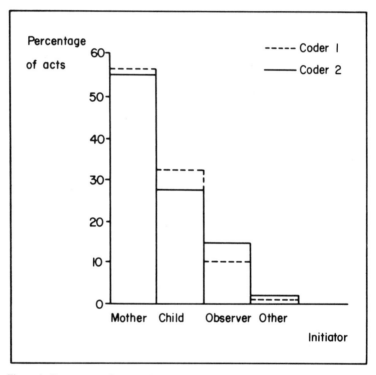

Figure 1. Percentages of acts attributed to the initiators by different coders (P family)

Comparison of the codings of the same transcript by three different coders identifies two important issues for the reliability and validity of participant observation studies. These are the roles of the observer/coder and the impact of previous experience on the information recorded.

The use of *different* people as observer and coder has several disadvantages. The method of recording observations by spoken account is liable to produce an imprecise description of events. If the observer also codes the transcript then useful clarification is possible and additional information may be recalled. Further, the use of two people may compound subjective biases. On the other hand, when the coder is also the observer there is further opportunity for the covert evaluation of events.

Prior information about a family may influence how events are observed and coded. A person's own experiences of family life may also have impact on observation and coding. In particular, the present study raises the suspicion that the experience of childrearing of an observer or coder may affect the information gathered. In the comparison of the three coders, Arlene and Claire have reared two children, while Kerry has no experience of parenting. There is a need for further research on these issues and, in participant observation study, a need to assess the results in relation to the experience of the observers/coders employed.

Conclusions and Guidance on Future Research

The data derived from the family study cannot be regarded as scientifically objective and highly reliable because of the problems outlined earlier in this chapter. This greatly limits the inferences which can be made from them and restricts their use as a descriptive tool for exploring patterns in family interactions. At worst the data derived from a participant observation session yield a highly subjective view of events in a specific family on a particular few days. Thus an account is derived which differs in the amount of detail and possibly also in emphasis from that obtained by asking the observer to answer, at the end of the visit, the question 'What did you think was going on in this family?' The data description offers considerable improvement on an observer's overall opinion, since it will not be known if this opinion has been shaped by a small subset of events. The data should not be viewed in isolation but in conjunction with other diagnostic procedures.

The family study raises several questions for future research:

1.   What levels of observer and coder agreement are achievable in a study of this kind by rigorous training and monitoring techniques?
2.   To what extent could simplification be made in the features of behaviour to be recorded and coded, without sacrificing the meaning and usefulness of the information gathered?
3.   Are the patterns of family interactions stable over time?
4.   Can the patterns be changed by therapy? Is it feasible to investigate changes using before-therapy and after-therapy observation sessions?

Two key features in setting up a participant observation study have emerged from this work:

1.   The careful definition, selection, training, and monitoring of 'expert' observers. Ideally this should involve simultaneous observation by pairs of observers. If participant observation in pairs is infeasible then some non-participating observation sessions using video film or actors could be useful for training and monitoring.
2.   The relation between coder and observer. If these are to be distinct then careful definition, selection, training, and monitoring of the coders are essential.

References

Bakeman, R. and Dabbs, J. M. (1976). Social interaction observed: Some approaches to the analysis of behaviour streams. *Personality and Social Psychology Bulletin, 2*, 335–345.

Brinker, R. P. and Goldbart, J. (1981). The problem of reliability in the study of early communication skills. *British Journal of Psychology,* **72**, 27–41.

Hartmann, D. P. (1977). Considerations in the choice of interobserver reliability estimates. *Journal of Applied Behaviour Analysis,* **10**, 103–116.

Johnson, S. M. and Bolstad, O. D. (1973). Methodological issues in naturalistic observation: Some problems and solutions for field research. In: L. A. Hamerlynck, L. C. Handy and E. J. Mash (Eds), *Behaviour Change: Methodology, Concepts and Practice.* Champaign, Illinois: Research Press.

Lincoln, Y. S. and Guba, E. G. (1985). *Naturalistic Inquiry.* Beverly Hills, California: Sage.

Mead, M. (1930). *Growing Up in New Guinea.* Harmondsworth: Penguin.

Whyte, W. F. (1955). *Street Corner Society: The Social Structure of an Italian Slum.* Chicago, Illinois: University of Chicago Press.

CHAPTER THIRTEEN
Conclusions and Recommendations for Future Research and Practice

Anthony Gale and Arlene Vetere

Introduction

This book describes family life as seen through the eyes of the observer. Each chapter describes the evolution of the methodology of participant observation as developed for our research purposes, and set within the context of a theoretical framework. We consider the problems of data analysis and the special ethical concerns of the family researcher. The issues raised are not only relevant to basic research into family structure and process but to the practice of family therapy. Within each chapter we have identified the costs and benefits of particular approaches and have made recommendations for the future development of the technique. The present chapter serves to summarize our key recommendations as they may be applied in the context of both research and clinical practice. We have not discussed other research methodologies in any depth because of our commitment to the participant observation technique. We believe that only by such methods can the true life of the family, and the meanings of family events for its members, be fully understood. Other methods of family research are considered by Straus and Brown (1978) and Miller (1986). The limitations of many of these methods are that they sample only subsystems of the family, typically in artificially created situations, and for sampling periods of short duration. We appreciate that our own technique of extended observation has the reverse problem of sampling too much veridical data, but our methods of data reduction and analysis, governed in part by a theoretical framework, help to synthesize and characterize continuity and pattern in family life.

Development and Use of Theory

General System Theory has clear benefits for the conceptualization of family life because it helps to organize notions of individual behaviour and interactions among individuals. Many therapeutic approaches in family therapy are based on this general conception. However, it is easy to imagine that by dressing up complex behaviours in technical terms one somehow captures reality in a more powerful fashion. It is also easy for therapists to slip into technical jargon without necessarily saying very much more than simpler language would convey; or even pretending to think or work in family terms while actually employing a loose mixture of eclectically derived practices. The misuse of General System terminology could be employed to bolster such a woolly approach. Thus General System Theory can be and has been abused. Our view, therefore, is that General System Theory is most powerful in family research and therapy when used as a *general orientative framework*.

None of the more specific theories, whether couched in system terms or not, is able to account for all family facts. Among the requirements for good theory we listed the following: clear definition of all key concepts and variables; specification of the relationships between variables; justification for the exclusion of variables; adoption of a motivational framework which does not falsely talk in terms of 'family needs, wishes, goals . . . and so on' *as if* the family is an individual; an account of conflict and its resolution; a specification of family roles and functions; a means of recognizing the different phenomenal views of individual family members; specifying and providing a means of exploring belief systems and their relationship to behaviour; giving an account of the ways in which the family changes over time; providing a framework for the description of repetitive behaviours; drawing a distinction between acts (as observed) and actions (the meanings imposed upon acts and recognized by family members); and, finally, description of atmosphere and situations as well as personal and interactional attributes. We recognize that the development of such a complete framework is unknown in general psychology; however, we fear that major components of and influences upon family life can be ignored by the theorist. The aim should be to seek to develop more comprehensive theory; unfortunately as Burr, Hill, Nye, and Reiss (1979) conclude, the need for such an achievement is yet to be acknowledged, never mind be initiated.

So far as clinical practice is concerned we appeal to therapists to cast off a narrow view of theory and its practical uses. In Chapter 9 we showed how the systematic application of three well-developed theories to each family under study, revealed facets of family life which were clouded by individual theories, because of their particular emphases. We are *not* suggesting a loose eclecticism but rather a *systematic* application of each theoretical approach, thus drawing upon its positive benefits.

Participant Observation

As psychologists, participant observation was a new experience for us. In the absence of systematic guidelines for practice, we had to devise our own procedures by an iterative process, becoming progressively more sensitive to the nuances of the technique. In the light of our experience, we are puzzled by the failure of Kantor and Lehr (1975) to consider the complexities of the method and the difficulties of interpretation; their account of method stands in strange contrast to the elaborate nature of their theory. We realized, after the event, that we ourselves were changed by the experience of participation, in a way that no laboratory scientist is changed by his or her experiments. The technique also offered new challenges in terms of the ethics of research; by getting near to the bone and into the lives of our subjects, we realized that they were in fact persons. Walking into and out of the home was simply not like walking into and out of the laboratory.

Yet in spite of this sense of personal involvement and personal change, in the interests of science we had to maintain an objective stance and to cut through the romance and excitement of the experience of sensing the inner lives of family members. We have attempted in our research to maintain objectivity, to be sensitive to bias, and to hold our own views and prejudices about family living in abeyance. In several places in this book we discuss the problem of reactivity, the myth of objectivity in social situations, and the need to rehearse the constraints of the participant observer's role.

In future we would recommend a long period of training for observers, *in vivo*, and in the thick of the experience of observation. We believe that the observer must be alone and that the presence of more than one observer and/or the introduction of elaborate equipment and recording devices, will disrupt the free and natural flow of events. Therefore the observers have to compare their own experience with that of others, in the absence of a common referent, as defined in terms of the *same* events, in the *same* circumstances, and at the *same* point in time. Somehow different observers have to share their experience, to search below the surface behaviours of the family, and to identify the common features of the deeper structure. Within-observer and between-observer consistency are crucial goals, but they can only be achieved by extensive practice. In this sense, therefore, our work is only a beginning. In principle, however, and with sufficient funds and resources, we believe the process could be refined. Observers need to experience scoring and re-scoring of their own and others' accounts and must be open to alternative interpretations of actions. Our methods can be extended.

But there is a theoretical limit to objectivity when the participants in the action which is observed *themselves* construe events in different ways from each other. Thus, there can be a danger of increasing reliability at the cost of validity. It must be doubted whether, in terms of the experience of a particular group of individuals with a long history of interaction, there can ever be a scale or taxonomy on which behaviours can be classified with reliable discrimination and in the absence of a level of interpretation. Each family has its own history and each family member has an investment in events.

Thus, family observation needs to be supplemented by techniques which seek out the individual viewpoints of family members. Here again, the notion of generalizability and the capacity to use the same set of constructs across families may be an unfulfillable dream. The realization that such existential uncertainty awaits the family researcher must be a source of anxiety and a possible cause of the neglect of family studies within psychology; complexity can be aversive.

Future Designs for Participant Observation

How then can our approach be improved upon? Can the method be used in a ready fashion by the clinician? Would such an investment in time and energy be cost-effective? To many therapists, active in their role as agents of change, the burden of passive observation may be too great to bear. Passive observation involves putting aside the role of expert and authoritative source of advice and guidance. In these days of public accountability and the search for the holy grail of effective service delivery, therapists need to ask whether current practices are actually doing what they are supposed to do. For example, the cost of keeping a difficult child in a special home is considerable. The puzzle of why such a child does not necessarily display difficult behaviour in a residential context may be resolved by examining the antecedent conditions which trigger off unacceptable behaviour in the home. Our view is that home observation and the detailed analysis of family behaviour in relation to the child may lead to the implementation of behavioural change on the part of the child and his or her parents. Only observation under a variety of natural circumstances, and in the ecological context within which the behaviour occurs, is likely to identify the maintaining factors and the emotions which events around them incur. The child guidance clinics with whom we worked on this project commented on the particular character and richness of the scenario diaries which arose as a result of our visits to the home. Other *personal* problems like smoking, alcoholism, and obesity, may be better understood by studying the client within their natural ecology. Sex therapists do not think it strange to treat the couple (rather than the individual); other personal habits and difficulties arise within an *interpersonal* context.

If therapists themselves find the role we describe too onerous or incompatible with their training and belief systems, then is it too outrageous to suggest that participant observers be trained as part of clinic teams? We believe there to be justification for the development of a profession of specialists in the field.

A weekend of observation might well be sufficient to give the observer an understanding of family dynamics, more indeed than several clinic interviews may achieve.

So far as research is concerned, however, much longer periods of observation are essential in order to capture repetitive actions, sequences, and temporal dependencies in a manner which allows them to be susceptible to a detailed statistical analysis. Moreover, the family needs to be observed under conditions which are sufficient enough to be able to measure variance attributable to particular members, to particular groupings, or indeed to interactions between observer and observed. Even after a week of observation and with some hundred pages of transcript for an individual family, there was rarely sufficient data to allow for averaging of events within particular subgroupings. This raises practical difficulties of voluntary consent and sufficient funding resources. It also imposes considerable strain on the observer as is apparent from Chapter 6. However, as some reviewers of family interaction research have commented, much of the resources spent in the heyday of family research in the 1960s were wasted upon ill-conceived theory and ill-executed partial research designs (Riskin and Faunce, 1972).

We have mentioned the use of repertory grids to elicit the phenomenal views of family members. We have also used the technique to tap the constructs used by the observer in her encounters with families. This technique may be extended to help therapists elaborate their construct systems, both in training and in practice; we believe that the discipline of having to compare *families* within a common framework is as valuable as eliciting individual personal constructs.

Conclusion

We have argued that family life is too important to be neglected by psychologists. While anthropologists and sociologists have devoted so much attention to the family, psychology seems to be almost blind to its influence, as witnessed by the index pages of introductory texts and the contents pages of learned periodicals. Our own attempts at research have been exposed in this volume and we have tried to be straightforward in our account of our successes and failures. There is no doubt that family research is harder than laboratory research. We hope that this book may help to trigger interest in others. It is a shame for clinicians to steal the show!

References

Burr, W. R., Hill, R., Nye, F. I. and Reiss, I. L. (1979). *Contemporary Theories About The Family*, vol. 1. *Research Based Theories*. New York: Free Press.

Kantor, D. and Lehr, W. (1975). *Inside the Family: Towards a Theory of Family Process*. San Francisco, California: Jossey-Bass.

Miller, B. C. (1986). *Family Research Methods*. Beverly Hills, California: Sage.

Riskin, J. and Faunce, E. E. (1972). An evaluative review of family interaction research. *Family Process,* **11**, 365–455.

Straus, M. and Brown, B. W. (1978). *Family Measurement Techniques*. Minnesota: University of Minnesota Press.

Author Index

The numbers in bold print indicate where the reference to the authors' work is cited in full

Subject Index